D0861437

THE FLORIDA LIGHTHOUSE TRAIL

THE FLORIDA LIGHTHOUSE TRAIL

SECOND EDITION

Josh Liller

Palm Beach, Florida

An imprint of The Rowman & Littlefield Publishing Group, Inc.
4501 Forbes Blvd., Ste. 200
Lanham, MD 20706
www.rowman.com

Distributed by NATIONAL BOOK NETWORK

Copyright © 2020 by the Florida Lighthouse Association

All rights reserved. No part of this book may be reproduced in any form or by any
electronic or mechanical means, including information storage and retrieval systems,
without written permission from the publisher, except by a reviewer who may quote
passages in a review.

British Library Cataloguing in Publication Information available

Library of Congress Cataloging-in-Publication Data available

Names: Liller, Josh, 1981- author. | Florida Lighthouse Association.
Title: The Florida LighthouseTrail / [edited by] Josh Liller.
Description: Second edition. | Palm Beach, Florida : Pineapple Press, 2020. | Includes
   bibliographical references. | Summary: "The histories of Florida's lighthouses
   by different authors, each an authority on a particular lighthouse. This book
   includes facts not covered in other books on Florida lighthouses such as dates of
   construction and operation, foundation materials, lighting equipment. Includes a
   preface by Wayne Wheeler, president of the United States Lighthouse Society. For
   each lighthouse directions, websites, contact information are given"—Provided by
   publisher.
Identifiers: LCCN 2019048601 (print) | LCCN 2019048602 (ebook) | ISBN
   9781561647101 (paperback) | ISBN 9781683340775 (epub)
Subjects: LCSH: Lighthouses—Florida.
Classification: LCC VK1024.F6 F58 2020 (print) | LCC VK1024.F6 (ebook) | DDC
   387.1/5509759—dc23
LC record available at https://lccn.loc.gov/2019048601
LC ebook record available at https://lccn.loc.gov/2019048602

♾™ The paper used in this publication meets the minimum requirements of
American National Standard for Information Sciences—Permanence of Paper
for Printed Library Materials, ANSI/NISO Z39.48-1992.

Dedicated to Florida's bright lights lost in the last twenty years:

Dennis Barnell
Hal Belcher
Paul Bradley
Ann Caneer
Hib Casselberry
Cullen Chambers
Candace Clifford
Dave D'Amicol
Gene Oakes
Tom Taylor

CONTENTS

SECTION II: THE FLORIDA KEYS

APPENDICES

CONTENTS

FOREWORD TO THE FIRST EDITION

Wayne Wheeler, President,
United States Lighthouse Society

The lighthouses of Florida reflect almost every style constructed in this country over the years: tall and short; brick, stone, and iron; screwpile and conical masonry towers; some located offshore and some on the coast. The Ponce de Leon Inlet and St. Augustine are among the tallest in this country. The skeletal towers of the Florida lighthouses are engineering marvels. Florida, along with Maine and Michigan, are premier lighthouse states.

Although several books have been written about the light stations of Florida, this book is refreshingly different. It is a collection of the histories of Florida's light stations by a number of different authors. Each author is, more or less, an expert on a particular light station. You'll find historical facts, interesting local history, and even directions and maps to locate the various lighthouses that dot the thousand-mile coast of Florida.

The entire work has been superbly edited by lighthouse historian Thomas Taylor, one of our nation's premiere experts on the subject. What follows is an interesting and accurate account of the lighthouses of the Sunshine State, as well as a handy reference book and guide to Florida's Lighthouse Trail. Sit back and enjoy, then go out and find Florida's lighthouses for yourself.

FOREWORD TO THE SECOND EDITION

Harry Pettit
Florida Lighthouse Association

It is only in retrospect that I realize what a significant and somewhat miraculous accomplishment it was when the Florida Lighthouse Association published the first edition of *The Florida Lighthouse Trail* in 2001. The FLA was not yet five years old. The project relied entirely on the volunteer effort and expertise of many of its dedicated members. The miracle was that these experts were available and willing to be enlisted in the cause. Among the contributors were lighthouse managers, historians, restorers, and local preservation enthusiasts. Several were founders of FLA. The result, managed and edited by Tom Taylor and illustrated by Paul Bradley, was a unique sort of guidebook, with a specific essay on each Florida lighthouse, including history, factual information, and directions.

I was delighted when Josh Liller told me that he was beginning work on a new edition of this book. The general layout and concepts of the original book held up well. However, for the book to remain useful, consideration had to be given to the many important changes that have occurred in the lighthouse community over the last two decades. The number of Florida lighthouses that have been restored and opened to the public increased dramatically during this time, reflecting in part the impact of significant seed money grants from the unique FLA grant programs.

Many of the original contributors, including Tom Taylor, Paul Bradley, and Hib Casselberry, have passed on. Their leadership and dedication are universally acclaimed. The publication of this edition marks the assumption of responsibility for this effort by the capable hands of a new generation, and we are indeed fortunate that Josh Liller has taken up this work. Building on the solid foundation of the original edition, he has produced a book of substantially enhanced value to all who are interested in Florida's lighthouses.

ACKNOWLEDGMENTS

FROM THE FIRST EDITION

The Florida Lighthouse Association is grateful to all of the authors who have contributed to this work, as well as artist Paul Bradley, whose superb talents greatly enhance the book. Thanks are also given to Hib Casselberry, Stuart McIver, Dr. Kevin McCarthy, James Dunlap, Neil Hurley, Richard Atwood, Linda Koestal, and Carol Moore for their proofreading assistance. Our great appreciation also goes to June Cussen and her staff at Pineapple Press for seeing the merit in this project and for so professionally editing, publishing, and marketing this book, and to Sandy Wright for her typesetting expertise.

FROM THE SECOND EDITION

The Florida Lighthouse Association is grateful to the many individuals who have worked so hard since the first edition of this book to restore, preserve, and interpret many of Florida's lighthouses and thus help necessitate a second edition. Thanks to the staff at Pineapple Press for being interested in a new edition rather than letting this guide go out of print.

The US Lighthouse Society's Light Lists and J. Candace Clifford Lighthouse Research Catalog were particularly helpful resources in updating and expanding the first edition. Kraig Anderson's LighthouseFriends.com was also a very useful secondary source.

For the chapters in which the main text received only some updates about recent events and small corrections that did not substantially change the content from the first edition, the author credit remains unchanged. Where the additions and corrections were more substantial, the author credit has been updated accordingly. The appendices have been substantially updated, and much of the content is completely new to this edition.

Whenever possible, staff or volunteers at each lighthouse were contacted to review their lighthouse's updates for accuracy. Proofreading and/or updated information for this edition provided by: Kate Aguiar, Kevin Begos, Chris Belcher, John Canetta, James Hargrove, Ellen Henry, Jon Hill, Barbara Holland, Terry Kemp, Billie Kinnett, Craig Kittendorf, Ralph Krugler, Eric Martin, Sharon McKenzie, Jessica Morgan, Betty Lowe Phelps, Richard Sanchez, and Sonny Witt. Special thanks go to FLA Historian Neil Hurley for additional research and fact checking.

INTRODUCTION

A BRIEF HISTORY OF FLORIDA LIGHTHOUSES

Josh Liller

The British and Spanish both established several daybeacons to mark key parts of the coast during their colonial rule of Florida in the late 1700s and early 1800s. This may have included a lighthouse near St. Augustine.

What is commonly called the Lighthouse Service was originally a civilian agency within the federal government, created by Congress in 1789. Until 1910, its formal name was the United States Light House Establishment (USLHE). The USLHE, under Stephen Pleasonton, began establishing lighthouses in Florida almost immediately after the United States acquired the territory from Spain in 1821. The first US lighthouse in Florida was established at St. Augustine on April 5, 1824. The first on the Florida Gulf Coast was Pensacola that December. The first lighthouse completed in the Florida Keys was Key West in March 1826.

Sixteen lighthouse towers were built in Florida at thirteen light stations between 1824 and 1845, but only two survive: Amelia Island (1839) and St. Marks (1842). The early lighthouses were mostly built to guide ships into the main harbors, although a few (like Cape Florida) warned of dangers. Winslow Lewis designed the majority of these early brick towers and provided his patented Lewis lamps for all of them. Unfortunately, these lighthouses nearly all proved inadequate in height and brightness, and most succumbed to hurricanes or erosion.

Twenty-one lighthouses were built in Florida between 1846 and 1860. Eleven of them survive today. During this period, many improvements occurred: most of the early towers were replaced, iron pile lighthouses allowed for lighting the Florida Reef, the Lighthouse Board formed in 1852 to better manage the Lighthouse Service, and Fresnel lenses replaced Lewis lamps. Sand Key Lighthouse received the first Fresnel lens used in Florida in 1853. A new system of Lighthouse Districts divided Florida among three districts—the sixth, seventh, and eighth.

Each lighthouse had one to three keepers responsible for the operation and maintenance of the station. Most keepers were joined at the lighthouse by their family, although some were bachelors. The Florida Keys lights were an exception. Isolated offshore and with very limited living space, they were designated "stag stations"—keepers only. Keepers were nearly always white men, but some women and African Americans did serve in Florida. In the Keys, many of the keepers were Cuban or Bahamian immigrants, or their descendants.

With the exception of those in the Keys, Florida's lighthouses were all darkened during the Civil War. None of them were destroyed outright by the war, although several were badly damaged. The Fresnel lenses were removed in haste and without properly trained laborers, usually resulting in damage that had to be repaired by the manufacturer in France. The prewar lights were nearly all reestablished by 1868. The 1860s also marked the transition from whale oil (spermaceti) to lard oil as the primary lamp fuel.

The 1870s and 1880s saw most of the gaps in coastal lighting filled, and more inadequate or lost lights replaced. Eighteen lighthouses were built in Florida between 1868 and 1895, and twelve are still standing. The five lighthouses from this period that did not survive were all riverine or offshore cottage-style wooden structures on pilings. Seven of the postwar lighthouses were skeletal iron designs. The last original brick Florida lighthouse (excepting the modern rebuilding of Cape St. George) was Ponce Inlet Lighthouse, completed in 1887. Ponce is also the tallest lighthouse in Florida and the second tallest brick lighthouse in the United States (after Cape Hatteras).

During the 1880s, "mineral oil" (kerosene) replaced lard oil in lighthouse lamps. The new highly flammable fuel necessitated the construction of new iron or brick oil houses at nearly every light station. Red sectors were added to most of the Florida Keys lighthouses in 1893 to mark the Florida Reef and other dangerous areas nearby. Around the turn of the century, ball bearings and mercury floats began to replace the old brass chariot wheels used to rotate Fresnel lenses, allowing for faster and smoother movement.

Only three lighthouses were built in Florida by the federal government during the twentieth century, and one of those (Boca Grande Rear Range Light) was relocated from another state. The last government-built Florida lighthouse was St. Johns in 1954.

Officially renamed the Bureau of Lighthouses in 1910, the Lighthouse Service began a new program of improvements: discontinuing lights deemed no longer necessary, automating some lights with acetylene, and converting all fixed lights to flashing lights. In the Florida Keys, the lighthouses were given new characteristics in sequence. Fowey Rocks flashed once, Carysfort Reef flashed twice, and so on. New incandescent oil vapor (IOV) lamps made lighthouses brighter than ever.

During World War I, some lighthouses came under the authority of the Navy Department. Many had Navy lookouts assigned during the war and received telephone connections so they could report suspicious activity.

In the 1920s and 1930s, electricity reached most lighthouses, either by commercial power lines or the installation of diesel generators. Electricity meant light bulbs instead of oil lamps, and an electric motor replaced a system of clockwork and weights to make the lenses rotate. For some lighthouses, it also meant the installation of a radio beacon as an extra aid to navigation.

On July 1, 1939, the entire Lighthouse Service merged with the US Coast Guard. Many lighthouse keepers enlisted in 1941 or 1942, but some chose to remain as civilian employees of the Coast Guard. The former keepers usually received some preferential treatment from their new service, but all those in Florida had retired by the 1950s. Coast Guard lookouts joined the keepers at nearly every Florida lighthouse during World War II.

After World War II, Florida's remaining manned lighthouses settled into a routine of three to five enlisted keepers each—usually a boatswain's mate, an engineman, and the rest junior enlisted men. The lighthouses were treated like any other military station; while servicemen could volunteer for or request lighthouse duty, they were usually transferred after only a year or two and rarely served at more than one lighthouse during their career.

Automation of lighthouses proceeded steadily during the postwar decades. Nearly all Florida lighthouses were automated by the 1970s. The last two, Dry Tortugas in 1987 and Egmont Key in 1989, were among the last two-dozen lighthouses to be automated in the entire country. Automation of a lighthouse often meant the removal of the Fresnel lens and replacement by a low-maintenance modern optic lacking the historical value and aesthetic beauty of its predecessor.

The first Florida lighthouse to be acquired for preservation and interpretation was the Key West Lighthouse in the 1960s. Ponce Inlet followed in the 1970s. The bicentennial in 1976 and the automation of the last lighthouses nationwide in the 1980s and 1990s drew increased attention to lighthouse history and the need for preservation. The formation of the Florida Lighthouse Association in 1996 and the National Historic Lighthouse Preservation Act of 2000 were major steps on the road toward saving Florida's lighthouses and opening them to the public (see the appendix about the Florida Lighthouse Association for further details).

USING THIS BOOK

This book is designed to provide comprehensive directions to the thirty surviving historic lighthouses in Florida, as well as the former sites of historic lighthouses lost through the years. This "trail" follows around the state clockwise, starting at Fernandina Beach. This is appropriate since the first lighthouse, Amelia Island Lighthouse, happens to be Florida's oldest extant tower. Also, many of Florida's out-of-state visitors often enter the state from the north by way of I-95. The trail can be followed continuously in this manner. Directions to each lighthouse follow from a major highway, so sections of the trail can be followed at different times.

The lighthouses in Section I: The Florida East Coast can be found off I-95, with the exception of the first few lighthouses that are more easily accessed by State Road A1A. Only US Highway 1, the Overseas Highway, provides access to the lighthouses in Section II: The Florida Keys, all but one of which are located offshore. For those lighthouses in Section III: The Florida Southwest Coast, access is from a combination of I-75, I-275, and US Highway 19. For the final leg, Section IV: The Florida Northwest Coast, main access is from US Highway 98, with I-10 as an alternative and the quickest return route.

Each chapter covers a different lighthouse or lighthouse site with a short history, basic facts, visiting information, directions, and a map. A few lighthouses located close together share maps. Several appendices give further information about Florida's light stations.

While the second edition of this book follows the same general layout as the first edition, each chapter has updated and expanded information. The appendices have also been updated and expanded. These changes give some indication about not only the changes (mostly for the better) during the last two decades, but also how much more we have learned about Florida's lighthouse history in the last two decades. Much serious archival research remains to be done so that the true and complete story of Florida's lighthouses can be told.

A little clarification may be helpful on a few of the Site Facts given for each lighthouse. Tower Height refers to the height of the structure from ground level (or sea floor, for offshore lighthouses) to the top of the lantern—excluding cupolas, vent balls, lightning rods, antennas, and more. Focal Height is the height of the center of the optic above sea level, accounting for both the tower and natural elevation, and it is the primary factor determining how far out to sea the light is visible. Number of Stairs counts those between the base of the tower and the lantern room. Handicapped Access refers only to whether a wheelchair could reasonably reach the base of the tower from the nearest parking. None of Florida's lighthouses have elevators, thus none of the towers themselves are handicapped accessible. Hours of operation given are the normal operating hours at the time of publication; holidays and special events may affect these hours.

For all lighthouses, children must be able to climb under their own power (they may not be carried) and are required to be accompanied by an adult when climbing. For safety reasons, some lighthouses have a minimum height for climbing the tower.

We at the Florida Lighthouse Association hope that the second edition of *The Florida Lighthouse Trail* will be of great assistance to our readers in locating and visiting the sites of Florida's great lighthouse heritage.

SECTION I
THE FLORIDA EAST COAST

AMELIA ISLAND LIGHTHOUSE

FERNANDINA BEACH, FLORIDA

Harold Belcher and Chris Belcher

At more than 180 years old, the Amelia Island Lighthouse is the oldest continuously operating lighthouse in Florida. It has been active since 1839 at this site, with the exception of the four years it was disabled during the Civil War. It is not only the oldest existing lighthouse in Florida, but, because of the curvature of the coast, it is also the lighthouse located furthest west of any US lighthouse along the Atlantic seaboard, excluding the western Florida Keys. This lighthouse also has the rare distinction of having been in active operation in two states.

The lighthouse was originally built in 1820 and was located across the St. Marys River on the south end of Cumberland Island, Georgia. In 1838, the original builder, Winslow Lewis, was contracted to remove and rebuild it on the highest point on Amelia Island, even though the site was more than three-fourths of a mile west of the ocean and two miles south of the river. Amos Latham, a seventy-eight-year-old veteran of the Revolutionary War, came with the lighthouse as keeper. He died four years later and was buried on the site; the remains of Latham and his wife were relocated to a family plot in nearby Bosque Bello Cemetery in 1964.

The lighthouse served as the rear light for the Amelia Island South Range until 1880. The South Range was one of five ranges used at various times to indicate the route into the mouth of the St. Mary's River leading to Fernandina, Florida, and St. Marys, Georgia. The others were the Amelia Island North Range, Amelia Island New North Range, Fort Clinch Range, and Tiger Island Range.

The original Lewis lamps were replaced several times before a third-order Fresnel lens was finally installed in 1856. The lens was removed during the Civil War, but later recovered. The lighthouse was relighted on May 1, 1865, with another third-order lens. In 1881, the tower received a new, larger lantern that extended the lighthouse's height by eight feet. The present rotating third-order Fresnel lens was first lighted on October 24, 1903, and is stamped with the manufacturer's name, "Barbier & Bénard, Paris." The light was finally electrified in 1933 but not automated until 1970.

The tower is a double-walled brick structure. The inner vertical cylinder is nine and a half feet in diameter, and the eight-inch-rise, hand-hewn, New England granite steps are embedded in that wall. They overlap slightly, forming a closed spiral much like an Archimedes' screw. The exterior wall is a tapered, truncated cone. The outside diameter is twenty-two feet at ground level, tapering to ten and a half feet at the top. Six window tunnels pierce the walls.

The original keeper's dwelling was replaced in 1860 by a two-story duplex. The second dwelling was in turn replaced in 1886. The building was auctioned off and removed from the station by the purchaser, with its subsequent where-abouts unknown. The 1886 dwelling was used until 1959 when the Coast Guard replaced it with a modern concrete block dwelling. An oil house was added to the station in 1890 and remains on the site.

The Amelia Island Lighthouse was placed on the Coast Guard Seventh District excess property list in late 1998. The City of Fernandina Beach acquired ownership through the National Historic Lighthouse Preservation Act in 2001. Unfortunately, the lighthouse is now located in a residential neighborhood, which severely limits public access. As of 2019, the light station is only open to the public on a very limited schedule, and the tower is not open for climbing.

SITE FACTS

Dates of Construction: 1838–1839 (present site)
First Lighted: 1839
Electrified: 1933
Automated: 1970
Deactivated: 1861–1865 (due to Civil War)
Tower Height: 64 feet
Focal Height: 107 feet
Designer/Architect: Winslow Lewis
Builder/Supervisor: Winslow Lewis
Type of Tower: conical brick
Foundation Materials: brick
Construction Materials: brick tower, granite stairs, iron lantern
Number of Stairs: 69
Status: active—public Aid to Navigation
Daymark: white tower, black lantern
Original Optic: 14 Lewis lamps with 15-inch reflectors on revolving apparatus
Other Optics Used: third-order revolving Fresnel lens (1856–1861), third-order revolving Fresnel lens (1865–1903), fourth-order Fresnel lens (1881, temporary)
Fresnel Lens Manufacturers: unknown, Henry-Lepaute (1860s), unknown
Current Optic: third-order revolving Fresnel lens (1903–present)
Current Optic Manufacturer: Barbier & Bénard (btwn. 1894–1901)
Characteristic: one white flash every 90 seconds (until 1903); one white flash every 10 seconds (since 1903)

Station Auxiliary Structures: keeper dwelling (1959), oil house (1890)
National Register of Historic Places: yes (part of Fernandina Beach Historic District)
Owner: City of Fernandina Beach
Operating Entity: City of Fernandina Beach (grounds), US Coast Guard, assisted by Coast Guard Auxiliary
Grounds Open to the Public: yes—limited schedule
Tower Open to the Public: no
Lighthouse Museum: no
Gift Shop: no
Lighthouse Passport Stamp: yes—Fernandina Beach Parks and Recreation
Hours: monthly bus tours (first and third Wednesday, departs 10 AM); Saturdays 11 AM–2 PM (grounds only, limited parking)
Adult Admission: $5 bus tour (including tower interior without climbing); free on Saturdays (grounds only)
Handicapped Access: no
Contact: Fernandina Beach Parks and Recreation Department, 2500 Atlantic Ave., Fernandina Beach, FL 32034
Phone: (904) 310-3350
Email: recinfo@fbfl.org
Website: https://www.fbfl.us/474/Amelia-Island-Lighthouse-Tour

DIRECTIONS

From I-95 (Exit 373), take State Road A1A / State Road 200 east into Fernandina Beach. Turn right on Atlantic Avenue to stay on A1A. Turn left (north) onto 20th Street. Turn right (east) at Highland Street, then left (north) onto Lighthouse Circle. Immediately after the street curves east, turn left (north) onto O'Hagan Lane, which leads to the front gate. This is also the closest place to view the lighthouse. Other observation points from across the adjacent marsh are available in Fort Clinch State Park.

The bimonthly guided bus tours to the lighthouse depart from the Atlantic Center at 2500 Atlantic Avenue.

You may also wish to visit the Amelia Island Museum of History in downtown Fernandina Beach (233 S. 3rd Street, (904) 261-7378, www.ameliamuseum.org), which has a small exhibit about the lighthouse.

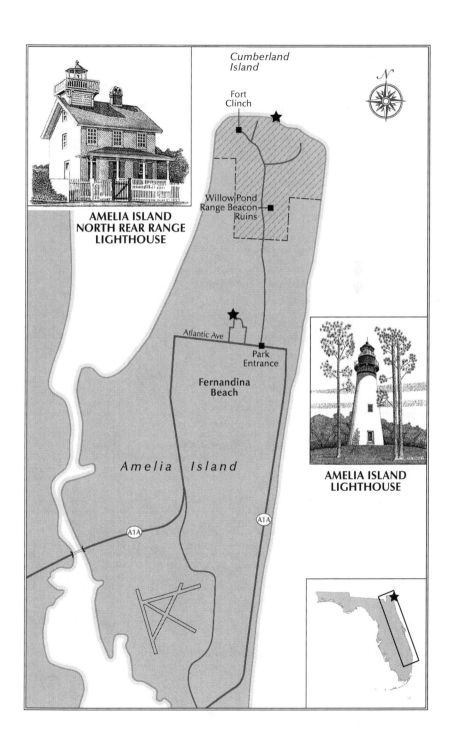

**AMELIA ISLAND
NORTH REAR RANGE
LIGHTHOUSE**

Cumberland
Island

Fort
Clinch

Willow Pond
Range Beacon
Ruins

Atlantic Ave

Park
Entrance

Fernandina
Beach

Amelia   Island

**AMELIA ISLAND
LIGHTHOUSE**

A1A

A1A

AMELIA ISLAND NORTH RANGE

FERNANDINA BEACH, FLORIDA
(Site Only)

Neil Hurley and Chris Belcher

In addition to the Amelia Island Lighthouse, in 1858 two navigational lights (one a small lighthouse) were needed to mark St. Marys Entrance, the channel just north of Fernandina Beach. By sailing on a course that brought both lights into alignment, ships' captains could be sure they were on a course that took them through the deepest part of the entrance channel. The front tower was the smaller of the two beacons. Further to the west, the lighthouse displayed its light from a lantern atop a wood-frame house, known as the Amelia Island North Rear Range Light. Both structures had sixth-order Fresnel lenses. The lighthouse is thought to have been located about eight hundred yards east of Fort Clinch in sand dunes along the beach. At the time, Fernandina Beach was one of the five largest cities in Florida.

With the start of the Civil War, the range lights were shifted to intermediate operation until the lenses were removed for safekeeping in mid-1861. Union forces seized the town of Fernandina in March 1862, and while it is not clear what happened to the structures, they did not survive the war.

The "growing navigation interest" called for the reestablishment of the range lights in 1870. Construction began in late 1871, and the rear range tower again consisted of a lantern on a frame dwelling. Throughout the operation of the range, shifting sand dunes required that frequent work be done to prevent the lighthouse from being buried. The front range light was originally a square pyramidal wooden structure, resembling a small shack, mounted on a north-south tramway so it could be moved easily whenever storms altered the bar. The wooden front light decayed rapidly and in 1876 was replaced with a new iron structure.

Construction began in 1880 on jetties at the north end of Amelia Island and south end of Cumberland Island. The jetties created new shipping channels, thus rendering the old ranges "useless." The South Range Front Light was moved and modified to become the New North Range Rear Light, also mounted on a tramway. The old North Rear Range Lighthouse was deactivated but continued to serve as the dwelling for the range keeper. An oil house was built in 1891 to store kerosene for the lights.

By December 1892 the channel across the bar shifted so often "that it was found impracticable to accommodate heavy structures to its frequent changes. The lights thus became a source of danger rather than assistance to navigation" and were discontinued. A new system of temporary range lights was devised using "light triangular structures carrying tubular lanterns, which could be easily and rapidly moved from place to place" as conditions warranted.

The range was permanently discontinued in 1899 when buoys were found to better mark the troublesome channel. Surveys of Amelia Island show an "old light house" along the north shore as late as 1924. In 1996, a local resident, Hal Belcher, found parts of a brick chimney base along the surf line in the approximate location of the old lighthouse. The spot was later covered over when the beach was replenished, but, at rare times, the brick foundation of the chimney can still be seen.

After the Amelia Island North Range was discontinued, two other ranges were established. The Fort Clinch Range had the rear range located atop the southeastern bastion of the fort. The Tiger Island Range Lights were located northwest of Fernandina Beach, just across the Amelia River on Tiger Island. Both ranges were tended by a keeper, at least in the early 1900s.

SITE FACTS

(Details are for the cottage-style North Rear Range Light)
Dates of Construction: 1858; 1871–1872
First Lighted: November 1, 1858; June 1, 1872
Electrified: never
Automated: never
Deactivated: March 15, 1880 (lighthouse); May 15, 1899 (range)
Tower Height: 40 feet
Focal Height: 53 feet
Designer/Architect: unknown
Builder/Supervisor: unknown
Type of Tower: cottage-style frame
Foundation Materials: unknown, but probably brick
Construction Materials: wood
Number of Steps: unknown
Status: no longer exists
Daymark: white house with red roof and black lantern
Original Optic: sixth-order Fresnel lens
Optic Manufacturer and Date: unknown
Other Optics Used: none
Current Optic: N/A
Characteristic: N/A
Station Auxiliary Structures: oil house (1891)
National Register of Historic Places: no
Owner: Florida Department of Environmental Protection (site)
Operating Entity: Fort Clinch State Park (site)

Grounds Open to the Public: yes
Tower Open to the Public: N/A
Lighthouse Museum: no
Gift Shop: no
Lighthouse Passport Stamp: no
Hours: 8 AM–sunset daily (park)
Adult Admission: $6/car (park)
Handicapped Access: no
Contact: Fort Clinch State Park, 2601 Atlantic Ave., Fernandina Beach, FL
   32034
Phone: (904) 277-7274
Email: none
Website: www.floridastateparks.org/fortclinch

DIRECTIONS

From the Amelia Island Lighthouse, retrace your route to Atlantic Avenue. Turn left (east) and drive a short distance to the entrance of Fort Clinch State Park on your left. There is an admission fee. The New North Range oil house and remnants of the tramway for the range lights is located on the right side of the park road; parking is available across the street at the Willow Pond Trailhead. For the (old) North Rear Range Light site, continue on the park road until you see the main parking area for Fort Clinch immediately ahead of you. Immediately before you enter the parking lot, turn right (northeast) onto a small dirt road. Park in the small lot at the end of this road, then use the short boardwalk to reach the beach. The site of the Amelia Island North Rear Range Light is about six hundred yards east-southeast along the beach.

   See previous chapter for map.

DAMES POINT LIGHTHOUSE

NEW BERLIN (JACKSONVILLE), FLORIDA (SITE ONLY)

Neil Hurley

One of two river lighthouses in Florida, the Dames Point Lighthouse formerly marked a sharp bend and a twelve-foot shoal in the St. Johns River between the river's mouth and Jacksonville. A small lightship that first marked the site in 1857 was equipped with both a bell and a horn for use as fog signals, and displayed a fixed white light from a small lens. The lightship was manned by a crew of three: the captain, a cook, and one crewman. During the Civil War, Confederate authorities ordered the lightship towed upriver to Jacksonville. A Confederate fort (at Yellow Bluff), which mounted as many as twelve cannons, guarded the Dames Point shoal. The Yellow Bluff fort was abandoned in 1863, and Jacksonville was later occupied by Union troops. It is not clear if the lightship survived the war.

It wasn't until 1870 that enough shipping returned to the river to merit a light on the shoal. The lightship had cost $9,500, but due to increases in crews' salaries and maintenance, it was more economical to build a pile lighthouse for $20,000. The lighthouse was framed at the Lazaretto Point Lighthouse Depot in Baltimore, Maryland, then disassembled, shipped south, and reassembled on the site over a three-month period in 1872. It was a wooden structure, mounted on five or six wooden piles in iron sleeves located in eight feet of water on the south side of the channel, opposite Dames Point. During the summer of 1875, Napoleon B. Broward, later governor of Florida, lived in the lighthouse while attending school in New Berlin.

Lightning is prevalent in Florida, and the tower of this lighthouse was struck by lightning several times in 1891. It survived, but the useful life of the Dames Point Lighthouse was soon to come to an end. Dredging and the construction of wooden "training walls," which used the river's current to keep the channel deep, removed the need for the lighthouse in the early 1890s. In 1893, the light was discontinued and the top of the lighthouse removed for use in another location. The lighthouse remained unused until it was destroyed by fire on Christmas Day 1913. Nothing remains of the tower today. As no known photographs or drawings of this lighthouse exist, the sketch accompanying this chapter was drawn from one made of a typical screwpile harbor light. Since then, a plan of the lighthouse has been found in the National Archives confirming the design matches the sketch.

SITE FACTS

Dates of Construction: 1872
First Lighted: July 15, 1872
Electrified: N/A
Automated: N/A
Deactivated: February 28, 1893
Tower Height: approximately 40 feet
Focal Height: 35 feet
Designer/Architect: unknown
Builder/Supervisor: unknown
Type of Tower: pile cottage
Foundation Materials: wooden pilings in iron sleeves
Construction Materials: wood and iron
Number of Stairs: unknown
Daymark: white structure (including lantern), red pilings
Status: destroyed by fire (1913)
Original Optic: fifth-order fixed Fresnel lens
Optic Manufacturer: unknown
Other Optics Used: none
Current Optic: N/A
Characteristic: fixed white
Station Auxiliary Structures: none
National Register of Historic Places: no
Owner: N/A
Operating Entity: N/A
Grounds Open to the Public: yes—open water
Tower Open to the Public: N/A
Lighthouse Museum: no
Gift Shop: no
Hours: N/A
Lighthouse Passport Stamp: no
Handicapped Access: N/A

DIRECTIONS

From Fernandina Beach, follow State Road A1A south to its juncture with State Road 105 (Heckscher Drive) near the ferry to Mayport. Continue west on Heckscher Drive just past the interchange with I-295. Turn left (south) on New Berlin Road. Yellow Bluff Fort Historic State Park is a small, free park located on this road with a marker about the fort. Turn right on Dames Point Road and follow it to a small park under the aptly named Napoleon Broward Dames Point Bridge. A fishing pier, here provides a view of the river. The lighthouse site was almost directly across the river near the bridge's south support pier. Looking east from the pier you will see the Fulton Cut that made the lighthouse unnecessary. You can imagine ships navigating around this point before that channel existed. There are no visible remains of this lighthouse, and it is not legal to stop on the bridge.

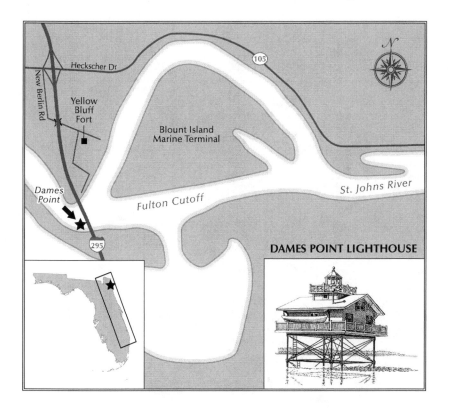

DAMES POINT LIGHTHOUSE

ST. JOHNS RIVER LIGHTHOUSE

MAYPORT (JACKSONVILLE), FLORIDA

Andrew M. Liliskis and Josh Liller

The entrance to the St. Johns River has challenged mariners since the early days of exploration. The forces and currents created by the river's meeting the ocean fashioned hazards for ships and shaped the fate of several lighthouse towers. The river and ocean meet at Mayport, the site of the settlement begun by French Huguenot Jean Ribault in 1565. Early Spanish explorers were so taken by the river's forces that they named it the River of Currents. The river eventually received its Anglicized name from the nearby Mission San Juan del Puerto.

Florida was still a territory in 1828 and 1829 when Congress made two appropriations totaling $10,550 for the construction of a lighthouse to assist vessels entering St. Johns River. The lighthouse was built in 1830 in the vicinity of the present-day south jetty, but erosion soon undermined the tower. The lighthouse was demolished in May 1833 and the lantern and material moved to a safe location; the Atlantic Ocean later claimed the site.

In 1834, Congress decided to rebuild the lighthouse. The second lighthouse was completed by Winslow Lewis in 1835 at a location one mile upstream, where the Navy turning basin is currently located. The second tower was sixty-five feet tall. It originally used fourteen Lewis lamps with 15-inch reflectors, replaced in the mid-1850s by a fourth-order Fresnel lens. In 1852, erosion began to threaten this lighthouse as well, and Congress appropriated an additional $10,000 to stabilize it.

By 1854, problems with erosion, sight lines, and land ownership concerns forced Congress to appropriate $15,000 to build a third lighthouse. In an attempt to avoid the fate of the previous lighthouses and to resolve the ownership issue, the new St. Johns River Lighthouse was built still further upriver. The new tower began operation on August 1, 1859. Its design loosely resembles a shorter version of the lighthouse built around the same time on Loggerhead Key, including granite stairs and a flared brick apron to support the gallery deck.

The Civil War erupted a little over a year after the light entered service. An oft-repeated story claims keeper John Daniels severely damaged the Fresnel lens to keep it out of Union hands, but this is most likely a myth. However, according to the Lighthouse Board, the lighthouse was "much damaged by the rebels" during the war and required a new third-order lens and lantern as part of the postwar repairs. It was relighted on July 4, 1867, with Daniels returning as lighthouse keeper for a short time.

In 1887, plans were made to raise the tower an additional fifteen feet, but these were canceled when the clearing of nearby trees rendered the work unnecessary. A brick oil house measuring 9 by 11 feet was built near the tower in 1890 with room for 450 cans of kerosene for the lighthouse's lamp. An IOV lamp was installed in 1912.

The lighthouse was electrified in 1920. A semiautomatic radio beacon was added in 1928, the first of its kind in the United States. A lightship was placed off the mouth of the St. Johns River in 1929, resulting in the lighthouse being discontinued. The radio beacon was moved to the lightship the following year. The last keeper, Charles Sisson, continued to reside at the station with his family until 1931, while serving as a relief keeper at other lighthouses in the 6th District. After Sisson was transferred, the station was abandoned.

Unlike its predecessors, the St. Johns River Lighthouse did not succumb to erosion; instead, the currents of human events have shaped its fate. In 1941, the US Navy built Mayport Naval Station as part of World War II military expansion. Almost all of the Village of Mayport was removed. The decommissioned light station and a nearby eighteenth-century cemetery did not fare any better. The keeper's house was demolished, the oil room attached to the lighthouse was removed, and eight feet of fill was placed on top of the entire site, burying the front door. The Navy wanted to raze the remaining lighthouse tower, but local citizens prevailed to preserve it.

Concerned citizens have repeatedly thwarted the Navy's efforts to destroy or move the lighthouse from its historic location. In a gesture of goodwill, the Navy made extensive repairs and helped place the structure on the National Register of Historic Places in 1982. In 1997, the non-profit Mayport Lighthouse Association (MLA) formed to open the site to the public. MLA sought to open a small lighthouse museum. They also made long-term plans to restore the lighthouse and build a replica of the keeper's house. Unfortunately, 9/11 resulted in the naval station being closed entirely to the public. MLA was unsuccessful in its efforts to have the Navy move the perimeter fence so that the tower would no longer be in a secure area and was likewise unable to raise funds for the tower to be moved to a park located a couple hundred yards away in Mayport. The organization quietly disbanded in 2011.

As of 2019, the lighthouse is without a local support organization or public access. Groundwater contamination issues will almost certainly require the lighthouse to be lifted out of the ground and moved to a new location as part of any future restoration effort. Florida Lighthouse Association meetings in Jacksonville are currently your best chance to see the lighthouse up close, although climbing was not permitted as of the last meeting there in 2016.

SITE FACTS

Dates of Construction: 1830; 1835; 1858–1859
First Lighted: 1830; 1835; August 1, 1859
Electrified: 1920
Automated: never
Deactivated: 1833–1835; 1929–present
Tower Height: 80 feet (reduced to 72 feet in 1941)
Focal Height: 75 feet (when active)
Designer/Architect: Winslow Lewis (1830 and 1835); probably W. H. C. Whiting (1859)
Builder/Supervisor: Winslow Lewis (1830 and 1835); unknown (1859)
Type of Tower: conical brick
Foundation Materials: brick
Construction Materials: brick and iron (1830 and 1835); brick, granite, and iron (1859)
Number of Steps: 90 (1859)
Daymark: red tower, white lantern (1859–present)
Status: inactive
Original Optic—Previous Towers: 14 Lewis lamps with 15-inch reflectors
Original Optic—Current Tower: third-order fixed Fresnel lens (1859–1861)
Other Optics Used: fourth-order fixed Fresnel Lens (1856?–1859); third-order fixed Fresnel lens (1867–1929)
Fresnel Lens Manufacturers: unknown; unknown; Henry-Lepaute
Current Optic: none
Characteristic: none (historically, fixed white)
Station Auxiliary Structures: none surviving
National Register of Historic Places: yes (1975)
Owner: US Navy
Operating Entity: US Navy
Grounds Open to the Public: no (active military base)
Tower Open to the Public: no
Lighthouse Museum: no
Gift Shop: no
Hours: N/A
Lighthouse Passport Stamp: yes—contact John Kennedy, Florida Lighthouse Association
Handicapped Access: no
Contact: none

DIRECTIONS

From Dames Point cross the river via I-295 and exit at Merrill Road (SR 116), go east on Merrill Road to SR A1A. Turn left (north) and follow A1A to Mayport. Alternatively, from Dames Point proceed east on Heckscher Drive (SR 105) to SR A1A and cross the St. Johns River via the Mayport Ferry ($6/vehicle). Either way, take Broad Street in Mayport, which will pass next to the Mayport Naval Station perimeter fence and provide the closest public view of the lighthouse.

If you are able to legally access Mayport Naval Station, the main gate is located on Mayport Road just north of Merrill Drive (see next chapter for directions). After entering the station, either turn left just before the helicopter display onto the perimeter road, or continue north and pass most of the ship basin before turning left onto the perimeter road. Either way, the lighthouse is along the perimeter road on the west side of the naval station, west of the runway.

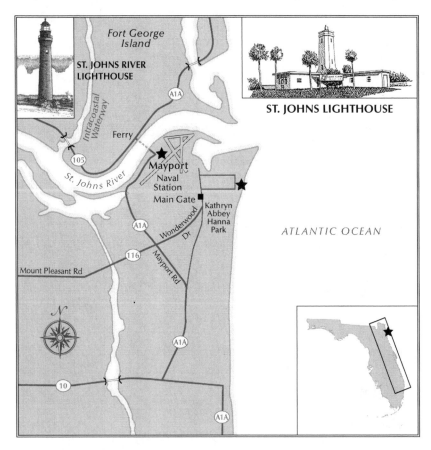

ST. JOHNS LIGHTHOUSE

MAYPORT NAVAL STATION (JACKSONVILLE), FLORIDA

Andrew M. Liliskis

The St. Johns Light Station is the fourth lighthouse to mark the treacherous entrance to the St. Johns River since 1830. It is located just over a mile from the old St. Johns River Lighthouse, yet these two structures are as different as the centuries in which they were built.

The older St. Johns River Lighthouse, located on the west side of the Mayport Naval Station, was built in 1859. It is a traditional, gently sloping, conical brick tower topped by a picturesque iron lantern, typical of its era. It readily appeals to those who wax nostalgic about lighthouses.

In contrast, the St. Johns Light Station, built in 1954, is an angular, monolithic, Art Deco–style structure originally topped by a small, drum-shaped lantern. By its fiftieth anniversary, the lighthouse began to attain its own significance and charm. It now represents the last manned lighthouse built in Florida and the latest in operating technology.

In the early 1900s, the maritime community began to pursue alternative ways to mark the treacherous entrance to the St. Johns River. Proposals for a major lighthouse on Mount Cornelia near the mouth of the river were never acted upon. Range lights were added in 1912 (Ward's Bank and Cross Over) and buoys were added and improved, but they proved insufficient. Ship captains and other maritime interests increasingly lobbied for a lightship. In particular, they argued that a lightship could guide ships into the port more effectively than a land-based lighthouse during fog and storms.

In 1929, after two nearly fatal ship groundings, the former Brunswick light-ship moved to a new station a few miles off the coast at the mouth of the St. Johns as a replacement for the old St. Johns River Lighthouse. The lightship remained in operation for the next twenty-five years, but new technology and increasing costs eventually made the lightship obsolete and too expensive to op-erate. The Coast Guard decided to return to a land-based operation, declaring that a new lighthouse would be six to ten times less expensive to operate than the lightship, which maintained a crew of fifteen.

The St. Johns Light Station was commissioned on December 15, 1954. The modern, sixty-four-foot concrete tower was built on a man-made beach dune, about three-fourths of a mile south of the jetties. It took fourteen months to build at a cost of $250,000. The newly built light station included the tower with two wings, its own water system, and an emergency electric generator. The radio beacon, formerly on the lightship, was moved ashore and broadcast from a 175-foot steel radio tower located two-thirds of a mile north of the light station. A fog signal station maintained by the light station crew was built on the south jetty. Two modern duplexes housed the crew of three to four people.

Besides the radio beacon with its two-hundred-mile range and the fog signal, the light station tower also had an aero marine beacon of 250,000 candlepower visible to ships up to twenty-two nautical miles away. The small, drumlike lantern had a Plexiglas cover and was designed to be lowered with chains and pulleys into the room below for repair and servicing. In September 1998, the Coast Guard removed the lantern, along with its 1950s-era optic, and replaced them with a flat roof and a state-of-the-art Vega VRB-25. The newer optic lacks the same power and range, but maintenance is simpler.

As of 2019, the lighthouse remains an active aid to navigation. The Coast Guard duplexes were demolished around 2005, but the two wings attached to the lighthouse still remain and are used by military personnel. Since it is sur-rounded by Mayport Naval Station, the lighthouse is not accessible to the pub-lic, but it can be visited and climbed when the Florida Lighthouse Association holds events in Jacksonville.

SITE FACTS

Dates of Construction: 1953–1954
First Lighted: December 15, 1954
Electrified: 1954 (from the beginning)
Automated: 1970
Deactivated: never
Tower Height: 64 feet
Focal Height: 80 feet
Designer/Architect: unknown
Builder/Supervisor: unknown
Type of Tower: square tower
Foundation Materials: concrete
Construction Materials: reinforced concrete
Number of Stairs: 71
Daymark: gray tower, no lantern, antennas on roof
Status: active—public Aid to Navigation
Original Optic: FB-61A rotating beacon (Crouse-Hinds, 1954)
Current Optic: Vega VRB-25 rotating beacon (Vega Industries, 1998)
Characteristic: four white flashes every twenty seconds
Station Auxiliary Structures: two integral wings attached to tower (1954)
National Register of Historic Places: no
Owner: US Coast Guard
Operating Entity: US Coast Guard
Grounds Open to the Public: no (active military base)
Tower Open to the Public: no
Lighthouse Museum: no
Gift Shop: no
Hours: N/A
Lighthouse Passport Stamp: yes—contact John Kennedy, Florida Lighthouse Association
Handicapped Access: yes—to base of tower
Contact: none

DIRECTIONS

From Mayport, take SR A1A south to Merrill Road (SR 116). Turn left (east) and follow Merrill Road past the intersection with Mayport Road (SR 101) and enter Kathryn Abbey Hanna Park ($5/car, open daily 8 AM–sunset). Park at the north end of the park and take the boardwalk over the dunes to the beach. Walk north a short distance to a line of large wooden poles across the beach that mark the south end of Mayport Naval Station. This is the closest public observation point to the lighthouse—about five hundred yards away.

If you are able to legally access Mayport Naval Station, the main gate is located on Mayport Road just north of Merrill Drive. After entering the station, turn right (east) on Moale Avenue then left (north) on Baltimore Street. The lighthouse is on the right before the Mayport Liberty Center.

See previous chapter for map.

ST. AUGUSTINE LIGHTHOUSE

ANASTASIA ISLAND, ST. AUGUSTINE, FLORIDA

Thomas W. Taylor

The St. Augustine Light Station was the first established in the state of Florida, and its original tower was the first one lighted in the state, on April 5, 1824. The original lighthouse was built with coquina limestone and wood using an extended Spanish watchtower, which itself had been rebuilt in 1737 at the location of an older tower. Notations on some maps suggest the watchtower may have been used as a lighthouse by the British and/or Spanish.

This first lighthouse served as a harbor light. The tower (excluding the lantern) was originally only thirty feet tall. This was extended to forty feet in 1848 and fifty-two feet in 1852. It received a fourth-order lens in the 1850s, which was removed during the Civil War. The tower was relighted on June 1, 1867.

The biggest issue with the original lighthouse was not its height, but an increasingly serious threat of erosion. In 1871, a new 165-foot tower was authorized six hundred yards southwest of the old tower on a site not as likely to be washed away. The architect for the new tower was Paul J. Pelz, who later designed the Library of Congress in Washington. His design was also used for 1870s lighthouses at Currituck and Bodie Island, North Carolina; Morris Island, South Carolina; and Sand Island, Alabama. The new lighthouse was completed and lighted on October 15, 1874. A new two-story duplex keeper's dwelling was built in 1876. In August 1880, the old tower collapsed. Today, its remains are under the waters of Salt Run, northeast of the present lighthouse.

The present lighthouse, that magnificent, black-and-white-spiral-striped tower with its red lantern, proved its sturdiness by withstanding three earthquakes in 1879, 1886, and 1893—all within the first fourteen years of its existence. The 1886 earthquake was centered in Charleston, South Carolina, and measured 7.2 on the Richter scale. It was the fourth most violent earthquake in American history and the strongest one recorded in the South in modern times. At the St. Augustine Light Station, head keeper William Harn reported that there was a loud "noise like a strong wind." Dogs and chickens barked and cackled. "Windows and doors rattled loudly and bird cages swung wildly. . . . Several persons were made sick by the motion of the earth. . . . The tower swayed in a violent manner" during a shock that lasted for about forty seconds, causing the lighthouse clock to stop its movement.

One problem with the lighthouse, which began only three weeks after it was first lighted, was that it attracted ducks and birds. Since it was located on the great Atlantic flyway, the lighthouse was often struck at night by flocks of migrating ducks and geese, which sometimes broke the lantern glass, causing the keepers some cleanup and repair work in the mornings. But it also gave them some sustenance beyond seafood and local crops. One time, the keeper reported picking up twenty-one dead ducks around the base of the tower.

Eventually, wire netting was put around the lantern to minimize the damage. Fortunately, this problem does not seem to exist today.

The St. Augustine Lighthouse has always been a stop for tourists. In the nineteenth century, many authors such as Sidney Lanier, Constance Fenimore Woolson (niece of author James Fenimore Cooper), R. K. Sewall, Margaret Deland, and Mrs. H. K. Ingram, visited and wrote about the lighthouse. It has also been the subject of countless paintings throughout the years.

Armed Coast Guard personnel were assigned to St. Augustine Lighthouse during World War II to keep a constant watch from the top of the tower. All ship sightings were reported to the local headquarters in St. Augustine's Government House. The 1941 coastal lookout dwelling where they lived at the station has recently been restored. It is one of the few such surviving structures in the country.

The keeper's dwelling was burned by vandals in 1970, but the light station was saved, restored, and opened to the public during a fifteen-year-long project undertaken by the Junior Service League of St. Augustine. The magnificent, original first-order Fresnel lens still operates today. It was restored in 1993 after having been shot by a teenager with a high-powered rifle in 1986, damaging nineteen prisms.

The nonprofit St. Augustine Lighthouse & Maritime Museum formed in 1988 and opened a new visitor center in 2000. In addition to preserving the lighthouse's history, the organization also started the Lighthouse Archaeological Maritime Program (LAMP) in 1999. The lighthouse was one of the first transfers of ownership under the National Historical Lighthouse Preservation Act of 2000. The lighthouse is one of the premier lighthouse museums in the country, and its historic Fresnel lens remains an active private aid to navigation.

SITE FACTS

(current tower only)
Dates of Construction: 1872–1874
First Lighted: October 15, 1874
Electrified: 1933
Automated: 1955
Deactivated: never
Tower Height: 165 feet
Focal Height: 168 feet
Designer/Architect: Paul J. Pelz
Builder/Supervisor: Hezekiah H. Pittee

Type of Tower: conical brick
Foundation Materials: coquina, stone, and brick
Construction Materials: brick and iron
Number of Stairs: 219
Daymark: black-and-white spiral stripes with a red lantern
Status: active—private Aid to Navigation
Original Optic: first-order FVF Fresnel lens (Sautter, Lemonnier, et Cie, 1874)
Other Optics Used: none
Current Optic: original Fresnel lens
Characteristic: fixed white light with one flash every thirty seconds
Station Auxiliary Structures: attached oil house (1874), two-story keeper's dwelling (1876), coastal lookout dwelling (1941)
National Register of Historic Places: yes
Owner & Operating Entity: St. Augustine Lighthouse & Maritime Museum (nonprofit)
Grounds Open to the Public: yes
Tower Open to the Public: yes
Minimum Height to Climb: 44 inches
Lighthouse Museum: yes
Gift Shop: yes
Hours: 9 AM–7 PM daily
Lighthouse Passport Stamp: yes—in gift shop
Adult Admission: $12.95 (lighthouse, museum, and grounds)
Handicapped Access: yes—to base of tower
Contact: St. Augustine Lighthouse & Maritime Museum, 100 Red Cox Drive, St. Augustine, FL 32084 (mailing address: 81 Lighthouse Ave., St. Augustine, FL 32084)
Phone: (904) 829-0745
Email: info@staugustinelighthouse.org
Website: www.staugustinelighthouse.org

DIRECTIONS

From St. Johns Light Station, go south on SR A1A. You will pass through St. Augustine and cross the Bridge of Lions onto Anastasia Island. Turn left on Red Cox Road—directly across from the St. Augustine Alligator Farm. The lighthouse is a few blocks north.

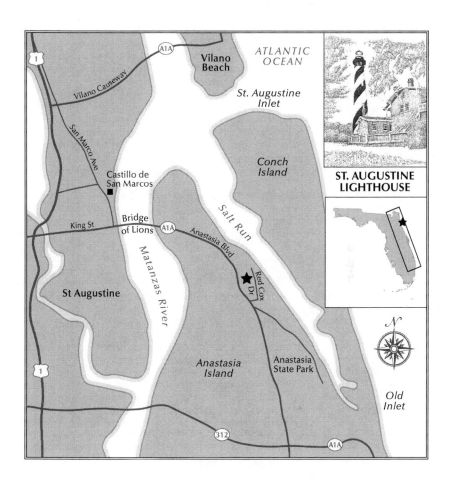

ATLANTIC OCEAN

Vilano Beach

St. Augustine Inlet

A1A

Vilano Causeway

1

San Marco Ave

Castillo de San Marcos

Conch Island

Salt Run

King St

Bridge of Lions

A1A

Anastasia Blvd

St Augustine

Matanzas River

Red Cox Dr

Anastasia Island

Anastasia State Park

1

Old Inlet

312

A1A

ST. AUGUSTINE LIGHTHOUSE

N

VOLUSIA BAR LIGHTHOUSE

LAKE GEORGE (NEAR ASTOR PARK), FLORIDA (SITE ONLY)

Thomas W. Taylor and Neil Hurley

When Florida became a territory of the United States in 1821, commerce along the upper St. Johns River was already so great that a petition requesting the construction of a navigational beacon at the south end of Lake George was sent to Congress in 1822. This beacon was needed to help vessels going south on the lake find the entrance to the river in an area where there were no navigational landmarks. The north-flowing St. Johns River also naturally produces a large sandbar (Volusia Bar) where it opens into the south end of the lake, just like a river does when it reaches the ocean. The channel through this sandbar was narrow, crooked, and shallow. There is no evidence that any beacon was constructed before the Civil War.

As steamboat traffic picked up again after the war, the DeBary Line established a private lighted beacon on the east side of the channel through Volusia Bar. An 1872 petition by St. Johns River steamboat pilots requested federal aids to navigation to mark Volusia Bar. Steamboats sometimes had to be dragged across Volusia Bar by chains hitched to teams of oxen on shore. Perhaps the most famous person to be stuck there was Ulysses S. Grant in 1880. The retired general and former president was vacationing in Florida in January 1880 with a party of family and friends. The steamer *Kelsey* grounded while bringing them up river, stranding them for two hours until they could be transferred to the steamer *Arrow*. Arriving five hours behind schedule, Grant and his party missed a reception and dance scheduled in their honor.

In March 1883, the Lighthouse Board was finally persuaded to request that Congress authorize a lighthouse to be built at the south end of Lake George. Jetties and "guide walls" were constructed through Volusia Bar in an effort to force the current to scour a deeper, straighter channel through the sand and mud. The new lighthouse would benefit some forty thousand people in five counties who were dependent for supplies upon ships that had to pass Volusia Bar.

Congress approved the new lighthouse project, but determining the exact site and gaining title to the submerged land for the structure took more time than planned, and work on the lighthouse did not begin until the fall of 1885. Iron piles and framework, brought down from Baltimore, were set up in four and a half feet of water. The white, five-room, frame dwelling, prefabricated in Charleston, was brought down with a working party and set on top of the iron piles. A fourth-order Fresnel lens was installed in the lantern room of this cottage-style lighthouse, and the entire structure was completed in March 1886. A large bell was installed as a fog signal. It would be struck once every ten seconds in foggy conditions. The lighthouse cost $8,635—not including the fog bell. Two post lanterns with fixed red lights were also established nearby to serve as range lights for the narrow channel.

The lighthouse soon served an additional purpose. Located right next to a waterway navigated by steamboats, the once-a-week mail parcels for the local residents would be dropped off at the lighthouse, and thus it became the post office for the people living at Silver Glen, Pat's Island, and in other local settlements within what is now Ocala National Forest. Sometimes, in addition to his lighthouse and mail duties, a keeper had to find additional income to support his family. Captain Frank Lansing, for example, who served at the lighthouse from 1913 to 1933, operated a commercial orange grove on Blue Creek Island.

River traffic decreased after the turn of the century, primarily due to railroads. The lighthouse and fog signal were discontinued in 1908, and the lantern was removed not long afterward. The Clyde Steamship Line repeatedly appealed for the fog signal to be reactivated and even paid temporarily for it to be manned at their expense. Volusia Bar was officially reestablished on February 1, 1915, as a manned, unlighted fog signal station.

In 1938, A. J. Anderson, keeper of the fog signal and nearby minor river lights, was found murdered and the lighthouse ransacked. The crime was never solved. That same year, the fog bell was replaced by a pair of Wallace & Tiernan FA-55 electric trumpet horns—one active, one backup. The Coast Guard discontinued the station entirely in 1943. The abandoned lighthouse was a popular temporary fishing camp for local residents, and it was also used as a summer residence for a local family in 1948. During this time, the structure was maintained by those who used it, but by 1954, it had started to deteriorate. It was damaged by Hurricane Dora in 1964 and burned down by vandals in 1974. Today the iron legs of this lighthouse mark its location.

WARNING: Beware of the many alligators in this area. Do not swim out to the lighthouse, even though it is in only four feet of water.

SITE FACTS

Dates of Construction: 1885–1886
First Lighted: March 1886
Electrified: never
Automated: never
Discontinued: 1908 (light); 1908–1915 and 1943 (fog signal)
Tower Height: 49 feet
Focal Height: 38 feet
Designer/Architect: Jared A. Smith
Builder/Supervisor: Jared A. Smith

Type of Tower: pile cottage

Foundation Materials: iron piles

Construction Materials: wood and iron

Number of Steps: unknown

Daymark: brown piles, white dwelling, black lantern

Status: destroyed—only pilings remain

Original Optic: fourth-order fixed Fresnel lens (1886–1899)

Other Optics Used: fifth-order fixed Fresnel lens (1899–1908)

Optic Manufacturers: unknown

Current Optic: N/A

Characteristic: fixed white (1886–1908)

Station Auxiliary Structures: none surviving

National Register of Historic Places: no

Owner: N/A

Operating Entity: N/A

Tower Open to the Public: N/A

Grounds Open to the Public: yes—open water

Lighthouse Museum: no

Gift Shop: no

Lighthouse Passport Stamp: yes—contact John Kennedy of the Florida
   Lighthouse Association

Hours: daylight hours (site only)

Handicapped Access: no

Contact: none

DIRECTIONS

From the St. Augustine Lighthouse, return to A1A and turn left (south). Turn
right (west) at State Road 312. Go past US Highway 1 then turn left (southwest)
onto State Road 207. At I-95, turn left onto the southbound onramp. Take Exit
268 for State Road 40 (Granada Blvd.). Go west toward Ocala. Cross the bridge
over the St. Johns River and pass through the small communities of Astor and
Astor Park. About four miles after the bridge and a mile after Astor Park, turn
right (north) on Blue Creek Lodge Road, a dirt road. Follow the road 2.5 miles,
and it will slowly curve east. Turn left (north) onto Lake George Road, also a
dirt road; look for a sign for "Volusia Bar Boat Ramp." Follow it 1.1 miles until
it ends at Lake George. A modern lighted beacon is about two hundred yards
off shore. The lighthouse pilings are a little over six hundred yards straight

out from the boat ramp, past the modern light and just west of the south end of the wooden guide jetty through Volusia Bar. They should be visible from shore. Local boaters using the ramp can sometimes be persuaded to give you a short ride out and around the piles, especially if you tell them the story of the lighthouse.

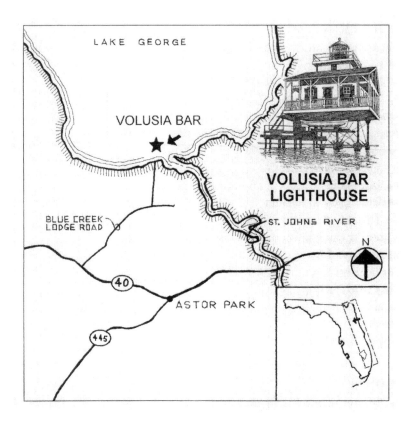

PONCE DE LEON INLET LIGHTHOUSE

PONCE INLET (NEAR DAYTONA BEACH), FLORIDA

Thomas W. Taylor

Ponce de Leon Inlet (often shortened to Ponce Inlet, and known until 1927 as Mosquito Inlet) is considered to be the seventh most dangerous inlet on the Atlantic Coast. Near this inlet, more than seventy shipwrecks have occurred since several vessels from Jean Ribault's French fleet washed ashore nearby during a hurricane in 1565.

In the 1770s, the British built a beacon (probably a fire basket on a pole) to help guide ships through Mosquito Inlet, but the first true lighthouse was not built there until 1835. That lighthouse, on the south side of the inlet, was never lighted (see Mosquito Inlet Lighthouse chapter) and was destroyed by coastal erosion after a little more than a year of existence. The Seminole Wars and the Civil War delayed the construction of a new lighthouse at this inlet.

In the 1870s, the Lighthouse Board noticed a large gap in the lighted coast between St. Augustine and Cape Canaveral and decided that Mosquito Inlet would be the best place to build a new lighthouse. On August 7, 1882, Congress first authorized the construction of this lighthouse with an appropriation of $30,000. Orville E. Babcock, district engineer (and Civil War general), selected the lighthouse site and designed the tower by modifying the Paul Pelz design used for St. Augustine. The changes included copying the "bell" lantern design from the Fowey Rocks Lighthouse. The noted architect, author, and painter Francis Hopkinson Smith is often mistakenly credited with designing the lighthouse.

In June 1884, General Babcock was being rowed ashore from the schooner *Pharos* to begin construction on the new Mosquito Inlet Lighthouse when his small boat overturned in the rough waters of the inlet; Babcock and three others drowned. Despite this tragedy, work stoppages due to a lack of funding, and mosquitoes, the lighthouse was completed under the supervision of his successor, Major Jared Smith, and first lighted on November 1, 1887. A massive hyper-radial Fresnel lens, built by Barbier & Bénard, was originally intended for the lighthouse, but a regular first-order fixed lens was installed instead.

In January 1897, author Stephen Crane was shipwrecked about ten miles off the coast. Stranded at sea in a ten-foot boat, he and three other men used the lighthouse as their guide to the shore. Crane immortalized the lighthouse in his short story "The Open Boat," one of the finest sea stories in the English language. During Prohibition, Bahamian rumrunners also used the light to navigate their cargoes into Daytona Beach, where federal agents waited in hopes of capturing the smugglers.

In 1933, the lighthouse's original first-order lens was replaced by a third-order revolving lens, and the light was electrified. A radio beacon was added in 1940. At the beginning of World War II, the keepers' families were removed from the light station, and it became a Coast Guard base from which to keep watch for enemy submarines. Several offshore sea battles took place, and many entries in the principal keeper's journal make note of military flotsam washing up on the beach.

The lighthouse was automated in 1952 and discontinued in 1970. Vandalism soon followed, and concerned local residents urged preservation. The Coast Guard deeded the lighthouse to the Town of Ponce Inlet, with the nonprofit Ponce de Leon Inlet Lighthouse Preservation Association formed to manage and restore the light station. Over the next four decades the lighthouse and all of the station buildings were restored. A gift shop, education center, administration building, and the Ayres Davies Lens Exhibit Building were added to the site. The latter building is home to one of the largest collections of Fresnel lenses in the world, including the original first-order lenses from Ponce Inlet and Cape Canaveral.

This light station is one of the most complete light stations in the nation, with all of its original buildings intact. It was placed on the National Register of Historic Places in 1972. In 1998, it was declared by the Secretary of the Interior to be a National Historic Landmark, the first lighthouse in Florida to receive this prestigious designation and one of only a handful in the nation. Much of this lighthouse's success can be credited to the leadership of the late Ann Caneer, one of the organization's early volunteers. She became operations manager in 1985 and later executive director. Caneer retired in 2007 and passed away in 2012.

SITE FACTS

Dates of Construction: 1884–1887
First Lighted: November 1, 1887
Electrified: 1933
Automated: 1952
Deactivated: 1970–1982
Tower Height: 175 feet
Focal Height: 159 feet
Designer/Architect: Paul Pelz & Orville E. Babcock
Builders/Supervisors: Orville E. Babcock, Jared A. Smith, James F. Gregory, and J. C. Mallery
Type of Tower: conical brick
Foundation Materials: brick

Construction Materials: brick, granite, and iron

Number of Stairs: 213

Daymark: red tower (with white ring near top), black lantern

Status: active—private Aid to Navigation

Original Optic: first-order fixed Fresnel lens (1887–1933)

Original Optic Manufacturer: Barbier et Fenestre (1867)

Other Optics Used: Carlile & Finch DCB-24 (1982), AmerAce FA-250-AC rotating beacon (1982–1991), Automatic Power FA-251 rotating beacon, (1991–1996), Vega VRB-25 (1996–2004)

Current Optic: third-order rotating Fresnel lens (1933–1970 and 2004–present)

Current Optic Manufacturer: Barbier, Bernard, et Turenne (1904)

Characteristic: fixed white light (1887–1933); six flashes in fifteen seconds followed by fifteen-second eclipse (1933–1970 and 2004–present); one white flash every ten seconds (1982–2004)

Station Auxiliary Structures: three brick keepers' dwellings with separate woodsheds/privies (1887), oil house, radio beacon transmitter building, pumphouse

National Register of Historic Places: yes—also a National Historic Landmark

Owner: Town of Ponce Inlet

Operating Entity: Ponce de Leon Inlet Lighthouse Preservation Association (nonprofit)

Grounds Open to the Public: yes

Tower Open to the Public: yes

Minimum Height to Climb: none

Lighthouse Museum: yes

Gift Shop: yes

Lighthouse Passport Stamp: yes—in gift shop

Hours: 10 AM–6 PM every day (until 9 PM Memorial Day through Labor Day); last admission one hour before closing

Adult Admission: $6.95

Handicapped Access: yes—to base of tower and throughout light station

Contact: Ponce de Leon Inlet Lighthouse & Museum, 4931 S. Peninsula Drive, Ponce Inlet, FL 32127

Phone: (386) 761-1821

Email: lighthouse@ponceinlet.org

Website: www.ponceinlet.org

DIRECTIONS

From the Volusia Bar Lighthouse, retrace your route to I-95 then continue south on that highway to Exit 256 (Dunlawton Avenue / SR 421). Take Dunlawton Avenue east across the Halifax River. Turn right (south) on Atlantic Ave. Go about five miles to Beach Street. Turn right (west) then turn left (south) on Peninsula Drive at the first stop sign. The lighthouse parking lot is two blocks south on the left.

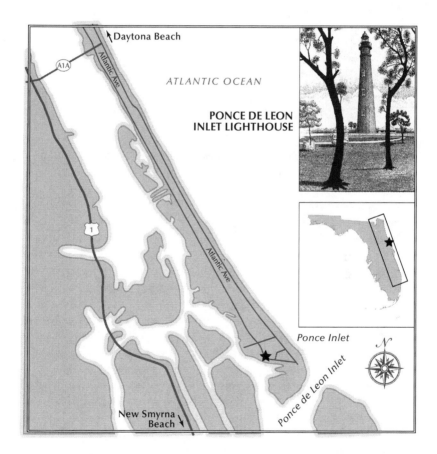

MOSQUITO INLET
LIGHTHOUSE

NEW SMYRNA BEACH, FLORIDA
(SITE ONLY)

Thomas W. Taylor

Since it was first explored by the Spanish in 1569, Mosquito Inlet (known since 1927 as Ponce de Leon Inlet) has been recognized as one of the most dangerous inlets on the east coast of Florida. The British erected a daybeacon on the north side of the inlet in 1774. In 1834, the US government authorized the construction of a lighthouse on the south side of the inlet for $11,000. This tower would be a forty-five-foot brick structure, surmounted by an iron lantern about ten feet tall. The site selected for the new lighthouse was on a twelve-foot-high, fifty-foot-wide sand dune near a second one on which a house had once stood. The location looked secure, but events would prove otherwise.

For $7,494 (much less than the appropriation), Winslow Lewis designed the lighthouse, contracted its construction, and outfitted it with eleven of his patent lamps with fourteen-inch reflectors. The new lighthouse and its brick keeper's dwelling were completed on February 2, 1835. Unfortunately, the whale oil fuel for the lighthouse lamps was lost when the schooner carrying it caught fire in Savannah. As the oil never arrived, the new lighthouse keeper found it impossible to light the lamps. This would not be the worst calamity to befall this lighthouse.

In September 1835, a hurricane struck. It did little damage except for blowing down a few trees and smashing a number of the glass panes in the lighthouse's lantern. To protect the remaining delicate lamps, the keeper removed them to the security of his dwelling until new glass could arrive with which to repair the lantern. Then, in October came the "high gale," which would spell the eventual end of the lighthouse. In this storm, the keeper's dwelling was completely destroyed, and the base of the dune upon which the lighthouse stood began to erode. The keeper fled with his family to the comfort of his nearby plantation, and the lighthouse was abandoned.

In late 1835, Seminole Indians went on the warpath, beginning the Second Seminole War. The nearby town of New Smyrna was a target, and on Christmas Day, under the war leader Coácoochee, "Wildcat," Indians attacked local plantations and then burned the town. The next day, they arrived at the abandoned lighthouse where they smashed the rest of the glass in the lantern. No oil was available to use in setting fire to the wooden parts of the lighthouse. Before leaving, they gathered some booty, which included the shiny reflectors from the lighthouse lamps. Three weeks later, Coácoochee was seen wearing one of these reflectors as a headdress during the Battle of Dunlawton Plantation. After the battle, a local settler found a reflector in the underbrush not far from the battlefield, and it is possible that this might be the same reflector that the famed Seminole leader had worn. The reflector remains a prized possession of the settler's descendants, long thought to be the only piece of an original Lewis lamp remaining in Florida. Today, an original Lewis lamp lens is on exhibit in the Lens Exhibit Building at Ponce Inlet Lighthouse, part of the lighthouse's collection and one of only a few known to exist.

Because of the Second Seminole War, engineers could not get to the lighthouse to repair it. In April 1836, its foundation thoroughly undermined, the structure collapsed into the sea. It is believed to have been the first lighthouse ever attacked by Indians in North America. Six months later, the first Cape Florida Lighthouse would suffer a similar fate.

SITE FACTS

Dates of Construction: 1834–1835
First Lighted: never (completed February 5, 1835)
Deactivated: n/a
Tower Height: 55 feet
Focal Height: 62 feet
Designer/Architect: Winslow Lewis
Builder/Supervisor: Timothy C. Knowlton and Elias Bourne
Type of Tower: conical brick
Foundation Materials: brick
Construction Materials: brick and iron
Number of Steps: unknown
Daymark: white tower
Status: destroyed (1836)
Original Optic: 11 Lewis Lamps with 14-inch reflectors
Other Optics Used: none
Current Optic: none
Characteristic: fixed white (never lighted)
Station Auxiliary Structures: none
National Register of Historic Places: no
Owner: Volusia County (site)
Operating Entity: Volusia County Parks (site)
Grounds Open to the Public: yes
Tower Open to the Public: N/A
Lighthouse Museum: yes—at Ponce Inlet Lighthouse
Gift Shop: yes—at Ponce Inlet Lighthouse
Lighthouse Passport Stamp: no
Hours: sunrise-sunset (site)
Handicapped Access: no
Contact: none

DIRECTIONS

From the Ponce de Leon Inlet Lighthouse, retrace your route to Dunlawn Avenue (SR 421). Cross the Halifax River bridge then turn left (south) on US Highway 1. Travel a little over nine miles to New Smyrna. Turn left (east) on Washington Street, which becomes North Causeway, then cross the North Indian River. Turn left (north) on Peninsula Avenue. Follow about two miles to Smyrna Dunes Park. The park entrance is next to the 1930s Coast Guard Station Ponce de Leon Inlet, which was responsible for the Ponce de Leon Inlet Lighthouse from 1952 to 1970 (the station is not open to the public). The exact site of the Mosquito Inlet Lighthouse is unclear and may be underwater; there are no ruins or markers to view. A long boardwalk around the park will give you a good idea of what the peninsula looked like when the lighthouse was here.

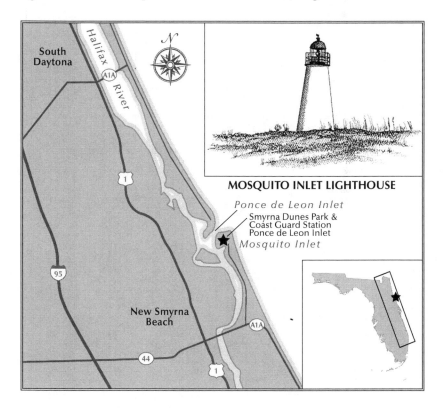

MOSQUITO INLET LIGHTHOUSE

CAPE CANAVERAL LIGHTHOUSE

CAPE CANAVERAL, FLORIDA

Neil Hurley and Josh Liller

Cape Canaveral was well known by early Spanish explorers and is one of the oldest named places in North America. European charts of Florida after 1513 show *Cabo de Canaveral* ("Cape of Cane"), named after the reeds or other long grasses that must have grown extensively on the cape. According to historian Sonny Witt, the Ais Indians make arrows and spears from the cane growing along the Banana River, hence why it made such a strong impression on the Spanish.

Sandy shoals lying off the southeast tip of the cape made the area dangerous for shipping. In 1848, a sixty-five-foot-tall brick tower was built by the federal government. First lit by fifteen lamps with twenty-one-inch reflectors, the lighthouse showed a flashing white light. Its first keeper, Nathaniel Scobie, abandoned the lighthouse during a Seminole Indian uprising in 1849. The third keeper of Cape Canaveral Lighthouse was Mills Olcutt Burnham, who served at the lighthouse for thirty-three years. Many of the keepers who served with or after him at the lighthouse were his descendants or relatives by marriage.

At the start of the Civil War, Cape Canaveral was the only Florida lighthouse still using Lewis lamps. During the war, Burnham obeyed the orders of the Confederate government to remove the lighthouse's lamps and reflectors, which he sent to St. Augustine. He carefully hid other lighthouse supplies in his nearby orange grove for the duration of the war. After the war, he returned the supplies and, in an unusual occurrence, was reinstated to federal service. The lighthouse was relighted on June 1, 1867, with a fourth-order lens.

Even before the Civil War began, a contract was let to build a taller tower that could be seen farther from land. No work could be done until the war was over, so the new tower—151 feet tall and built of cast iron with a brick lining—wasn't completed and first lighted until 1868. The West Point Foundry in New York produced the ironwork. The tower was constructed with living quarters inside for the assistant keepers (the head keeper remained in the original 1849 dwelling), but the Florida climate made this impractical, so they lived in small wooden dwellings instead. In 1878, a new dwelling was built for the head keeper, with a dwelling of identical design constructed in 1883 for the assistant keepers.

The lighthouse's distinctive daymark—black and white horizontal bands—was added in 1873. An 1879 earthquake shook the lighthouse badly enough to throw oil from the lamp onto the lens. During the Great Freeze of 1894, assistant keeper Frank Wilson "heard several reports like a gun" while on watch and in the morning found that the freezing temperatures cracked two of the iron brackets supporting the upper deck.

Shoreline erosion threatened the tower in the late 1880s. After several years of attempting to halt the erosion, the lighthouse was disassembled piece by piece and moved over a mule-drawn tramway to a site one and one quarter miles inland. During the move, a fourth-order lens on a temporary wooden structure served as a substitute for the lighthouse. The relocated and rebuilt tower was first lighted on July 25, 1894. Both keeper dwellings were demolished and rebuilt at the new site and a third dewelling added. A brick oil house was constructed to store kerosene for the lamp. Ironically, the erosion problem soon abated and the original site is still dry land.

In 1931, a radio beacon transmitter and diesel generator were installed in the base of the lighthouse. The generator provided electricity to the station for the first time. A door was also installed on the ground floor of the tower at this time, providing easier access to both the transmitter and generator. Until this time, keepers would have to ascend the exterior staircase to the main door on the third floor, then descend the interior stairs to the lower floors.

The lighthouse reservation, which had been expanded to eight hundred acres as part of the 1894 relocation, made an excellent location for missile and rocket tests. Most of the reservation was transferred to the Air Force after World War II. The new Cape Canaveral Air Force Station would eventually encompass seventeen thousand acres. Construction on the first launch pads began in 1949, with the first launch in July 1950. The space program remains active on the Cape, both NASA and private companies, and numerous past and present launch sites are visible from the lighthouse or along the road leading to it.

Cape Canaveral and its lighthouse were briefly renamed Cape Kennedy (1963–1973) after the assassination of President John F. Kennedy, a major proponent of the space program. The lighthouse was automated in 1967, and soon thereafter the Coast Guard permitted the keeper's dwellings to be burned down in firefighter training exercises. Due to the damage caused by decades of nearby rocket launches, the lighthouse's Fresnel lens was removed in 1993. The restored lens is on display in the Ayres Davies Lens Exhibit Building at Ponce Inlet Lighthouse.

The lighthouse was transferred to the US Air Force in 2000 and restored in 2003. The nonprofit Cape Canaveral Lighthouse Foundation formed in 2002 to assist in the preservation and interpretation of the lighthouse. Unfortunately, post-9/11 security issues cut off almost all public access for many years. Monthly bus tours to the lighthouse started again in 2017 and, as of 2019, van tours are also available. A replica of one of the keeper dwellings was completed in 2019 as an interpretive center, with plans to rebuild the other two dwellings in the future.

SITE FACTS

Dates of Construction: 1848 (original tower); 1867–1868 (current tower); 1894 (moved and rebuilt)

First Lighted: 1848; May 10, 1868; July 25, 1894

Electrified: 1931 (diesel generator); 1949? (Commercial power)

Automated: 1967

Discontinued: never

Tower Height: 55 feet (1848); 145 ft (1868 and 1894)

Focal Height: 65 feet (1848); 139 feet (1868); 155 feet (1894); 57 feet (1893–1894 beacon)

Designer/Architect: unknown (1848); probably William F. Smith (1868)

Manufacturer: West Point Foundry, West Point, NY (1868)

Builder/Supervisor: Nathaniel Scobie (1848); unknown (1868 and 1894)

Type of Tower: conical brick (original); conical iron with interior brick lining (current)

Foundation Materials: brick and stone

Construction Materials: brick and iron

Number of Stairs: 179

Daymark: alternating white and black horizontal bands (since 1873), with a black lantern

Status: active public aid to navigation

Original Optic (original tower): 15 Lewis Lamps with 21-inch reflectors

Original Optic (current tower): first-order revolving Fresnel lens (1868–1993)

Original Optic Manufacturer (current tower): Henry-Lepaute (1860)

Other Optics Used: fourth-order fixed Fresnel lens (1867–1868); fourth-order revolving Fresnel lens (temporary, 1893–1894)

Current Optic: DCB-224 (1993–present)

Characteristic: flashing white (1849–1861); one white flash every minute (1868–1931); one white flash every fifteen seconds (1931–1950s); three white flashes every sixty seconds (1950s–1993); dual flash every twenty seconds (1993–present)

Station Auxiliary Structures: oil house (1894); replica of 1894 keeper dwelling (2019)

National Register of Historic Places: yes

Owner: US Air Force

Operating Entity: 45th Space Wing (USAF) & Cape Canaveral Lighthouse Foundation (nonprofit)

Grounds Open to the Public: yes, but limited access requiring advance tour registration

Tower Open to the Public: yes, but limited access requiring advance tour registration

Lighthouse Museum: yes

Gift Shop: yes

Lighthouse Passport Stamp: yes—at gift shop

Hours: during bus tours and special events

Handicapped Access: yes

Contact: Cape Canaveral Lighthouse Foundation, PO Box 1978, Cape Canaveral, FL 32920

Phone: (321) 307-2900

Website: www.canaverallight.org (CCLF); www.canaverallighthouse.tours (tours)

DIRECTIONS

From Mosquito Inlet Lighthouse at Smyrna Dunes Park, take Peninsula Avenue south to South Causeway (SR 44) and turn right (west). Take SR 44 to I-95 and turn left onto the southbound on-ramp. Take the ramp for Exit 205A (Martin Anderson Beachline Expressway / SR 528) and head east. The Expressway crosses the Indian River and Banana River.

For regular bus or van tours of the lighthouse (reservations must be made in advance), take the last exit for George King Blvd (sign for Port Canaveral: Cruise Terminal B and South Cargo Piers; no exit number). Make a left from the off-ramp (east), then take the first left on Dave Nisbet Drive. Tours depart from the Exploration Tour, a large and unmistakable sail-shaped building.

To reach the main gate for Cape Canaveral AFB, instead take the exit for SR 401 (sign for Port Canaveral: Cruise Terminal A and North Cargo Piers; no exit number). SR 401 leads directly to the base. However, at this time there is no public drive-up access to the lighthouse. The Sands Space History Center is on the right just before the base main gate; it has free exhibits about the various missiles and rockets tested at Cape Canaveral near the lighthouse.

You may also wish to visit the Brevard Museum of History and Natural Science, which has a scale model of the lighthouse in the lobby. If so, take Exit 45 from the Beachline Expressway onto Industry Road southbound; make an immediate left onto SR 501; and make a right on Michigan Avenue. The museum will be on the left at 2201 Michigan Avenue and is open 10 AM–5 PM Thursday–Saturday. (Lobby is free; $9 adult admission to the whole museum.)

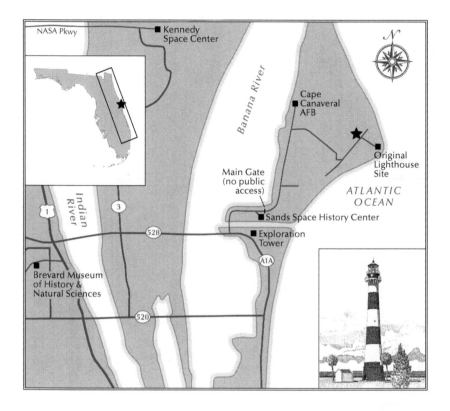

JUPITER INLET LIGHTHOUSE

JUPITER, FLORIDA

Josh Liller

Maritime shipping interests called for a seacoast lighthouse near the Jupiter Inlet at least as early as 1850. The Lighthouse Board's 1852 report listed Jupiter as the top priority for the entire Atlantic and Gulf coasts. George Meade selected a location on a sand hill a half-mile inland from the Jupiter Inlet in 1854 and created the original design for the lighthouse and keeper's dwelling. Congress allocated $35,000 for the project, and an executive order designated 61.5 acres as a lighthouse reservation.

The Third Seminole War delayed construction for several years. William Raynolds succeeded Meade as district engineer and made several improvements to Meade's design: extended the tower's height, added a double wall, and used granite brackets (instead of iron) to hold up the gallery deck.

Work finally resumed in early 1859, but Jupiter Inlet proved too shallow to use and supplies had to be shipped via the Indian River from the next inlet to the north. Progress was slow, and the workers departed in the summer due to the harsh climate. Work resumed in January 1860 and was completed in May. Jupiter Inlet Lighthouse was first lighted in July 1860.

Following the outbreak of the Civil War, Jupiter's remote location initially protected it. However, in August 1861, local Confederate sympathizers chased off the head keeper and disabled the lighthouse. They removed the lamp, fuel, and other vital supplies but left the lens in place and intact. Blockade runners used the Jupiter Inlet to travel between the Indian River and Bahamas, resulting in the Union Navy blockading the inlet. Union and Confederate personnel made several visits to the lighthouse, which made a convenient observation post.

The lighthouse was repaired and returned to service in June 1866 with a new first-order lens. The climate and location caused numerous problems in the early years for supply, maintenance, and hiring keepers. Seminoles made many visits to trade, and tourist parties on hunting and fishing trips to the Florida wilderness became an increasingly common sight. The three keepers initially shared one house, but a separate home for the head keeper was built in 1883. The lighthouse converted from lard oil to kerosene in 1886. Starting around 1905, the tower was painted dark red, having been unpainted brick until that time.

In 1925, a new survey of the lighthouse reservation found that it comprised 122 acres—not 61.5 as originally thought. A fire destroyed the original keeper's house in late 1927. The lighthouse was electrified early the next year and a radio beacon added. The light's characteristic was altered at this time by rearranging some of the lens panels and installing blanking panels. During a major hurricane in September 1928, the backup generator failed and the lens had to be turned by hand for several days. One of the bullseye lens panels broke during the storm and was repaired with a metal crossbar, which remains in place today. A new duplex for the assistant keepers was built in 1929 to replace the one destroyed by fire. A ficus tree was planted at the site of the old keeper's house in the early 1930s and remains standing as of 2019, having grown to substantial size.

The Coast Guard heavily renovated the station in 1959 to 1960, replacing the 1883 keeper dwelling with two modern concrete block houses and removing many auxiliary buildings. In 1962, nine additional houses were added near the lighthouse for personnel assigned to LORAN Station Jupiter, located eight miles to the north. Besides the LORAN Station housing, the lighthouse also shared the site over the years with a weather bureau station (1888–1911), a naval radio station (1905–1947), and a tracking station for missile tests (1951–1980s).

The former oil house was converted to a small museum in 1973, operated by the local historical society. In 1987, the lighthouse was automated. In 1994, the nonprofit Loxahatchee River Historical Society (LRHS) received a lease from the Coast Guard to open the lighthouse for tours and to be responsible for its restoration and maintenance. The lighthouse and oil house were restored in 1999 to 2000, returning to the dark red tower and black lantern daymark. A new museum opened in 2006 in the last surviving naval radio station building.

In 2008, LRHS led a successful campaign to have the lighthouse reservation designated by Congress as Jupiter Inlet Lighthouse Outstanding Natural Area, part of the Bureau of Land Management's National Conservation Lands system. The Coast Guard began the process of closing their station in 2013, with the transfer to the Bureau of Land Management completed in 2019. LRHS remains the lead partner, providing historical interpretation and preservation of the lighthouse and site.

SITE FACTS

Dates of Construction: 1859–1860
First Lighted: July 1860
Electrified: 1928
Automated: 1967 (partly); 1987 (fully)
Tower Height: 108 feet
Focal Height: 146 feet
Designer/Architect: George G. Meade and William F. Raynolds
Builder/Supervisor: Edward A. Yorke
Type of Tower: conical brick

Foundation Materials: brick and coquina
Construction Materials: brick, granite, and iron
Number of Steps: 105
Daymark: red tower with black lantern
Status: active—public Aid to Navigation
Original Optic: first-order revolving Fresnel lens (1860–1866)
Original Optic Manufacturer: L. Sauter (1854)
Other Optics Used: flashing 190 mm beacon (temporary 1999–2000)
Current Optic: first-order FVF Fresnel lens (1866–present)
Current Optic Manufacturer: Henry-Lepaute (1863)
Characteristic: prolonged white flashes (1860–1861); fixed white light var-
    ied by flashes (1866–1928); two flashes followed by an eclipse, repeating
    every thirty seconds (1928–present)
Station Auxiliary Structures: oil house (1860), radio beacon transmitter and
    generator building (1929), pump house and workshop (1929), three-
    bay garage (1929), two keeper dwellings (1960), nonlighthouse historic
    structures
National Register of Historic Places: yes (1975)
Owner: Bureau of Land Management
Operating Entity: Loxahatchee River Historical Society (nonprofit)
Grounds Open to the Public: yes
Tower Open to the Public: yes
Minimum Height to Climb: 48 inches (4 feet)
Lighthouse Museum: yes
Gift Shop: yes
Lighthouse Passport Stamp: yes—in gift shop
Hours: Daily 10 AM–5 PM. Last admission 4 PM. Closed Mondays May–
    Christmas.
Adult Admission: $12 (lighthouse, grounds, and museum)
Handicapped Access: museum and main grounds, but not to base of light-
    house
Contact: Jupiter Inlet Lighthouse & Museum, 500 Captain Armours Way,
    Jupiter, FL 33469
Website: www.jupiterlighthouse.org

DIRECTIONS

From I-95, take Exit 87A and go east on Indiantown Road to Alternate A1A. Turn left (north); the road crosses a bridge and curves east to intersect with US Highway 1. Go straight through the intersection, then take the first right into Lighthouse Park. The museum and gift shop are at the south end of the park on the riverfront. The lighthouse is a quarter-mile walk on a brick path from the museum.

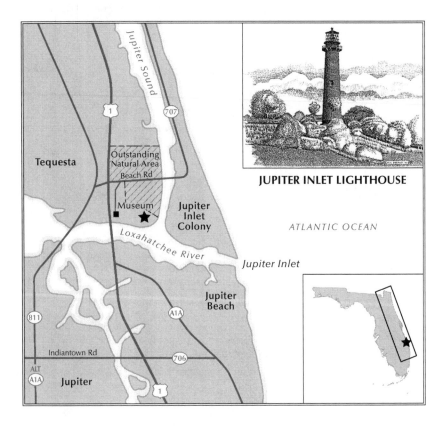

JUPITER INLET LIGHTHOUSE

HILLSBORO INLET LIGHTHOUSE

POMPANO BEACH, FLORIDA

Hibbard Casselberry

As ships sailing south often hugged the coast to avoid the north flow of the Gulf Stream, they could strike one of three offshore reefs. This is the north end of the coral reefs along the south Florida coast.

The Lighthouse Service first recommended a lighthouse near Hillsboro Inlet in 1852. The US Coast & Geodetic Survey team surveyed the area in 1884, which further indicated the need for a seacoast light between Jupiter and Fowey Rocks. It was not until 1902 that Congress began allocating funds for the project. Construction of the lighthouse on the north side of the inlet lasted from 1905 until early 1907 and finished under the $90,000 budget.

The beauty of this iron, skeletal lighthouse is its lantern room, which houses the beautiful bivalve Fresnel lens. The curved-glass exterior of this room—with diamond-shaped glass panes held by brass fittings—was something quite new and elegant in 1906. The combination of lens and panes gave the lighthouse its nickname, "Big Diamond."

The Hillsboro Inlet area has had a colorful history. The Great Miami Hurricane of 1926 washed away six hundred feet of land between the lighthouse and shore with its 132 mph winds, exposing the lighthouse foundation. To protect the foundation from future storms, a 260-foot stone breakwater was built in 1930.

Thomas Knight was by far the lighthouse's longest-serving principal keeper, from 1911 until 1936, except for six months at Jupiter Inlet Lighthouse in 1919. During Prohibition, Knight's brother built a restaurant on an island west of the inlet. Much of the illegal booze aboard rum-running boats entering the inlet was served at this restaurant, Club Unique (still in business as "Cap's Place"). During World War II, Club Unique was rumored to have been a secret meeting place for President Franklin Roosevelt, Prime Minister Winston Churchill, Prime Minister Anthony Eden, and others. They would often spend some R&R near the lighthouse, as would General MacArthur and Admiral Nimitz. To this day, top brass in the Coast Guard still use the keeper's cottages for vacations.

During World War II, battles were fought in the shadow of the lighthouse. German subs patrolled offshore; one grounded on the reefs. In May 1942, the tanker *Lubrofol* was torpedoed off Hillsboro Beach. A naval patrol boat rescued all but two of the crew. Some stories claim U-boats were sunk or captured nearby, but this has never been verified from official documents.

In 1992, the lens stopped rotating because of a broken gear. Some of the 450 pounds of mercury (on which the lens floated and revolved) evaporated, contaminating the air inside the lighthouse. The decision was made to remove all the mercury and discontinue use of the lens. To replace the lens, a 190 mm rotating beacon was attached to the east railing as a "temporary light," but this failed in 1998 and was replaced by a Vega VRB-25 optic. In 1996, the Coast Guard performed a Section 106 review, which recommended that the Fresnel lens be removed from the lighthouse and displayed in a historical museum. Local lighthouse enthusiasts persuaded the Coast Guard to keep the lens in the lighthouse and suggested a new design using ball bearings. With great fanfare, the Hillsboro Light shone again in its glory at the relighting ceremony on January 28, 1999. The new system lasted only a month before the weight of the massive lens crushed the bearings. Commercial-grade bearings were installed in July 2000 and have proven durable and effective ever since.

Restoration work in the 2010s included new panes of lantern glass and a replica of the lighthouse's historic entrance walkway and handrails. The tower's skeletal structure underwent a multiyear three-phase restoration project. Some of the iron parts were so badly corroded by the humid, salty air that replacements had to be fabricated. A small lighthouse museum and gift shop opened across the inlet in 2012.

As of 2019, the Coast Guard continues to use the former keeper dwellings as vacation rental homes. Access to the lighthouse remains limited to one Saturday each month, with visitors brought in by boat from a nearby marina.

SITE FACTS

Dates of Construction: 1905–1907
First Lighted: March 8, 1907
Electrified: February 26, 1932
Automated: 1973
Deactivated: never
Tower Height: 144 feet
Focal Height: 136 feet
Designer & Manufacturer: Russell Wheel & Foundry, Detroit, MI
Builder/Supervisor: J. H. Gardiner of New Orleans
Type of Tower: octagonal pyramidal skeletal
Foundation Materials: concrete footers with lead and steel bolts into limestone bedrock
Construction Materials: iron
Number of Stairs: 175
Daymark: bottom half white, top half black (including lantern)
Status: active—public Aid to Navigation
Original Optic: second-order bivalve Fresnel lens

Optic Manufacturer: Barbier, Bénard, & Turenne (1904)

Other Optics Used: 190 mm rotating beacon (1992–1997), Vega VRB-25 (1997–2000)

Current Optic: original lens

Characteristic: one white flash every twenty seconds

Station Auxiliary Structures: two wooden keeper dwellings (1907), two storehouses (1907), radio beacon building (1944)

National Register of Historic Places: yes (1979)

Owner: US Coast Guard

Operating Entity: Hillsboro Lighthouse Preservation Society (nonprofit) & USCG Auxiliary

Grounds Open to the Public: yes—limited schedule

Tower Open to the Public: yes—limited schedule

Minimum Height to Climb: 48 inches

Lighthouse Museum: yes—Hillsboro Inlet Park, 2700 N. Ocean Blvd., Pompano Beach, FL

Hours: museum open all tour days 10 AM–3 PM, and Thursday–Sunday and Tuesday 11 AM–3 PM; lighthouse usually open one Saturday per month (check website or contact museum for schedule)

Gift Shop: yes—in museum

Lighthouse Passport Stamp: yes—in museum

Handicapped Access: museum yes, light station grounds partly

Contact: Hillsboro Lighthouse Preservation Society, PO Box 326, Pompano Beach, FL 33060

Phone: (954) 942-2102

Email: information@hillsborolighthouse.org

Website: www.hillsborolighthouse.org

DIRECTIONS

From Jupiter Inlet Lighthouse, retrace your route to I-95 and take the southbound flyover on-ramp. Take Exit 36A (Atlantic Blvd / SR 814) and go east, crossing the Intracoastal Waterway.

If you are taking a HLPS boat tour to visit the lighthouse, take your first left after the bridge onto North Riverside Drive. Tours usually depart from the north end of the dock at Sand Harbor Resort & Marina (fee parking lot available across the street), but check the tour schedule to be certain.

To visit the lighthouse museum, instead take the second left after the bridge onto North Ocean Blvd. Proceed north just over two miles to Hillsboro Inlet Park on the right. The only building in the park is the museum. There is also an excellent view from the park of the lighthouse and inlet. There is no public drive-up access to this light station.

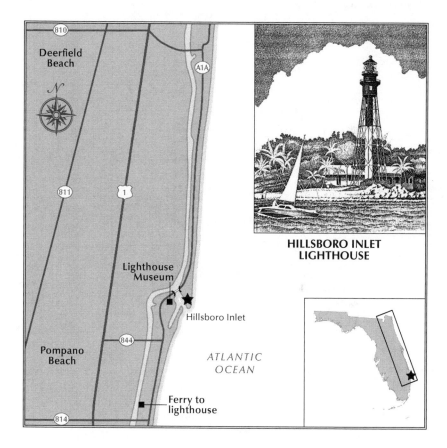

HILLSBORO INLET
LIGHTHOUSE

CAPE FLORIDA LIGHTHOUSE

KEY BISCAYNE, FLORIDA

Joan Gill Blank

The Cape Florida Lighthouse, located at the southern tip of the barrier island of Key Biscayne, is the second oldest surviving structure in southeast Florida (only the 1844 Fort Dallas barracks is older).

It was originally built in 1825. Shipwrecks and piracy obstructed international trade and commerce along the sparsely settled territory, prompting Congress to appropriate $8,000 in 1821 and an additional $16,000 in 1824 to build a navigational light at the northern end of the Great Florida Reef. It was lighted by keeper John DuBose on December 17, 1825.

In July 1836, during the Second Seminole War, more than forty Seminole Indian warriors attacked and set fire to the lighthouse and keeper's dwelling, injuring a temporary keeper and killing his assistant. In 1838, a military fort and hospital were established near the burned-out lighthouse. A new lighthouse at the same location was completed and lighted in October 24, 1846. The surviving Cape Florida Lighthouse is frequently described as an 1825 structure. However, historical documents make it clear the original tower was completely demolished, thus what stands today is an 1846 structure.

The lighthouse soon proved to have inadequate range. In 1855, Lt. George G. Meade sought to solve the problem by extending the tower from sixty-five to ninety-five feet and adding a new lantern with a second-order Fresnel lens. The improved tower was first lighted on April 15, 1856.

In August 1861, Confederate sympathizers traveled from Jupiter to Key Biscayne and smashed the Fresnel lens. Cape Florida Lighthouse was repaired and returned to service on April 15, 1866, with a new lens.

For the next twelve years, the beacon was tended by keepers and their families, braving tropical hurricanes, rattlesnakes, and mosquitoes on the remote sand island. On June 15, 1878, the onshore light was superseded by the Fowey Rocks Lighthouse five and a half nautical miles away on the Florida Reef. The last of Cape Florida's keepers, John Frow, moved offshore to the new lighthouse. The decommissioned Cape Florida tower was conscripted during the Spanish-American War as the Cape Florida Signal Station. It was briefly leased to the Biscayne Bay Yacht Club until descendants of the first landowners purchased the light station. Beach erosion in the early twentieth century endangered the base, and a "maximum security" foundation was privately rebuilt for $10,000. When the owners died, Cape Florida was again abandoned.

After a bridge was built to Miami, development threatened Key Biscayne. Happily, Cape Florida was bought and preserved as public park land, with its coastal landmark owned and protected by the state of Florida at Bill Baggs Cape Florida State Park, which opened in 1967. The Coast Guard reactivated the lighthouse in 1978—a century after it had been abandoned—to help ships navigating into the Port of Miami, but they discontinued it again in 1987. Listed on the National Register of Historic Places, the tower underwent a million-dollar restoration to its 1856 condition in 1996. The deteriorated ironwork was replaced by steel replicas. The 1856 iron lantern and other artifacts from the lighthouse are now an outdoor display near the lighthouse. A replica keeper's cottage and cookhouse serve as an interpretive museum.

The southern end of Key Biscayne has been steadily eroding away since the lighthouse was built. It originally stood a quarter mile from the ocean, but now a seawall and jetty are all that keep the lighthouse safe. Out of Florida's surviving lighthouses, Cape Florida is the one most endangered by sea level rise.

SITE FACTS

Dates of Construction: 1825 (original); 1846 (current); 1855–1856 (extension)

First Lighted: December 17, 1825 (original); October 24, 1846 (current)

Electrified: 1978 (when relighted)

Automated: 1978 (when relighted)

Discontinued: 1878–1978 and 1987–1996

Tower Height: 95 feet

Focal Height: 100 feet

Designer/Architect: probably Winslow Lewis (1825 and 1846); George G. Meade (1855)

Builder/Supervisor: Samuel B. Lincoln and Noah Humphries (1825); Leonard Hammond (1846); George G. Meade (1855)

Type of Tower: conical brick

Foundation Materials: brick

Construction Materials: brick, iron, and wood (1825); brick, granite, and iron (1846); brick, granite, and steel (1996)

Number of Stairs: 112

Daymark: white tower, black lantern

Status: active—private Aid to Navigation

Original Optic: seventeen Lewis lamps with 21-inch reflectors

Other Optics Used: second-order fixed Fresnel lens (1856–1861), second-order fixed Fresnel order lens (1866–1878), fifth-order (375 mm) drum lens (1978–1987)

Fresnel Lens Manufacturers: Henry-Lepaute (1855?)

Current Optic: 300 mm aero beacon

Characteristic: fixed white light (1800s); one white flash every five seconds

Station Auxiliary Structures: replica keeper's dwelling (1970), replica summer kitchen (1970), replica cistern (1970), replica outhouse

National Register of Historic Places: yes

Owner: State of Florida

Operating Entity: Bill Baggs Cape Florida State Park

Grounds Open to the Public: yes—daily

Tower Open to the Public: yes, on a limited schedule

Minimum Height to Climb: 42 inches

Lighthouse Museum: yes—in keeper's dwelling

Gift Shop: no

Lighthouse Passport Stamp: yes—at state park ranger station

Hours: park open daily 8 AM–sunset; museum open 9 AM–5 PM, Thursday–Monday; tower open for climbing at 10 AM and 1 PM, Thursday–Monday

Handicapped Access: yes

Adult Admission: $8/car park admission; no additional cost for lighthouse and museum

Contact: Bill Baggs Cape Florida State Park, 1200 S. Crandon Blvd., Key Biscayne, FL 33149

Phone: (305) 361-8779

Email: none

Website: https://www.floridastateparks.org/index.php/parks-and-trails/bill-baggs-cape-florida-state-park/cape-florida-light

DIRECTIONS

From Hillsboro Inlet Lighthouse, retrace your route to I-95. Head south through Miami to Exit 1A. From the off-ramp go straight, then turn left at the second intersection onto Rickenbacker Causeway (SR 913). The causeway has a $2.25/car toll. Follow the causeway to and through Key Biscayne where it becomes Crandon Blvd. The entrance to Bill Baggs State Park is the south end of Crandon Blvd. The park has an $8/car admission fee. Follow the main park road to the south end of the park. The light station area is gated with a covered seating area if you need to wait for the lighthouse to open. The lantern and other outdoor displays are outside the station gate.

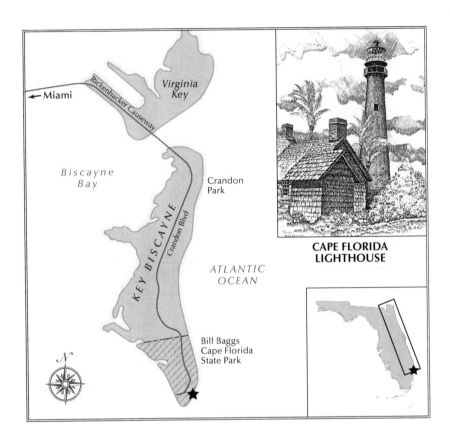

Miami ←

Rickenbacker Causeway

Virginia
Key

Biscayne
Bay

Crandon
Park

KEY BISCAYNE

Crandon Blvd

ATLANTIC
OCEAN

Bill Baggs
Cape Florida
State Park

N

**CAPE FLORIDA
LIGHTHOUSE**

SECTION II
THE FLORIDA KEYS

FOWEY ROCKS LIGHTHOUSE

OFF MIAMI, FLORIDA

Love Dean and Josh Liller

Fowey Rocks Lighthouse is one of a series of six iron-pile lighthouses in the Florida Keys known as the Reef Lights. Built between 1852 and 1880, these navigational aids mark the only living barrier coral reefs in North America. Although these historic lighthouses are not open to the public, most can be seen from shore and are easily reached by boat.

In 1873, the Lighthouse Board noted that Cape Florida Lighthouse "is so situated as to be almost useless as a guide to navigators." They recommended a new lighthouse be built seven miles to the southeast on a portion of the Florida Reef known as Fowey Rocks. The site chosen was named, as were so many reefs in the Keys, for a shipwreck. The HMS *Fowey*, a twenty-gun British warship commanded by Capt. Francis William Drake, sank in this area in 1748. Named after a city in Cornwall, England, Fowey is pronounced "foh-wee," but Americans often pronounce it "fow-ee" instead.

This was the fifth and most difficult of the Reef Lights to build. The Lighthouse Board successfully requested $100,000 for the project in 1874, but difficulties with the open-water site—particularly delays caused by rough seas—resulted in a final cost of $163,015.60. Due to the hard coral rock at the site, the lighthouse's nine iron piles were driven ten feet into the sea floor with a pile driver rather than using screwpiles. There were also delays in the manufacture of the superstructure. The builders chose Soldier Key, a small island four miles from the lighthouse site, as project headquarters. A work platform was built on the reef site, and launches transferred the workmen back and forth. When bad weather set in, the work crew remained out on the platform. They were provided with tents, provisions, and building materials.

During the first month the men lived and worked under these conditions, there was only one day of good weather. The seas crashed constantly against the pilings under the men's precarious perch. Twice, steamers headed in their direction, threatening to demolish the platform. The *Arratoon Apcar* hit the reefs just yards from the platform and was wrecked. The *Carondelet* is also reported to have run aground on Fowey Rocks during the construction.

After three years of difficult construction, the lighthouse was finally lighted on June 15, 1878. Thousands of people had already seen the lantern and lens. The Lighthouse Board had featured both as part of a special display at one of the greatest exhibitions of the century—the 1876 Philadelphia Centennial Exposition. The display proved so popular that the board decided to prepare another exhibit for the 1892 to 1893 World's Columbian Exposition held in Chicago. Featured were a painting and a model of the Fowey Rocks Lighthouse.

The lighthouse switched from lard oil to kerosene lamps in 1886, and three red sectors were added to the lantern in 1893 to better mark the dangerous reefs nearby. In 1898, an oil house was built on a platform under the dwelling. In 1915, the light was changed from fixed to occulting with a double white flash, but retained its red sectors. A diesel generator was added in 1931, providing electricity for both the light and a new radio beacon that sent out its signal from an antenna on the lantern roof.

Fowey Rocks Lighthouse was automated in 1975, and the radio beacon moved ashore to the local Coast Guard station. The Fresnel lens was removed in 1982 and placed on display at the Coast Guard's Aids to Navigation School in Yorktown, Virginia. A RACON (radar beacon) was installed on Fowey Rocks in 1999. Biscayne National Park gained ownership of the lighthouse through the NHLPA process in 2012. The lighthouse still awaits restoration by NPS as of 2019. In the meantime, the Florida Lighthouse Association and Florida Keys Reef Lights Foundation have funded several stabilization projects, including the installation of sacrificial anodes to protect the iron piles.

The 115-foot lighthouse is the first navigational light seen by ships approaching the city of Miami from the south. Neil Hurley, historian for the Florida Lighthouse Association, suggests that this is why Fowey Rocks Lighthouse was nicknamed "The Eye of Miami."

SITE FACTS

Dates of Construction: 1875–1878
First Lighted: June 15, 1878
Electrified: 1931 (diesel generator)
Automated: 1975
Deactivated: never
Tower Height: 115 feet
Focal Height: 110 feet
Designer/Architect: unknown
Manufacturer: Paulding, Kimble, & Company, Cold Spring, NY (foundation); Pusey, Jones, & Company, Wilmington, DE (tower)
Builder/Supervisor: Jared A. Smith
Type of Tower: octagonal skeletal
Foundation Materials: driven iron piles
Construction Materials: iron
Number of Stairs: 77
Daymark: white dwelling with green shutters, white cylinder, brown frame, black lantern

Status: active

Original Optic: first-order fixed Fresnel lens (1878–1982)

Optic Manufacturer & Date: Henry-Lepaute (1876)

Other Optics Used: flash tube array (1982–1983), 300 mm optic (1983–1985), 190 mm optic (1985–1997)

Current Optic: Vega VRB-25 (1997–present)

Characteristic: fixed white (1878–1893); fixed white with three red sectors (1893–1915); occulting with two flashes every ten seconds, with three red sectors (1915–1950s); occulting white with two flashes every ten seconds, with two red sectors (1950s–1982); one flash every ten seconds, with two red sectors (1982–present)

Station Auxiliary Structures: structure includes dwelling

National Register of Historic Places: yes (2011)

Owner: National Park Service

Operating Entity: Biscayne National Park

Grounds Open to the Public: yes—open water

Tower Open to the Public: no

Lighthouse Museum: no

Gift Shop: yes—Dante Fascell Visitor Center, Homestead, FL

Hours: N/A

Lighthouse Passport Stamp: yes—at Dante Fascell Visitor Center or mail Florida Keys Reef Lights Foundation

Handicapped Access: no

Contact: Biscayne National Park, 9700 SW 328th Street, Homestead, FL 33033

Phone: (305) 230-1144

Email: bisc_information@nps.gov

Website: www.nps.gov/bisc/

DIRECTIONS

The best place to view Fowey Rocks Lighthouse from land is the top of Cape Florida Lighthouse. Fowey is located about seven miles to the southeast. The lighthouse is only accessible by boat. The nearest public boat ramp is at Crandon Park on the north end of Key Biscayne. Crandon Park Marina, Rickenbacker Marina on the causeway to Key Biscayne, several marinas in Coconut Grove, and Homestead Marina are all possible locations for charter, fishing, or dive boats that may take you to Fowey Rocks.

Biscayne National Park's Dante Fascell Visitor Center is near the Homestead Marina. From southbound Florida Turnpike Homestead Extension or US 1, take Tallahassee Road (Exit 6) south, then turn left (east) on 328th Street and go almost to the end. Just before the marina, turn left at the large park entrance sign.

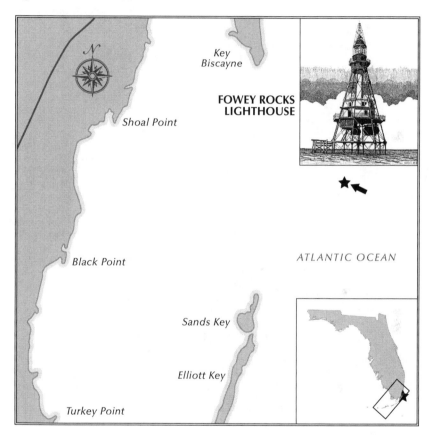

CARYSFORT REEF LIGHTHOUSE

OFF KEY LARGO, FLORIDA

Love Dean and Josh Liller

CARYSFORT REEF FLA.

This easternmost section of the Florida reefs was named for the twenty-eight-gun frigate HMS *Carysford*, which ran aground here in 1770. Years later, the name was misspelled "Carysfort," and it has remained that way ever since. Charts noted the position of the reef as early as 1775, but it remained unmarked until 1826 when the US Lighthouse Service stationed the lightship *Caesar* on the ocean side of the reef. The wooden vessel suffered severe dry rot and had to be replaced by the new lightship *Florida*. Violent storms often blew the lightship off station, and mariners deemed its lights inadequate. A lighthouse was badly needed to mark this navigational hazard.

Funding was first allocated for Carysfort Reef Lighthouse in 1837. Winslow Lewis proposed a masonry tower could be built in the water (akin to the later Minot's Ledge Lighthouse). It was not until Englishman Alexander Mitchell invented the iron screwpile design that building a lighthouse on the submarine site was feasible. Ironically, screwpiles proved ill suited to the seafloor at Carysfort Reef, so straight piles were used instead. Each of the nine pilings was made of wrought iron eight inches thick, encased in a two-inch-thick cast iron sleeve. They were driven ten feet into the sand, with foot plates six feet in diameter providing additional stability.

A Philadelphia foundry was contracted to manufacture the prefabricated iron structure. The lighthouse was first assembled at the foundry, then disassembled and shipped to the reef site along with trained workmen and all needed supplies. The lighthouse had a circular keeper's dwelling with a balcony, in contrast to the more angular dwellings found on the other Reef Lights.

Work on the site began in 1848, with installation of the structure beginning late the following year. The first supervisor, Capt. Stansbury, was reassigned to a survey expedition, and the second, Maj. Linnard, died of natural causes. I. W. P. Lewis, Winslow Lewis's nephew, had created the original design and oversaw some of the early work. Lt. George G. Meade oversaw the completion of the project, the first of several he would be involved with in Florida. The entire lighthouse cost $105,069.

Carysfort Reef was intended to be the first US lighthouse to use a Fresnel lens from the beginning. However, mistakes by the New York Customs Office resulted in the lens being tied up in legal issues, so the lighthouse was instead first lighted with Lewis lamps. It was not until 1858 that a revolving first-order Fresnel lens was installed, and apparently not the one originally intended for the lighthouse since the frame is stamped with the year 1857. The new lens was first lighted on March 17, the same day Sombrero Key Lighthouse was first lighted.

The tropical climate proved extremely harsh on the iron structure, and annual reports frequently mention problems with oxidation. Kerosene lamps were installed in 1884, which were in turn replaced by IOV lamps in 1912. Red sectors were added in 1893 to mark the Florida Reef. The characteristic was further altered in 1912 with the placement of a blanking panel over every fourth bull's-eye lens. A diesel generator provided electricity beginning in 1938.

In September 1945, a major hurricane made landfall in the Homestead area, where it did serious damage to several military bases. The eye of the hurricane passed over Carysfort Reef Lighthouse where pressure dropped as low as 953 millibars, sustained winds peaked at 123 mph, and gusts were as high as 138 mph. Hurricane Donna buffeted Carysfort in 1960 and destroyed the wooden balcony around the upper story of the keeper's dwelling.

In 1960, the light was automated and the first-order lens replaced by a third-order lens. Although it was a fixed lens, the electric light allowed the characteristic to remain flashing. In 1975, Carysfort was the first Reef Light converted to solar power. A modern optic replaced the Fresnel lens in 1982. The last optic used was a solar-powered Vega VRB-25 rotating beacon. A RACON was added in 1999. The lighthouse was last repainted in 1996.

Even with the most modern technology, the living coral reefs in the Keys have sustained enormous damage from ships. From 1984 to 1989, there were four major groundings near Carysfort Reef Lighthouse, one causing a twenty-thousand-square-foot gouge in the reef, which is still evident. The shock and dismay caused by these preventable accidents were shared by people throughout the country. On November 16, 1990, President George Bush signed a bill that created a thirty-five-hundred-square-mile Florida Keys National Marine Sanctuary stretching from Biscayne National Park to the Dry Tortugas, including both the Atlantic and Gulf of Mexico sides.

In the 1990s, the Pennekamp Coral Reef Institute tried to establish a research station at Carysfort but fundraising proved difficult and the Coast Guard was reluctant to allow the lighthouse to be repurposed. The Coast Guard discontinued Carysfort Reef Lighthouse in 2014, citing safety concerns with the tower, and replaced it with a nearby forty-foot modern ATON with an LED beacon. The lighthouse was released through the NHLPA process in 2019.

Both Fresnel lenses formerly used in Carysfort Reef Lighthouse are on display, although only one to the public. The first-order Fresnel lens has been prominently exhibited at History Miami (formerly the Historical Society of South Florida Museum) since the 1960s. The third-order lens was originally displayed at Coast Guard Station Islamorada, but in recent years has been moved to Coast Guard Station Miami, where it can be seen in the base cafeteria.

SITE FACTS

Dates of Construction: 1848–1852
First Lighted: March 10, 1852
Electrified: 1938 (diesel generator)
Automated: 1962
Deactivated: 2014
Tower Height: 112 feet
Focal Height: 106 feet
Designer/Architect: I. W. P. Lewis & Howard Stansbury
Manufacturer: Merrick & Towne, Philadelphia, PA
Builders/Supervisors: Howard Stansbury, I. W. P. Lewis, Thomas B. Linnard, and George G. Meade
Type of Tower: octagonal pyramidal skeletal
Foundation Materials: iron piles
Construction Materials: wrought iron
Number of Stairs: unknown
Daymark: dark red structure with white roof and white dwelling shutters (1852–1870s); dark brown structure, white lantern (1870s–1890?); dark brown structure, black lantern (1890?–1910s); brown (1910s–1990s); dark red with white dwelling shutters and white roof (1990s–present)
Status: inactive
Original Optic: 18 Lewis lamps with 21-inch reflectors (1852–1858)
Other Optics Used: first-order revolving Fresnel lens (1858–1962), third-order fixed Fresnel lens (1962–1982), flash tube array (1982–1983); 300 mm optic (1980s), 190 mm revolving optic (1980s–1990s), Vega VRB-25 (1990s–2015)
Fresnel Lens Manufacturers: Henry Lepaute (1857); unknown
Current Optic: none
Characteristic: fixed white (1852–1858); one white flash every thirty seconds (1858–1893); one white flash every thirty seconds, with three red sectors (1893–1912); three flashes every twenty seconds, with three red sectors (1912–1982); three flashes every sixty seconds, with three red sectors (1982–2015)
Station Auxiliary Structures: integral keeper's dwelling
National Register of Historic Places: yes (1984)
Owner: General Services Administration (pending transfer or auction)
Operating Entity: none
Grounds Open to the Public: yes—open water

Tower Open to the Public: no
Lighthouse Museum: no
Gift Shop: no
Hours: N/A
Lighthouse Passport Stamp: yes—Florida Keys Reef Lights Foundation
Handicapped Access: no
Contact: Florida Keys Reef Lights Foundation

DIRECTIONS

From Cape Florida, return to the mainland. Turn left (south) on US Highway 1. Turn right (west) onto the ramp for the Snapper Creek Expressway (SR 878). Snapper Creek will merge onto the Don Shula Expressway (SR 874) southbound then onto the Florida Turnpike Homestead Extension southbound, which ends on US Highway 1 southbound in Florida City. You can avoid the toll roads and remain on US 1, but it will usually be a much slower drive. Either way, from Florida City, continue south on US 1 to Key Largo. Carysfort Reef Lighthouse is only visible by land from the Ocean Reef Club, a private community; there is no public viewing location.

The offshore lighthouse is only accessible by boat. The closest public boat ramp is John Pennekamp State Park. Many charter fishing and dive boats operate from Key Largo, including Amy Slate's Amoray Dive Resort (305-451-3595; www.amoray.com) and Captain Slate's Scuba Adventures (305-451-3020; www.captainslate.com).

ALLIGATOR REEF LIGHTHOUSE

OFF ISLAMORADA, FLORIDA

Love Dean and Josh Liller

ALLIGATOR REEF FLA.

Alligator Reef Lighthouse is situated on a reef named for a schooner that went hard aground here in 1822. Because of the activity of pirates along the Florida Keys, the commander of the USS *Alligator* decided to scuttle his ship rather than leave anything that could be used by the marauders. Both the lighthouse and the wreck of the USS *Alligator* have been nominated to the National Register of Historic Places.

The area near Islamorada is excellent for fish but hazardous for marine navigation. A lighthouse was first proposed for Indian Key in 1837. A thirty-six-foot-high iron screwpile daymark was erected in 1852 to mark the dangerous reef. Serious plans for a lighthouse at Alligator Reef were first made in 1857, with an estimated cost of $130,000. The Civil War intervened, but afterward the Lighthouse Board revisited the matter of sufficiently lighting the Florida Reef. Alligator Reef was the most important of three lighthouses proposed for that purpose in 1867. Congress allocated $100,000 for the project in 1870, but further funding was required. The final cost for the lighthouse was $185,000.

Engineers selected an area thirty yards from the 1852 daybeacon and about two hundred yards from the deep water of the Gulf Stream as the most suitable site for a lighthouse. The first step was the construction of a supply depot and work camp four miles away on Indian Key. Material and equipment for the lighthouse began arriving at Indian Key in January 1872.

Because of the exposed position of the site, with the sea breaking heavily on the reefs at times, many delays occurred during the construction of the foundation. Workmen used a piledriver powered by a portable steam engine to drive the twenty-six-foot-long iron foundation piles through disks and into the coral. The hammer on the piledriver weighed two thousand pounds, and the hammer fell on the piles from an average distance of about eighteen feet. Each blow forced the piles anywhere from one-half inch to one-and-one-half inches into the coral. The piles had to be driven ten feet deep into the reef. It took workers a year to complete the lighthouse.

Once the lighthouse was in service, the Lighthouse Board wrote, "This is one of the finest and most effective lights on the coast." The board considered the light tower to be the most gracefully designed iron-pile structure in the Keys. Wrought iron had also proven to be a durable building material. Other than the lantern, Alligator Reef is a very similar design to Sombrero Key Lighthouse.

The lighthouse switched to kerosene lamps in 1884, and shortly thereafter an oil storage room was hung underneath the dwelling to safely store the fuel. The apparatus was upgraded again in 1913 with an IOV lamp. Alligator Reef had a revolving Fresnel lens from the beginning, but the specific characteristic changed several times. It used a combination of white and red flashes, with red sectors added in 1891 to denote the position of the Florida Reef. In 1914, the red flashes were discontinued although the red sectors remained.

On September 2, 1935, Alligator Reef Lighthouse found itself directly in the path of a Category 5 hurricane. "The Labor Day Hurricane" remains the most intense hurricane in US history, in terms of both barometric pressure and sustained winds at time of landfall. Gusts exceeded 200 mph. All the glass in the lantern was blown out, and the first-order Fresnel lens was destroyed. Two glass panes from the lighthouse's red sectors were reportedly found on the beach at Islamorada, somehow still intact. Doors and windows blew out on the keeper's dwelling, the landing platform and boats washed away, and the two keepers were forced to seek shelter on the central column stairs. The keepers witnessed a twenty-foot storm wave sweep past the lighthouse on its way to Upper Matecumbe Key. Almost everything along the shore was wiped out. In the Islamorada area, 423 people were killed.

In 1960, Hurricane Donna hit the upper Keys. As the storm wave surged toward the lighthouse, the Coast Guardsmen on duty climbed to the lighthouse's highest platform and lashed themselves to the iron structural braces to keep from being blown away. Luckily, no one had to endure the hardship or terror of being aboard Alligator Reef Lighthouse during Hurricane Betsy in 1965—the light was automated in June 1963.

In the 1960s, Dr. Walter Starck conducted a scientific study at Alligator Reef for *National Geographic Magazine*. Dr. Starck identified a total of 517 species of fish on Alligator Reef, including nineteen new species and sixty other species previously unknown in North American waters.

The first annual Swim for Alligator Reef was held in 2013. More than four hundred participants make an eight-mile open-water roundtrip journey from the south end of Islamorada to Alligator Reef Lighthouse and back. The event raises funds for local groups, and also raises awareness of Alligator Reef and the other Reef Lights.

A RACON was added to Alligator Reef in 1999. The light was discontinued in 2015, replaced by a small modern beacon on a thirty-foot tower nearby. The lighthouse was released through the NHLPA process in 2019.

SITE FACTS

Dates of Construction: 1871–1873
First Lighted: November 25, 1873
Tower Height: 150 feet

Focal Height: 136 feet

Designer/Architect: unknown—probably Charles E. Blunt

Manufacturer: Paulding, Kemble, & Company, West Point Foundry, Cold Spring, NY

Builder/Supervisor: unknown—probably Charles E. Blunt

Type of Tower: octagonal skeletal

Foundation Materials: iron piles

Construction Materials: wrought and cast iron

Number of Stairs: unknown

Daymark: white dwelling, cylinder, and frame; black lantern and pilings

Status: inactive

Original Optic: first-order revolving Fresnel lens (1873-1935)

Other Optics Used: second-order bivalve Fresnel lens (1935-1982), flash tube array (1982-1983), 190 mm rotating beacon (1983-1990s), Vega VRB-25 (1990s-2015)

Fresnel Lens Manufacturers: unknown; Henry-Lepaute (1928)

Current Optic: none

Characteristic: one flash every five seconds, alternating white and red (1873-1880); one flash every five seconds, two white followed by one red (1880-1891); one flash every five seconds, two white followed by one red, with two red sectors (1891-1914); four white flashes every fifteen seconds, with two red sectors (1914-2015)

Station Auxiliary Structures: integral dwelling

National Register of Historic Places: yes (2011)

Owner: General Services Administration (pending transfer or auction)

Operating Entity: none

Grounds Open to the Public: yes—open water

Tower Open to the Public: no

Lighthouse Museum: no

Gift Shop: no

Hours: N/A

Lighthouse Passport Stamp: yes—Florida Keys Reef Lights Foundation

Handicapped Access: no

Contact: Florida Keys Reef Lights Foundation

DIRECTIONS

From Key Largo, continue south on US Highway 1 to Islamorada. The lighthouse is only accessible by boat, but it is the closest to land of all six Reef Lights (3.5 miles offshore). It can be seen from the Indian Key Fill Causeway connecting Upper and Lower Matecumbe Keys. Several marinas offer rental, fishing, and dive boat trips to Alligator Reef. Your best options are Robbie's at the south end of the causeway (305-664-8080 / www.robbies.com) or Bud & Mary's Marina at the north end of the causeway (305-664-2461 / www.budnmarys.com).

Florida Keys History & Discovery Center (82100 Overseas Hwy., Islamorada; 305-922-2237; www.keysdiscovery.com) has a small exhibit about Alligator Reef Lighthouse, including the prism from the lighthouse's lens.

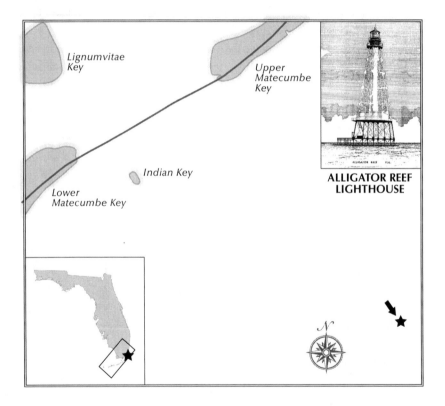

SOMBRERO KEY LIGHTHOUSE

OFF MARATHON, FLORIDA

Love Dean and Josh Liller

Sombrero Key, named Cayo Sombrero ("Hat Island") by the Spanish, is about seven miles offshore from the town of Marathon in the Middle Keys. The foundation pilings of Sombrero Key Lighthouse, the tallest of the Reef Lights, sink deep into a shallow plain of elkhorn and staghorn coral. On the Gulf Stream side, there are large, parallel coral formations reaching out like fingers. At other places on the reef, there are caves and surprising, twisting channels between coral heads, rising twenty-five feet from the bottom. Brightly colored tropical fish are always plentiful on this diverse reef formation.

In 1852, Congress began appropriating funds for a lighthouse near an area of the Florida Reef known as Coffins Patches shoal, about halfway between the lighthouses at Carysfort Reef and Sand Key. Before beginning construction of the Sombrero Key Lighthouse, George Meade had insisted that the nine, twelve-inch iron foundation pilings be galvanized, a fairly new process at the time. He also used thicker pilings with wider footers than had been used at Carysfort or Sand Key. Meade predicted that these pilings would last two hundred years. Meade's plans for the lighthouse were approved in 1854. Although Meade worked on several South Florida lighthouses, Sombrero Key was the only one for which he deserves sole credit for the design.

Construction did not begin until late 1855 due to the need for further funding. The work suffered two setbacks in 1856: Meade's transfer to a survey project in the Great Lakes and the damage done to the work site by a hurricane passing through the Florida Straits in August 1856. Meade's successor, William Raynolds, reconsidered the location in the aftermath of the storm. When work resumed late that year, it was at a new location nearly ten miles west on the Florida Reef, a sporadic island known as Dry Banks or Sombrero Key. Raynolds brought Meade's design to completion and lighting in 1858 with a first-order Fresnel lens. The final cost was $153,156.17. The lighthouse was officially known as Dry Banks until 1873, at which time it was renamed Sombrero Key.

The lighthouse upgraded to kerosene lamps in 1884 and IOV lamps in 1913. An oil room suspended under the dwelling was added in 1889, and red sectors were added to the lantern in 1893. Rotating blanking panels were installed inside the fixed lens in 1914 to make the characteristic a series of five flashes. The Coast Guard manned Sombrero Key Lighthouse from 1939 until it was automated in 1960. The original first-order Fresnel lens, removed in 1982, is on display at the Key West Lighthouse Museum.

Sombrero Key was deactivated in 2015 and released through the NHLPA process in 2019.

SITE FACTS

Dates of Construction: 1855–1858
First Lighted: March 17, 1858
Electrified: 1938 (diesel generator)
Automated: 1960
Deactivated: 2015
Tower Height: 149 feet
Focal Height: 142 feet
Designer/Architect: George G. Meade
Manufacturer: Merrick & Towne, Philadelphia, PA
Builder/Supervisor: George G. Meade and William F. Raynolds
Type of Tower: square pyramidal skeletal
Foundation Materials: galvanized iron piles
Construction Materials: galvanized iron
Number of Stairs: 133
Daymark: red (1858–1870s); brown structure, white lantern (1870s–1890s);
    brown structure, black lantern (1890s–1990s); red (1990s–present)
Status: inactive
Original Optic: first-order fixed Fresnel lens (1858–1982)
Optic Manufacturer: Henry-Lepaute (1857)
Other Optics Used: flash tube array (1982–1983); 300 mm beacon (1980s);
    190 mm rotating beacon (1990s); Vega VRB-25 (1990s–2015)
Current Optic: none
Characteristic: fixed white (1858–1893); fixed white with three red sectors
    (1893–1914); five flashes every fifteen seconds, with three red sectors
    (1914–1982); five flashes every minute (1982–2015)
Station Auxiliary Structures: integral dwelling
National Register of Historic Places: yes (2012)
Owner: General Services Administration (pending transfer or auction)
Operating Entity: none
Grounds Open to the Public: yes—open water
Tower Open to the Public: no
Lighthouse Museum: no
Hours: N/A
Gift Shop: no
Lighthouse Passport Stamp: yes—Florida Keys Reef Lights Foundation
Handicapped Access: no
Contact: Florida Keys Reef Lights Foundation

DIRECTIONS

Continue south on US Highway 1 (Overseas Highway) to Marathon. At Mile Marker 50, turn left on Sombrero Beach Road (CR 931) and follow that road to its terminus at Sombrero Beach. The lighthouse is visible four-and-one-half miles to the south, with a sign pointing it out. An alternative view is available from near the east end of the Seven Mile Bridge.

The lighthouse is only accessible by boat. There are a number of dive boats and fishing charters available in Marathon that make regular trips to Sombrero Key, including Captain Hooks Marina and Dive Center (11833 Overseas Hwy.; 305-743-2444; www.captainhooks.com). There are also several public boat ramps, including Mile Marker 54 and the end of 33rd Street.

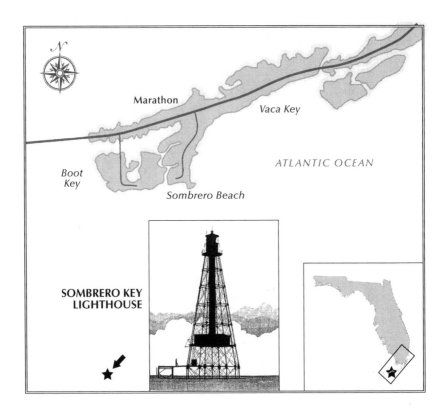

AMERICAN SHOAL LIGHTHOUSE

OFF SUGARLOAF KEY, FLORIDA

Love Dean and Josh Liller

AMERICAN SHOAL FLA.

American Shoal Lighthouse was the final iron screwpile lighthouse built on the Florida Reef. The site originally chosen for the light was Looe Key, named for the HMS *Looe*, a frigate of the Royal Navy that sank on the reef in 1744. The area still contains some remains of the frigate and other wrecks. Looe Key, designated a National Marine Sanctuary in 1981, is a prime example of reef life at its fullest. In an area just over five square nautical miles, Looe Key embodies the diversity of plant and animal life that snorkelers as well as advanced divers come to see. The American Shoal Lighthouse, southwest of Looe Key, is almost identical in design to the Fowey Rocks Lighthouse off Miami, without the Victorian flourishes or bell-shaped dome.

The need for a navigational marker on American Shoal was recognized in 1850, when a thirty-six-foot-high iron screwpile was erected as a daymark. But more than daymarks and lighted aids were needed to prevent vessels from going aground on the coral reefs. Following the completion of Alligator Reef Lighthouse in 1873, the Lighthouse Board sought funding for a lighthouse on or near Looe Key to fill the last remaining unlighted gap in the Keys. Congress finally appropriated $75,000 for the lighthouse in 1878 and an additional $50,000 the following year. Phoenix Ironworks manufactured the entire iron structure in 1879. Construction began late that year, and the lighthouse was ready by the summer of 1880, making it by far the quickest and easiest construction project of the six Reef Lights. The final cost was $93,665.48, which also made it the cheapest of the six.

American Shoal Lighthouse switched to kerosene lamps in 1886 and an IOV lamp in 1913. Three red sectors were added to the lantern in 1893, marking the nearby reefs. An oil house hanging under the dwelling was added in 1899. The lighthouse was electrified in the 1930s using a diesel generator and automated in 1963.

The lighthouse served not only as an important navigational aid, but also as a Coast Guard radar/visual station during the Cuban refugee exodus of 1980. Six Coastguardsmen were assigned to the lighthouse during that time, and the lighthouse continued to operate automatically as a lighted beacon. At the completion of the exodus, Lt. R. C. Eccles reported, "There is no doubt in my mind that these lights can be effectively utilized to put another small dent in the tremendous flow of illegal maritime activity that transpires in and around the Keys."

Ironically, American Shoal Lighthouse would be the scene of a small immigrant crisis when twenty-one Cubans attempting to flee to the United States sought refuge on the unmanned structure. A legal battle ensued over whether the lighthouse was legally equivalent to actual dry land, and thus whether they would be allowed to remain in the United States or be sent back to Cuba.

In 1999, Coast Guard Aid to Navigation personnel installed radar beacons (RACONs) on American Shoal Lighthouse and the other five Reef Lights. RACONs produce a distinctive image on the screens of radar sets and are visible to most commercial shipboard radar systems six to twenty miles from the lighthouses. These devices are of great benefit to mariners in preventing groundings and provide valuable protection for the living reef and marine environment.

This stark and sturdy-looking lighthouse was honored by the US Postal Service in its American lighthouses postage stamp series issued on April 26, 1990. American Shoal Lighthouse was deactivated in 2015. Two years later it suffered serious lantern damage from Hurricane Irma. The lighthouse was released through the NHLPA process in 2019.

SITE FACTS

Dates of Construction: 1879–1880
First Lighted: July 15, 1880
Electrified: 1938 (diesel generator)
Automated: 1963
Deactivated: 2015
Tower Height: 115 feet
Focal Height: 109 feet
Designer/Architect: unknown
Manufacturer: Phoenix Iron Company, Trenton, NJ
Builder/Supervisor: unknown (probably William H. Heuer)
Type of Tower: octagonal pyramidal skeletal
Foundation Materials: iron screwpiles
Construction Materials: iron
Number of Stairs: unknown
Daymark: brown, with white cylinder (1880–1890s and 1910s–1990s); brown framework and dwelling, white cylinder, black lantern (1890s–1910s); red (1990s–present)
Status: inactive
Original Optic: first-order revolving Fresnel lens (1880–1982)
Optic Manufacturer: Henry-Lepaute (1874)
Other Optics: flash tube array (1982–1983), 190 mm rotating beacon (1983–1990s), Vega VRB-25 (1990s–2015)
Current Optic: none

Characteristic: one white flash every five seconds (1880–1893); one white
flash every five seconds, with three red sectors (1893–2015)
Station Auxiliary Structures: integral keeper's dwelling
National Register of Historic Places: yes (2011)
Owner: General Services Administration (pending transfer or auction)
Operating Entity: none
Grounds Open to the Public: yes—open water
Tower Open to the Public: no
Lighthouse Museum: no
Hours: N/A
Gift Shop: no
Lighthouse Passport Stamp: yes—Florida Keys Reef Lights Foundation
Handicapped Access: no
Contact: Florida Keys Reef Lights Foundation

DIRECTIONS

From Marathon, continue south on US Highway 1 across the Seven Mile Bridge
to Sugarloaf Key. Turn left on Sugarloaf Boulevard (CR 939). Go just over five
miles to Sammy Creek Landing, on the left just before the bridge over Sugarloaf
Creek. The lighthouse is visible to the south.

The lighthouse is only accessible by boat. Various charter boats from Big
Pine Key, Little Torch Key, Cudjoe Key, and Sugarloaf Key make trips to Looe
Key and American Shoal. Your best option is probably Captain Hook's Looe
Key Reef Adventures & Strike Zone Charters, 29675 Overseas Hwy., Big Pine
Key (305-872-9863 / www.captainhooks.com).

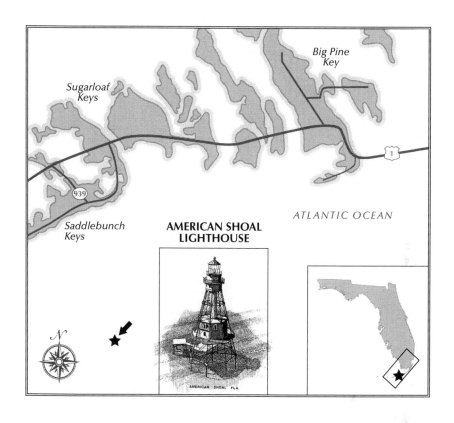

Sugarloaf
Keys

Big Pine
Key

Saddlebunch
Keys

939

1

ATLANTIC OCEAN

**AMERICAN SHOAL
LIGHTHOUSE**

AMERICAN SHOAL FLA.

N

KEY WEST
LIGHTHOUSE

KEY WEST, FLORIDA

Thomas W. Taylor

Although known today primarily as a tourist destination, Key West is one of the oldest cities in Florida. During most of the nineteenth century, it was the largest port and largest city in the territory/state. It was also the headquarters for the Seventh Lighthouse District.

The first lighthouse at Key West was lighted on March 10, 1826. It was built on Whitehead Point, which was then the southwestern corner of the island (not to be confused with the modern "Southernmost Point"). Described by the local superintendent of lights as "unquestionably one of the best lights" in the country, this tower was destroyed by a hurricane in 1846. The foundation of the tower, long believed to have been washed out to sea, was found in the 1990s. The site is now within the grounds of the NAS Key West Truman Annex.

A second lighthouse was built further inland on a more sheltered hill, fifteen feet above sea level, about halfway up today's Whitehead Street. This was the first lighthouse built within the limits of a city. Its thirteen whale oil lamps were first lighted on January 15, 1848. The replacement lighthouse cost $25,317.28. In 1858, a magnificent third-order Fresnel lens, which serves in the tower to this day, was installed.

The keeper of the new lighthouse, Barbara Mabrity, had succeeded her husband as keeper of the old lighthouse in 1832. She served at the new lighthouse until 1863, possibly when pro-Confederate statements were attributed to her and, at the age of eighty-two, she was encouraged to retire from her position by federal officials. The Coast Guard honored Barbara Mabrity by naming a new buoy tender after her in 1999.

During the nineteenth century, there were many changes at the Key West Lighthouse. It received a new lantern in 1873. In 1887, a new keeper's dwelling was constructed and an oil house added in 1891, both of which still exist. In early 1895, the tower was extended twenty feet, and another new lantern was mounted on top. In 1898, the lighthouse witnessed the arrival of the battleship *Maine* on its way to Havana harbor and its tragic destiny.

Hurricanes devastated Key West many times in the past century, but the lighthouse endured them all. In 1915, the lighthouse was automated with acetylene. The keeper's dwelling, no longer inhabited by keepers, became the home of William W. Demeritt, superintendent of the Seventh Lighthouse District.

Throughout the twentieth century, the lighthouse was a destination for many visitors. One who came to visit decided to stay. He purchased a house across the street from the lighthouse, and the fixed white light would shine into his bedroom window. The new Key West resident was Ernest Hemingway. Legend later reported that he sometimes wrote under the huge false banyan tree next to the lighthouse tower.

The lighthouse was decommissioned in 1969, after 121 years of service. The light station became "Key West Lighthouse and Military Museum" until 1990 when it became a dedicated lighthouse museum. Thanks to the Key West Art and Historical Society, the tower and keeper's dwelling have been restored and are open to the public. The historic Fresnel lens is still in the lighthouse, although it no longer serves as a navigational aid. The lighthouse is a sight every visitor to Key West must see.

SITE FACTS

Dates of Construction: 1825–1826, 1847, and 1895

First Lighted: March 10, 1826; January 15, 1848

Electrified: 1930s

Automated: 1915 (with acetylene)

Deactivated: 1969

Tower Height: 83 feet (1826); 60 feet (1848); 86 feet (1895)

Focal Height: 70 feet (1826); 67 feet (1848); 72 feet (1873); 91 feet (1895)

Designer/Architect: Smith, Keeney, and Hollowday Company (1848)

Builder/Supervisor: Duncan Cameron (1848)

Type of Tower: conical brick

Foundation Materials: brick

Construction Materials: brick, granite, and iron

Number of Stairs: 88

Daymark: white tower, black lantern

Status: inactive, but lens still in place

Original Optic: 15 Lewis lamps with 15-inch reflectors (1826–1847); 13 Lewis lamps with 21-inch reflectors (1848–1858)

Other Optics Used: none

Current Optic: third-order fixed Fresnel lens (1858–present)

Fresnel Lens Manufacturer: Henry-Lepaute (1857)

Characteristic: fixed white light (1826–1893); fixed white light, with three red sectors (1893–1915); one flash every twenty-four seconds, with three red sectors (1915–1969)

Station Auxiliary Structures: keeper's dwelling (1887), oil house (1891)

National Register of Historic Places: yes

Owner & Operating Entity: Key West Art & Historical Society (nonprofit)

Grounds Open to the Public: yes

Tower Open to the Public: yes

Minimum Height to Climb: none
Adult Admission: $12
Lighthouse Museum: yes
Gift Shop: yes
Lighthouse Passport Stamp: yes—in gift shop
Hours: 9:30 AM–4:30 PM every day except Christmas
Handicapped Access: yes—to base of tower and in keeper's dwelling
Contact: Key West Lighthouse & Keeper's Quarters Museum, 938 White-
    head Street, Key West, FL 33040 (mailing address only; entrance is on
    Truman Avenue, not Whitehead Street)
Phone: (305) 294-0012
Email: kwahs@kwahs.org
Website: www.kwahs.org/museums/lighthouse-keepers-quarters/visit

DIRECTIONS

From Sugarloaf Key, return to US Highway 1 (Overseas Highway) and continue south to Key West. Turn right on Roosevelt Boulevard, which later
becomes Truman Avenue. Parking for the lighthouse is just past Whitehead
Street on the right. The parking lot is free for lighthouse visitors but cannot accommodate RVs, trailers, or other oversize vehicles. (Although the lighthouse's
mailing address is Whitehead Street and your GPS may try to take you there,
the parking lot is only accessible from Truman Avenue.)

The site of the original lighthouse cannot be visited as it is located within an
active Navy base. There are also no markers or landmarks on the base to identify
the site. The closest the public can get would be the corner of Fort Street and
Amelia Street. From the Key West Lighthouse parking, continue west on Truman Avenue. Turn left on Emma Street then right on Julia Street (one way),
then left on Fort Street. Keep in mind that almost everything west of Fort Street
only became dry land in the twentieth century.

While in Key West you may also want to visit the former Key West Lighthouse Depot, which served the Seventh Lighthouse District. The building
(at 291 Front Street) is now Clinton Square Market and is located next to the
Customs House Museum (also operated by the Key West Arts & Historical Society). From the current lighthouse parking lot, turn right on Truman Avenue,
right on Thomas Street, right on Olivia Street, and left on Whitehead Street.
(From the viewing location toward the site of the first lighthouse, follow Amelia
Street east then turn left on Whitehead Street.) Go north on Whitehead Street

until it ends at Front Street; the lighthouse depot is the large stone building across the street to the left. For the nearest parking, turn left on Front Street then turn right into the parking garage at 201 Front Street.

SAND KEY LIGHTHOUSE

SAND KEY
(OFF KEY WEST), FLORIDA

Love Dean and Josh Liller

Unlike the other Reef Lights, the Sand Key Lighthouse has never been considered an isolated station. It is located nine miles south southwest of the harbor of Key West on a small, white, sandy islet that often changes shape and sometimes disappears completely. As Key West developed, shipping activity in the vicinity of the light increased. Turtlers, fishermen, and wreckers often stopped on the island to collect birds' eggs and to socialize. It has always been an enticing spot to picnic.

The first brick light tower on the island, built in 1827, survived the officially recorded hurricanes of 1835, 1841, 1842, and 1844. But in 1846, storm waves surged over the island. The keeper's house and the light tower collapsed, killing the keeper and five others who had fled to the tower for safety. Sand Key disappeared, and the lightship *Honey* was moored nearby from 1847 to 1852.

Knowing the instability of the site, I. W. P. Lewis designed a wrought-iron screwpile lighthouse on Sand Key, with seventeen foundation piles (by far the most of any Florida lighthouse) secured to the underwater coral reefs. Lt. George Gordon Meade, who would eventually build or work on seven lighthouses in Florida, arrived in 1852 to take over the project. Meade's work at Sand Key earned him great praise from the Lighthouse Board. It has given him a measure of immortality, as the lighthouse has withstood all subsequent hurricanes even though the island has been washed away many times. Meade did not use the original lantern design for the lighthouse but instead substituted one of his distinct style also used at Sombrero Key, Cape Florida, and Jupiter. He also successfully introduced a hydraulic lamp of his own design and corrected some weaknesses in the original design.

Upon completion of the new tower, the Lighthouse Board dramatically described it as "one of the most important lights on the coast of the United States, constructed upon a plan comparatively novel in this country, and upon a site presenting many difficulties for the engineer."

Although the lighthouse itself could withstand hurricanes, auxiliary structures were not so fortunate. The station's wharf and boathouse had to be rebuilt many times. The dwelling and part of the tower were damaged by a pair of hurricanes in 1870 and a severe hurricane in September 1875. Insufficient maintenance in the harsh tropical climate also resulted in serious rust problems. The entire thirty-eight-square-foot dwelling was rebuilt in 1875 to 1876, along with numerous other repairs to the lighthouse.

The lighthouse upgraded to kerosene lamps in 1886 and to IOV lamps in 1913. In 1891, red sectors were added to the lamp and the characteristic changed to something unusual: fixed for one minute, then a twenty-five-second eclipse, then a ten-second flash, then a twenty-five-second eclipse.

The federal government constructed a weather bureau station on pilings at Sand Key in 1903. The weather station was destroyed by a 1909 hurricane, rebuilt in 1912, and severely damaged by another hurricane in 1919 before being discontinued in 1925.

What almost destroyed the Sand Key Lighthouse was a devastating fire in 1989. The damage was concentrated in the central core of the tower. The Coast Guard concluded that the lighthouse was still serviceable and should be salvaged. Renovations finally began in 1994 and were completed in 1999 at a cost of $500,000. The Sand Key Lighthouse still stands in 2019, sans stairwell and keeper's house. The lighthouse was discontinued in 2015, with a fifty-foot-tall modern ATON replacement built nearby. In 2018, Sand Key Lighthouse was released through the NHLPA process. No government sought ownership, and the only nonprofit applicant was denied. The federal government put the lighthouse up for auction in 2019.

SITE FACTS

Dates of Construction: 1827 and 1851–1853

First Lighted: 1827 and July 20, 1853

Electrified: 1930s

Automated: 1943

Deactivated: 1847–1853; 1989–1999; 2015–present

Tower Height: 65 feet (1826); 121 feet (1853)

Focal Height: 70 feet (1826); 110 feet (1853)

Designer/Architect: I. W. P. Lewis (original design) and George G. Meade (lantern and improvements)

Manufacturers: John F. Riley Ironworks, Charleston, SC (tower) and J. V. Merrick & Son, Philadelphia, PA (lantern)

Builders/Supervisors: I. W. P. Lewis, Thomas B. Linnard, and George G. Meade

Type of Tower: square pyramidal skeletal

Foundation Materials: brick (1826); iron screwpiles (1853)

Construction Materials: brick and iron (1826); iron (1853)

Number of Stairs: none currently (formerly 122)

Daymark: brown structure, white lantern (1858–1890s); brown structure, black lantern (1890s–1910s); brown structure and lantern (1910s–1997); brown structure and white lantern (1997–present)

Status: inactive

Original Optic: 14 Lewis lamps with 15-inch reflectors (1826–1840s); first-order FVF Fresnel lens (1853–1967)

Fresnel Lens Manufacturer: unknown

Other Optics Used: 14 Lewis lamps with 21-inch reflectors (1840s–1847); fourth-order fixed Fresnel lens (1967–1982); flash tube array (1982–1983); 300 mm flashing beacon (1983–1987); Vega VRB-25 (1999–2015)

Current Optic: none

Characteristic: one white flash every fifty-four seconds (1826–1847); fixed varied by one flash every two minutes (1853–1891); fixed varied by one flash every two minutes, with two red sectors (1891–1893); fixed varied by one flash every two minutes, with four red sectors (1893–1913); fixed light varied by one flash every minute, with red sectors (1914–1916); two white flashes every ten seconds, with two red sectors (1916–1982); two white flashes every fifteen seconds, with two red sectors (1983–2015)

Station Auxiliary Structures: none surviving

National Register of Historic Places: yes

Owner: General Services Administration (pending conclusion of auction)

Operating Entity: none

Grounds Open to the Public: yes—open water

Tower Open to the Public: no

Lighthouse Museum: no

Gift Shop: no

Hours: N/A

Lighthouse Passport Stamp: yes—at Key West Lighthouse Gift Shop or contact Florida Keys Reef Lights Foundation

Handicapped Access: no

Contact: Florida Keys Reef Lights Foundation

DIRECTIONS

The best place to see Sand Key Lighthouse from land is the top of the Key West Lighthouse, or alternatively, from the top of Fort Zachary Taylor or the Edward Knight Pier. Sand Key is 7 to 8 miles southwest of Key West, depending on your vantage point. The lighthouse is also visible in the distance from the ferry to the Dry Tortugas.

The Sand Key Lighthouse is only accessible by boat. The nearby reefs are a popular snorkeling spot, so a number of charter boat options exist from Key West. If you have your own boat, the nearest public ramps are 11th Street in Key West and Key Haven Boat Ramp between Mile Markers 5 and 6.

NORTHWEST PASSAGE LIGHTHOUSE

OFF KEY WEST, FLORIDA
(Lighthouse Site Only)
Neil Hurley

As early as 1833, mariners were petitioning Congress for a lighthouse to mark the Northwest Passage into Key West. The twelve-foot-deep natural channel could be used as a shortcut for vessels going from the Atlantic to ports in the Gulf of Mexico. The outer entrance to the channel is in open water, with no island or other point of reference nearby.

In 1838, a 145-ton lightship named the *Key West* was anchored to mark the entrance to the channel, located about seven miles from Key West. The lightship was poorly built, and the light had a bad reputation during most of its operation. In the hurricane of 1846, the anchor chain broke and the ship was pushed sixty miles to the north before it could sail back to its station.

By 1850, the high cost of maintaining the lightship made a lighthouse preferable. A plan for the new lighthouse was approved in early 1854. The dwelling section of the structure was prefabricated in Philadelphia and shipped to Key West, but a yellow fever outbreak delayed construction. Work began in November 1854 and, after further delays caused by rough seas, the lighthouse was first lighted on March 5, 1855. The light was a wooden cottage on wrought iron piles and with a galvanized iron roof. The fifth-order lens was visible ten miles away.

Although small and exhibiting a nonrevolving light, the isolated location necessitated two keepers. Like other Keys lighthouses, the Northwest Passage Lighthouse remained in operation throughout the Civil War. Because of wood rot, the entire wooden part of the lighthouse was replaced in 1879. The Lighthouse Board originally wanted $20,000 to build an entirely new lighthouse but settled for $6,000 to rebuild the dwelling. The light was upgraded to a fourth-order lens as part of this project. Kerosene lamps were installed in 1882. A small beacon was erected nearby in 1885 to form a range with the lighthouse. An oil house was added in 1899, hung under the dwelling on iron rods.

During an inspection of the lighthouse in 1911, it was recommended that the light be converted to acetylene gas and the station be unmanned. The light continued to operate until around 1921, when the iron lantern was removed and the hole roofed over. The deserted structure remained standing alongside the channel. Local rumor eventually erroneously labeled it as one of Ernest Hemingway's homes. In 1971, it was destroyed by fire, and today only the iron foundation pilings remain. It's easy to see the pilings, which lie in four feet of water on the west side of the channel entrance, about seven miles northwest of Key West.

SITE FACTS

Dates of Construction: 1854–1855; 1879
First Lighted: March 5, 1855; June 30, 1879
Electrified: never
Automated: 1913 (with acetylene)
Deactivated: June 30, 1921
Tower Height: 55 feet
Focal Height: 50 feet
Designer/Architect: George G. Meade
Builder/Supervisor: George G. Meade
Type of Tower: pile cottage
Foundation Materials: wrought iron pilings
Construction Materials: wood and iron
Number of Stairs: unknown
Daymark: white dwelling and lantern (1855–1879); white dwelling, black
    lantern (1879–1921); white dwelling, no lantern (1921–1971)
Status: destroyed (August 30, 1971)
Original Optic: fifth-order fixed lens (1855–1879)
Other Optics Used: fourth-order fixed lens (1879–1921)
Optic Manufacturers: L. Sautter (1854); unknown
Current Optic: N/A
Characteristic: fixed white light (1858–1886); fixed white light, one red
    sector (1886–1893); fixed white light, two red sectors (1893–1913); two
    flashes every ten seconds (1913–1921)
Station Auxiliary Structures: none surviving
National Register of Historic Places: no
Owner: N/A
Operating Entity: N/A
Grounds Open to the Public: yes—open water
Tower Open to the Public: N/A
Lighthouse Museum: no
Gift Shop: no
Hours: N/A
Lighthouse Passport Stamp: no
Handicapped Access: no
Contact: none

DIRECTIONS

The ruins of this lighthouse (the iron pilings) are located about 7 miles north-west of Key West. They can only be reached by boat and are not visible from land. The ferry to the Dry Tortugas often uses this channel and will pass within sight of the pilings. Charter boats or charter seaplanes from Key West may be able to bring you here.

REBECCA SHOAL LIGHTHOUSE

WEST OF KEY WEST, FLORIDA
(Lighthouse Site Only)

Thomas W. Taylor

Rebecca Shoal is an area of shallow water between Key West and the Dry Tortugas, just west of the Marquesas Keys. By passing west of the Marquesas, ships could save time compared to going around the west side of the Tortugas, but they had to be careful not to run aground. So dangerous was the area that the Life Saving Service considered building a House of Refuge on the uninhabited Marquesas.

The lighthouse on Rebecca Shoal was the last and most difficult of those built in the Florida Keys. It was located forty-three miles west of Key West at the west end of its namesake shoal in very turbulent waters. Efforts to construct a daybeacon there began in 1854 under Edward A. Yorke, who would later supervise construction of the Jupiter Inlet Lighthouse. The beacon was nearly completed when, on May 17, 1855, a violent storm washed the entire structure away. Work restarted several times, only for the work platform and unfinished beacon to be wrecked each time. Lt. George Meade reported that no beacon or lighthouse "has been erected, in this country or in Europe, at a position more exposed or offering greater obstacles." After appropriations totaling $25,000 and several years of frustration, the shoal was finally marked with buoys rather than a daybeacon.

The Civil War delayed any further work. A daybeacon was finally completed in May 1873, only to be destroyed by a hurricane that October. The Lighthouse Board decided that a major structure was needed here rather than just a daymark. In the meantime, a new seventy-five-foot daybeacon was erected in 1878. Congress finally allocated funds for a lighthouse at Rebecca Shoal in 1884. In May 1886 the daybeacon was taken down, and work began on the lighthouse. The new cottage-style lighthouse on screwpiles was first lighted on November 1, 1886, sending out a light that flashed alternately red and white.

The lighthouse consisted of three floors, with the lantern incorporated into the roof of the structure. Supplies were lifted onto the first floor by a small crane. The three keepers—all men without their families—lived on the second floor. The small third floor, with four dormer windows, consisted of the watch room.

This lighthouse survived many severe storms. In 1889, one storm rocked the lighthouse so badly that the lens was damaged. In 1893, a red sector was installed so the flash over the nearby shoal was always red. Steel tanks were added to the lighthouse in 1914 for kerosene storage.

A hurricane damaged the lighthouse in September 1919. The same storm sank the Spanish ocean liner *Valbanera* with all hands (nearly five hundred passengers and crew). The wreck was eventually located six miles east of the lighthouse in forty feet of water.

On August 1, 1925, the Rebecca Shoal Lighthouse was automated with acetylene, and keepers no longer had to risk their lives there. Deterioration and vandalism took their toll on the structure, and the lighthouse was removed in 1953. In 1985, the entire structure was replaced with an automated modern beacon mounted directly on a new screwpile foundation. Years of storm impacts culminating in 2017's Hurricane Irma caused the Coast Guard to deem the structure unstable and unsafe. A lighted buoy now marks the shoal and the ruined beacon.

SITE FACTS

Dates of Construction: 1886
First Lighted: November 1, 1886
Electrified: 1953? (Modern ATON)
Automated: August 1, 1925 (with acetylene)
Deactivated: 1953 (lighthouse); 2017 (modern ATON)
Tower Height: approx. 70 feet (lighthouse)
Focal Height: 66 feet (lighthouse)
Designer/Architect: George G. Meade (1850s daybeacon); unknown (lighthouse)
Builder/Supervisor: unknown
Type of Tower: screwpile cottage
Foundation Materials: iron screwpiles
Construction Materials: wood and iron
Number of Stairs: unknown
Daymark: white dwelling, green shutters, brown pilings, black lantern (1886–1953)
Status: demolished (1953); replaced by a modern ATON
Original Optic: fourth-order revolving Fresnel lens (1886–1925)
Optic Manufacturer: unknown
Other Optics Used: fourth-order fixed Fresnel lens (1925–1953); Amerace 190 mm rotating beacon (modern ATON); 250 mm lantern (modern ATON)
Current Optic: none
Characteristic: two flashes every ten seconds, alternating white and red (1886–1893); two flashes every ten seconds, alternating white and red, with red sector (1893–1914); three white flashes every fifteen seconds,

with red sector (1914–1990s); one white flash every six seconds, with red
sector (1990s–2017)
Station Auxiliary Structures: none surviving
National Register of Historic Places: no
Owner: US Coast Guard (modern ATON)
Operating Entity: US Coast Guard (modern ATON)
Grounds Open to the Public: yes—open water
Tower Open to the Public: no
Lighthouse Museum: no
Gift Shop: no
Hours: N/A
Lighthouse Passport Stamp: yes—Florida Keys Reef Lights Foundation
Handicapped Access: no
Contact: none

DIRECTIONS

The modern ATON at the former lighthouse site is not visible from land and
only accessible by boat. The daily ferry to the Dry Tortugas frequently passes
within sight of it. Boat ramps, charter boats, and charter seaplanes are available
in Key West.

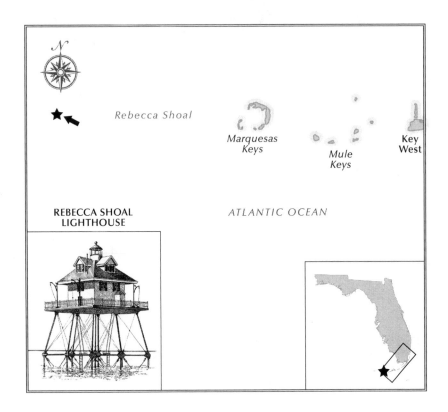

OLD DRY TORTUGAS LIGHTHOUSE

GARDEN KEY, DRY TORTUGAS, FLORIDA (Lighthouse Site Only)

Neil Hurley

Tortugas is the Spanish word for turtles. It was the presence of large numbers of sea turtles and a lack of fresh water that gave this island group its name when it was discovered by Spanish explorer Ponce de León in 1513. The island group is the westernmost of the Florida Keys and has historically been a great danger to ships moving from the Gulf of Mexico to the Atlantic.

Although the British considered building a lighthouse in the Dry Tortugas in 1773, the first lighthouse was built under American ownership. Congress first appropriated funds in 1822, and the tower was constructed in 1825. The sixty-five-foot-tall brick lighthouse and its detached keeper's dwelling were the first permanent buildings in the Dry Tortugas. The tower showed a white light from twenty-three lamps, each with a fourteen-inch reflector. The buildings were located on Garden Key, which was in the center of the island group and also had the advantage of being next to one of the best anchorages around. The lighthouse was first lighted on July 4, 1826, the fiftieth anniversary of the signing of the Declaration of Independence and the same day that Thomas Jefferson died. Coincidentally, the huge fort built around the lighthouse twenty years later would bear Jefferson's name.

The lighthouse's first keeper, retired Major John Flaherty, had a hard time keeping a good light and was transferred to the less remote Sand Key Light near Key West, in part due to a request from his wife to the president of the United States. The loneliness of Garden Key ended when construction of Fort Jefferson was started in 1847. A new keeper's dwelling was also built that year.

Fort Jefferson eventually surrounded the lighthouse. It was garrisoned for the first time in 1861 due to the outbreak of the Civil War and remained firmly under Union control throughout the war. Just after the Civil War, the cries of a prisoner being tortured at the fort kept the keeper's family awake all night. Dr. Samuel Mudd was held at the fort after he was implicated in the conspiracy to assassinate Abraham Lincoln. Dr. Mudd saved numerous lives during the 1867 yellow fever epidemic and was pardoned in 1869. Visitors today can see his cell.

The lighthouse on Garden Key was downgraded in importance after a taller light was built on nearby Loggerhead Key in 1858. By 1874, some people thought the old Garden Key tower detracted from the appearance of the parade ground of the fort. The combined effects of years of hurricanes also made the tower unsafe. In 1876, a new lighthouse was built on the wall of Fort Jefferson, and the old tower was torn down soon after.

Today, the foundation of the 1826 Dry Tortugas Lighthouse tower remains visible inside Fort Jefferson.

SITE FACTS

Dates of Construction: 1825
First Lighted: July 4, 1826
Electrified: never
Automated: never
Deactivated: 1873
Tower Height: 65 feet
Focal Height: 70 feet

Designer/Architect: Winslow Lewis?
Builder/Supervisor: Noah Humphries
Type of Tower: conical brick
Foundation Materials: brick
Construction Materials: brick tower, wooden stairs, iron lantern
Number of Stairs: 70 (approximate)
Daymark: white tower, black lantern
Status: demolished
Original Optic: 15 Lewis lamps with 14-inch reflectors (1826–1840s)
Other Optics Used: 17 Lewis lamps with 23-inch reflectors (1840s–1858),
    fourth-order fixed Fresnel lens (1858–1873)
Current Optic: N/A
Characteristic: fixed white light (1826–1873)
Station Auxiliary Structures: none surviving
National Register of Historic Places: yes (as part of Dry Tortugas National
    Park)
Owner: National Park Service (site)
Operating Entity: Dry Tortugas National Park (site)
Grounds Open to the Public: yes
Tower Open to the Public: N/A
Lighthouse Museum: no
Gift Shop: yes—Garden Key Visitor Center
Hours: site open at all times; visitor center open daily 8:30 AM–4:30 PM
Adult Admission Fee: $15 park admission (included in $180 ferry cost)
Lighthouse Passport Stamp: no
Handicapped Access: no
Contact: Dry Tortugas National Park, PO Box 6208, Key West, FL 33041
Email: none
Phone: 305-242-7700 (park) and 800-634-0939 (ferry)
Website: www.nps.gov/drto (park) and www.drytortugas.com (ferry)

DIRECTIONS

Garden Key is 65 miles west of Key West and only accessible by boat or sea-plane. Enter the Fort Jefferson main gate to the fort's parade ground. The circular foundation of the old lighthouse is located on your right, just west of the fort's bastion with the second lighthouse.

The catamaran ferry *Yankee Freedom* (www.drytortugas.com) is the official park concessionaire providing daily roundtrip service from Key West to Garden Key. Seaplane Adventures—www.keywestseaplanecharters.com—is another official park concessionaire.

Private boats are allowed but must be fully self-sufficient with water, fuel, and supplies. The park has no boat moorings or slips. Overnight anchorage is limited to the designated area within 1 nautical mile of Fort Jefferson.

A small primitive campground on Garden Key outside the fort allows overnight stays. Campsites are available on a first-come, first-served basis except the group site.

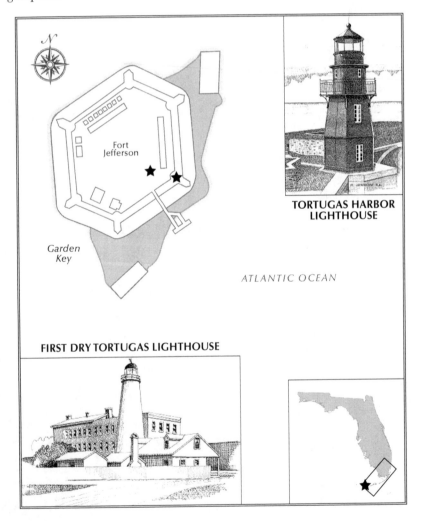

TORTUGAS HARBOR LIGHTHOUSE

FIRST DRY TORTUGAS LIGHTHOUSE

TORTUGAS HARBOR LIGHTHOUSE

GARDEN KEY, DRY TORTUGAS, FLORIDA

Neil Hurley

FT. JEFFERSON FLA.

After the old 1826 lighthouse tower on Garden Key was heavily damaged by an 1873 hurricane and reported to be an unsafe eyesore, a new lighthouse tower was built on the walls of Fort Jefferson in 1876. The new tower was constructed of boilerplate iron since a brick lighthouse could cause dangerous fragments if hit by enemy gunfire. The tower has six sides and originally showed a light from the same fourth-order Fresnel lens used in the old lighthouse. Like its predecessor, the Garden Key lighthouse was officially known as the Dry Tortugas Harbor Light. This changed in 1883 to Tortugas Harbor Light.

In 1888, a new keeper's dwelling was built in the same location as the old one, adjacent to the parade ground inside the walls of Fort Jefferson. The fort had been abandoned by the army in 1874, but after 1889 a quarantine station and buoy depot shared the island with the lighthouse keeper and his family. The army returned to Fort Jefferson for a short time beginning with the Spanish-American War of 1898. The fort was abandoned again after 1910 because of damage caused by a hurricane. During the early 1900s, the Navy also made use of Garden Key as a coaling station (pilings from two coaling docks are still visible), a wireless telegraph (radio) station, and a seaplane base.

The fort's value as a military post ended in 1912. A fire started in the lighthouse's outhouse at around 2:30 in the morning, quickly spreading to another shed, then to the lighthouse keeper's home and a three-story brick barracks. Kitchen buildings behind the barracks also caught on fire. Only the wooden drawbridge leading into the fort was saved. The lighthouse was automated with acetylene later that year, and the keeper's house was never rebuilt.

The Tortugas Harbor Light was discontinued as unnecessary in 1921, but the tower was left standing. Fort Jefferson National Monument was created in 1935, and it became part of the new Dry Tortugas National Park in 1992. The National Park Service made periodic repairs to the lighthouse beginning in 1939. A structural assessment in 2013 to 2014 determined the tower needed extensive restoration work. The lighthouse was extensively photographed and laser scanned in 2017. The NPS plans to disassemble the tower in late 2019 for restoration at an off-site facility, with the restored lighthouse expected back in place in 2021.

SITE FACTS

Dates of Construction: 1876
First Lighted: April 5, 1876
Electrified: never
Automated: 1912 (with acetylene)
Deactivated: 1921

Tower Height: 25 feet
Focal Height: 67 feet
Designer/Architect: unknown
Builder/Supervisor: unknown
Type of Tower: cast iron hexagonal pyramidal
Foundation Materials: brick (bastion of Fort Jefferson)
Construction Materials: boilerplate iron with wooden steps
Number of Steps: 50
Daymark: brown tower, black lantern (Lighthouse Service); black tower and
    lantern (NPS)
Status: active—ornamental light
Original Optic: fourth-order fixed Fresnel lens
Optic Manufacturer & Date: Henry-Lepaute (1858)
Other Optics Used: none
Current Optic: three light bulbs (no lens or reflectors)
Characteristic: fixed white light (1876–1893 and 1901–1912); fixed white light,
    three red sectors (1893–1901); one flash every two seconds (1912–1921)
Station Auxiliary Structures: none surviving
National Register of Historic Places: yes (as part of Fort Jefferson)
Owner: National Park Service
Operating Entity: Dry Tortugas National Park
Grounds Open to the Public: yes
Tower Open to the Public: no
Lighthouse Museum: no
Gift Shop: yes—Garden Key Visitor Center
Lighthouse Passport Stamp: yes—in gift shop
Hours: site open at all times; visitor center open daily 8:30 AM–4:30 PM
Adult Admission: $15 park admission (included in $180 ferry cost)
Handicapped Access: no
Contact: Dry Tortugas National Park, PO Box 6208, Key West, FL 33041
Email: none
Phone: 305-242-7700 (park) and 800-634-0939 (ferry)
Website: www.nps.gov/drto (park) and www.drytortugas.com (ferry)

DIRECTIONS

See previous chapter for information about reaching Garden Key and a map of both lighthouse sites. The lighthouse is atop the fort's southeast bastion just east of the site of the first lighthouse.

DRY TORTUGAS LIGHTHOUSE

LOGGERHEAD KEY, DRY TORTUGAS, FLORIDA

Neil Hurley

As early as 1836, mariners complained about the lighthouse tower on Garden Key. Despite a number of shipwrecks in the intervening years, it wasn't until 1856 that funds were approved for a new, larger lighthouse to be built closer to the most dangerous reefs on Loggerhead Key.

The new Dry Tortugas Lighthouse was first lighted on July 1, 1858. The first-order Fresnel lens was maintained by a head keeper with two assistant keepers. Sharing a two-story brick duplex, they were the only residents of the mile-long island.

When Benjamin Kerr, the first keeper, moved from his old job at the Tortugas Harbor Lighthouse on Garden Key, he brought his wife and two daughters with him. All was well until one of Kerr's daughters fell in love with one of the assistants. With Kerr and one of his daughters on one side and his wife, other daughter, and the two assistant keepers on the opposing side, a fight ensued. Clubs, chairs, and knives were used before Kerr and his daughter escaped to Fort Jefferson. The two assistant keepers were later removed from their posts, and Kerr and his wife separated, Mrs. Kerr moving to Key West.

The lighthouse bricks were unpainted until late 1869 when the tower gained the daymark it still carries today: lower half white, upper half black. Hurricane winds in 1873 caused the tower to vibrate so much that the top of the lighthouse was nearly blown off. Plans were made to replace the entire tower with a stronger, all-iron one, but temporary repairs held through another hurricane in 1875, so the plan for a new tower was abandoned. A 1909 thunderstorm killed thousands of migratory birds on the island and left the newly painted lighthouse "literally plastered with brilliant feathers." A hurricane in 1910 blew windowpanes out from around the lens. After the storm, bits of wind-blown seaweed were found at the top of the tower, more than 160 feet above sea level. As part of the post-hurricane repairs, new second-order bivalve lens replaced the first-order lens that had been damaged by the storm. This required modifications to the lantern interior and was accompanied by the installation of IOV lamps.

A separate dwelling for the head keeper was completed in 1923 and is still used by park personnel today. A radio beacon was added in 1927, the first in Florida. The radio equipment was located in the old oil house at the base of the lighthouse. However, the light was not electrified until 1931, at which time newspapers declared it the brightest lighthouse in the country.

From 1904 until 1939, lighthouse keepers shared Loggerhead Key with scientists from the Carnegie Marine Biological Laboratory. The lab conducted some of the first research on coral reefs and mangroves in the Western Hemisphere and also took the first ever black-and-white and color underwater photographs. A 1960s fire destroyed the remaining buildings, but some of the ruins can still be found on the north end of the island.

During World War II, the Coast Guard posted additional servicemen at Loggerhead Key to act as lookouts. One of these lookouts may have been responsible for the accidental fire that destroyed the two-story brick keeper's dwelling in 1945.

In late 1986, a problem with the mercury float for the lens resulted in the installation of a modern optic. The historic lens was sent to the Coast Guard Aids To Navigation School in Yorktown, Virginia. The lighthouse was automated the following year, making it the second-to-last manned lighthouse in Florida.

The National Park Service assumed ownership of Loggerhead Key in 1992, but the Coast Guard retained ownership of the lighthouse. After the solar-powered modern optic stopped working in 2014, the lighthouse was decommissioned the following year. Final transfer of the lighthouse to NPS has been repeatedly delayed and was still pending as of 2019. The NPS hopes to begin restoration work on the lighthouse in 2022, including relighting with a modern optic and providing limited access to the tower.

SITE FACTS

Dates of Construction: 1857–1858
First Lighted: July 1, 1858
Electrified: 1931 (diesel generator)
Automated: 1987
Tower Height: 157 feet
Focal Height: 151 feet
Designer/Architect: Horatio G. Wright and Daniel P. Woodbury
Builder/Supervisor: Daniel P. Woodbury
Type of Tower: conical brick with attached oil house
Foundation Materials: brick and stone
Construction Materials: brick tower, granite stairs, iron lantern
Number of Steps: 204
Daymark: red unpainted brick (1858–1869); lower half white, upper half black (1869–present)
Status: inactive
Original Optic: first-order fixed Fresnel lens (1858–1911)

Other Optics Used: second-order bivalve Fresnel lens (1911–1986), DCB-24 (1986–1995), VRB-25 (1995–2014)

Optic Manufacturers: L. Sautter (1857), Henry-Lepaute (1909?)

Current Optic: none

Characteristic: fixed white light (1858–1893); fixed white light, one red sector (1893–1911); one flash every twenty seconds (1911–2014)

Station Auxiliary Structures: attached oil house / radio beacon room (1858), kitchen/dwelling (1858), keeper's dwelling (1923), oil house (1926), cisterns (1858 and 1922)

National Register of Historic Places: yes (as part of Dry Tortugas National Park)

Owner: National Park Service

Operating Entity: Dry Tortugas National Park

Grounds Open to the Public: yes

Tower Open to the Public: no

Lighthouse Museum: no

Gift Shop: yes—Garden Key Visitor Center

Hours: site open at all times; visitor center open daily 8:30 AM–4:30 PM

Adult Admission Fee: $15 park admission (included in $180 ferry cost)

Lighthouse Passport Stamp: yes—in gift shop

Hours: island open daily sunrise–sunset; visitor center open daily 8:30 AM–4:30 PM

Handicapped Access: no

Contact: Dry Tortugas National Park, PO Box 6208, Key West, FL 33041

Email: none

Phone: 305-242-7700 (park) and 800-634-0939 (ferry)

Website: www.nps.gov/drto (park) and www.drytortugas.com (ferry)

DIRECTIONS

The lighthouse is located 2.5 miles west of Fort Jefferson and is clearly visible from the fort. See section on Tortugas Harbor Lighthouse for directions to Fort Jefferson. Park concessionaires do not currently stop at Loggerhead Key, only Garden Key, but this may change once the lighthouse is restored. Visitors can get to Loggerhead Key via private or charter boats, or paddling over from Garden Key on a sea kayak.

N

Loggerhead Key

Fort Jefferson

Garden Key

DRY TORTUGAS

DRY TORTUGAS LIGHTHOUSE

Section III

THE FLORIDA SOUTHWEST COAST

SANIBEL ISLAND LIGHTHOUSE

SANIBEL ISLAND (NEAR FORT MYERS), FLORIDA

Charles LeBuff

In 1833, a group of New York investors platted a settlement on the island known as "Sanybel." Their elaborate plan indicated the future location of a lighthouse to aid in commerce, but their hopes for long-term settlement of the island were short-lived. A harsh environment with hordes of mosquitoes, frequent hurricanes, and the threat of Indian attack during the Second Seminole War caused settlers to abandon "Sanybel" Island by 1836.

By midcentury, nearby Punta Rassa, on the opposite side of San Carlos Harbor from Sanibel, became a busy cattle-shipping port. Before the Civil War, the shippers asked the Lighthouse Board to approve a lighthouse for the entrance to the harbor. Their request was denied because the Board determined maritime traffic did not justify a lighthouse. However, by the early 1870s, as many as sixteen thousand head of Florida scrub cattle left Punta Rassa each year on vessels bound for Cuba.

The small seaport at Punta Rassa continued to grow, and in 1878, the Lighthouse Board finally requested funding for a lighthouse between the Dry Tortugas and Egmont Key. Congress appropriated $50,000 between 1881 and 1882 to establish Sanibel Island Light Station. However, obstacles delayed the station's construction. The state of Florida had been granted title to public domain lands on Sanibel Island in 1845 when it entered the Union, and this included East Point (now Point Ybel), the selected construction site. Quick diplomacy on the part of the federal government resulted in Florida agreeing to relinquish any land title claims to the island. The Sanibel Island Lighthouse Reservation was established by an executive order on December 9, 1883.

Construction of the station began in March 1884. In May, when the parts for the light tower were being delivered by schooner from New Jersey, the vessel foundered on an enormous sandbar in the Gulf of Mexico south of Point Ybel. Salvagers recovered some of the unique cargo. Working parties from two lighthouse tenders, including a hardhat diver, managed to retrieve everything else, except for two gallery brackets that were reproduced in New Orleans. Sanibel was first lighted on August 20, 1884.

The iron skeletal tower and two square keeper dwellings were mostly typical of the era. The main exception was that the stairs to the bottom of the tower came from the porches of both houses rather than the ground. The original station also included a 162-foot wharf on the bayside of the island. The dwellings and their cisterns were placed on pilings to make them more resistant to storms.

When first lighted in 1884, the lamp inside the lighthouse's lantern was fueled by kerosene. Upgraded in 1923, it was retrofitted with a new burner that ignited timed releases of acetylene gas. The US Coast Guard took over responsibility for lighthouses and other aids to navigation in 1939. Because of major damage to the station's buildings and water supply during a 1948 hurricane, it was determined that the quarters were unsafe to be used by Coast Guard personnel. In early 1949, the lighthouse was fully automated. It would not be electrified until 1962 when the construction of the first Sanibel Causeway brought electrical lines to the island. At that time, a 300 mm drum lens replaced the original third-order Fresnel lens.

In April 1949, the US Fish and Wildlife Service negotiated a revocable lease with the Coast Guard and assumed responsibility for the land and structures (excluding the lighthouse itself) as the headquarters of the Sanibel National Wildlife Refuge, renamed the J. N. "Ding" Darling National Wildlife Refuge in 1967. The light station was added to the National Register of Historic Places in 1974.

Within months of the departure of NWR staff in 1982, the City of Sanibel secured a lease with the Coast Guard to manage the light station and have city staff members reside in the dwellings, a practice that continues as of 2019. The area around the lighthouse became Lighthouse Beach Park. The Coast Guard relinquished the lighthouse to the Bureau of Land Management in 2000, and the City of Sanibel acquired ownership in 2010. The lighthouse underwent a $269,563 restoration in 2013 funded by beach parking funds and a state historic preservation grant.

Unfortunately, due to liability concerns, the City of Sanibel does not currently allow climbing of the lighthouse. The grounds are open as part of the city park. Sanibel Historical Museum and Village displays the 300 mm drum lens formerly used in the lighthouse.

SITE FACTS

Dates of Construction: 1884
First Lighted: August 20, 1884
Tower Height: 112 feet
Focal Height: 98 feet
Designer/Architect: unknown
Manufacturer: Phoenix Ironworks, Camden, NJ
Builder/Supervisor: unknown
Type of Tower: pyramidal skeletal
Foundation Materials: concrete
Construction Materials: iron
Number of Stairs: 127
Daymark: brown tower and lantern
Status: active
Original Optic: third-order FVF Fresnel lens (1884–1923)
Optic Manufacturer: unknown
Other Optics Used: third-order fixed Fresnel lens (1923–1962), AGA fourth-order drum lens (1962–1982)

Current Optic: 190 mm aerobeacon (1982–present)

Characteristic: fixed white light varied by a flash every two minutes (1884–1923); two flashes every ten seconds (1923–1982); double flash every six seconds (1982–present)

Station Auxiliary Structures: two wooden keeper dwellings (1884), oil house (1884)

National Register of Historic Places: yes (1974)

Owner: City of Sanibel

Operating Entity: City of Sanibel

Grounds Open to the Public: yes—public park

Tower Open to the Public: no

Lighthouse Museum: none at light station; exhibit at Sanibel Historical Museum & Village

Gift Shop: no

Lighthouse Passport Stamp: yes—Sanibel Historical Museum & Village (see Directions below) or Sanibel-Captiva Chamber of Commerce (1159 Causeway Road, Sanibel Island, FL 33957; 239-472-1080)

Hours: lighthouse not open to the public; surrounding park always open

Handicapped Access: no

Contact: City of Sanibel, 800 Dunlop Road, Sanibel, FL 33957

Phone: (239)472-3700

Email: none

Website: www.sanibellighthouse.com

DIRECTIONS

From Key West, return north on US 1 to Homestead. Take the Florida Turnpike Homestead Extension north to I-75 (Exit 39). Keep left at Exit 19 to stay on I-75 as it turns west and becomes Alligator Alley ($3/car toll). (For a longer, slower, but free and scenic alternative route take US Highway 41 aka the Tamiami Trail.) Continue on I-75 toward Fort Myers and take Exit 131 (Daniels Pkwy / CR 876). Turn left from the off ramp, then go west about 2.5 miles. Turn left on Six Mile Cypress Parkway (CR 865). Pass US Highway 41 then at Summerlin Road (CR 869), keep left to take the flyover ramp. Summerlin Road will merge with McGregor Road (CR 867), then becomes the Sanibel Causeway ($6/car toll). At the first stop sign on Sanibel Island, turn left (east) on Periwinkle Way, which leads to Lighthouse Beach Park.

From the park entrance, the Gulf parking lot is directly ahead with a short trail leading to the lighthouse. Or turn left, following signs for "Historic Lighthouse & Fishing Pier," which will allow you to drive directly to the lighthouse, but with very limited parking. The fishing pier is near the original lighthouse wharf site but is not the same. Note that as of 2019 the parking fee at Lighthouse Beach Park is $5/hour.

To see the drum lens formerly used in the lighthouse, take Periwinkle Way west from Lighthouse Beach Park for almost four miles to Palm Ridge Road. Turn right, then take the right lane onto Wooster Lane (which becomes Dunlop Road) immediately after the shopping plaza. Sanibel Historical Museum and Village will be on your left (950 Dunlop Road, $10 admission, seasonal hours; info@sanibelmuseum.org; www.sanibelmuseum.org).

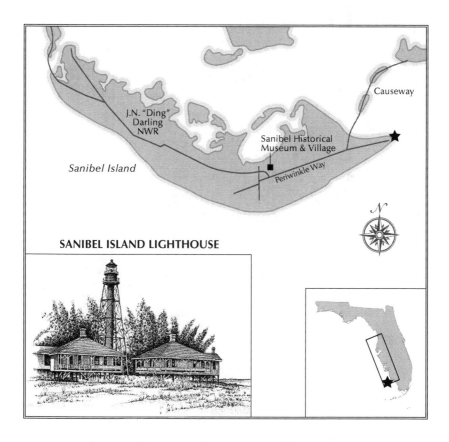

CHARLOTTE HARBOR LIGHTHOUSE

NEAR PUNTA GORDA, FLORIDA
(Lighthouse Site Only)

Neil Hurley and Josh Liller

Charlotte Harbor is a large bay on Florida's west coast. It was described in the 1880s as possessing greater natural advantages than any other harbor on the Gulf Coast, and has been pronounced by competent authority to be the best harbor between Port Royal (South Carolina) and Pensacola. Despite this grand description, the shallow depths of the inner part of the bay prevented development of a port for large seagoing ships.

In 1886, a railroad reached Punta Gorda at the head of the bay. This made the town important as a cattle-shipping port in need of a lighthouse. Funded by part of the same $35,000 congressional appropriation that funded the Port Boca Grande Lighthouse, a small cottage-style lighthouse was built in water nine feet deep near the center of the bay in 1890. It marked a turning point in the twelve-foot-deep channel.

The lighthouse consisted of three rooms in the lower story, two rooms on the second floor, and a lantern on the roof. A keeper and one assistant manned the lighthouse, which had a fifth-order Fresnel lens with a fixed red light. Locals sometimes called it the Cape Haze Lighthouse after the nearest part of the mainland.

In addition to the lighthouse in the middle of the harbor, three beacon lights were also built further up the harbor: Mangrove Point, marking the intersection of the Myakka River and Peace River; Peace Creek, marking the last turn in the harbor channel; and Live Oak Point, across from the Punta Gorda railroad wharf. The trio of square, pyramidal wooden skeletal structures were completed in September 1890, but they were not immediately lighted. Mangrove Point and Peace Creek Beacons were finally lighted with lens lanterns on February 20, 1893 (Live Oak Point was removed). Although these small structures were not lighthouses, they were built and operated by the Lighthouse Service, and each had an assigned keeper (who lived ashore) until they were automated with acetylene in the 1910s.

In 1900, the Charlotte Harbor Lighthouse's characteristic changed from red to white and an oil house was added, hanging underneath the main house on iron rods. When another railroad line reached the deep-water port at the south tip of Gasparilla Island in 1906, Charlotte Harbor's days as an important port were numbered. On October 1, 1912, the lighthouse was automated with an acetylene gas flasher, but it remained active until the early 1930s. In 1943 the structure was described as "badly deteriorated and unsightly from lack of proper maintenance." As a result, the lighthouse was torn down and replaced with an iron skeletal tower. The lighthouse's original pilings were removed in 1975. Today, Cape Haze Shoal Light 6, a single-pile structure with a red triangular daymark and a flashing red light, stands watch at the lighthouse's former location

SITE FACTS

Dates of Construction: 1890
First Lighted: December 31, 1890
Electrified: never
Automated: 1912
Discontinued: early 1930s
Tower Height: 50 feet (approximate)
Focal Height: 36 feet
Designer/Architect: unknown
Builder/Supervisor: unknown
Type of Tower: screwpile cottage
Foundation Materials: iron screwpiles
Construction Materials: wood and iron
Number of Steps: unknown
Daymark: white house with green shutters, red roof, and black lantern
Status: demolished (1943)
Original Optic: fifth-order fixed Fresnel lens (1890–1930s)
Optic Manufacturer: unknown
Other Optics Used: none
Characteristic: fixed red (1890–1900), fixed white (1900–1912), one white
    flash every second (1912–1930s)
Station Auxiliary Structures: none
National Register of Historic Places: no
Owner: N/A
Operating Entity: US Coast Guard (modern ATON)
Grounds Open to the Public: yes—open water
Tower Open to the Public: N/A
Lighthouse Museum: no
Gift Shop: no
Lighthouse Passport Stamp: no
Hours: N/A
Handicapped Access: no
Contact: none

DIRECTIONS

From Sanibel Island, return to the mainland. Continue straight onto Summerlin Road (follow signs for I-75 and US 41). Go a little more than 11 miles to

Colonial Boulevard (SR 884). Turn left (west) and cross the Midpoint Bridge ($2/car westbound toll). The road becomes Veterans Parkway, continues west for several miles, then turns north. Turn left (west) on Pine Island Road (SR 78) and cross the Matlacha Pass Bridge to Pine Island. Turn right (north) at Stringfellow Road (CR 767). Follow the road to Bokeelia where it turns west along the bayfront and becomes Main Street. Park at the Bokeelia Fishing Pier. The former lighthouse site is 5 miles northeast of the pier bearing 43 degrees. However, due to the distance, Charlotte Harbor Light 6 (the present structure) may not be visible.

This lighthouse site (N 26 45.583 W 82 06.483) can be reached only by boat. It is two-and-one-half miles ESE of Cape Haze (the geographic cape, not the municipality of the same name) and about eight-and-a-half miles east of Port Boca Grande Lighthouse. For those who wish to visit the site of this vanished lighthouse, a free public boat ramp is located at the north end of the Boca Grande Causeway at Placida Park. Boat rental establishments are available in Boca Grande and on Pine Island.

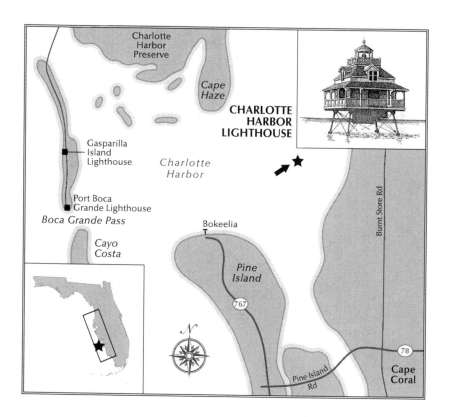

GASPARILLA ISLAND LIGHTHOUSE

GASPARILLA ISLAND, FLORIDA

Marilyn Hoeckel

The Gasparilla Island Lighthouse (formerly Boca Grande Entrance Rear Range Light) is one of only a handful of lighthouses that have had active service in two states. This tower was originally built in 1881 to serve as the Delaware Breakwater Rear Range Lighthouse, north of Lewes, Delaware, and was known locally as the Green Hill Lighthouse (although no hill actually exists). A nearly identical tower was built in 1877 and still exists as the Liston Range Rear Light, near Taylor's Bridge, Delaware. The Delaware Breakwater Rear Range Lighthouse was originally painted black but was changed to brown around 1890. It displayed a fixed white light from its third-order Fresnel lens (uncommonly large for a range light) at a focal plane of 108 feet. However, due to shoreline changes, this lighthouse was discontinued in 1918.

In 1919, the Seventh Lighthouse District in Florida notified the superintendent of the Delaware station that there was a need for the tower in Florida. However, funding for moving the lighthouse to Florida was not available until 1921. The tower was dismantled, with each part marked and numbered for easy reassembly, then shipped by railroad to Miami. Again, funding problems delayed the reassembly of the lighthouse, but finally, in 1927, the Lighthouse Service erected the skeletal, 105-foot-tall rear range light on Gasparilla Island about a mile north of the Port Boca Grande Lighthouse at the southern tip of the island.

The tower was painted white, and a fourth-order lens was installed and lighted in 1932. No dwelling was ever constructed at this light station. Instead, the light was maintained by the keepers of the nearby Port Boca Grande Lighthouse. It was of great commercial importance during the heyday of Port Boca Grande in the third quarter of the twentieth century, guiding ships from all over the world through the treacherous waters of the Boca Grande Navigation Channel into Charlotte Harbor.

It is the rear range light that was mainly used by ships to proceed safely into Port Boca Grande. A ship's captain can tell which of the two Boca Grande lighthouses he is seeing because of the difference in the characteristic. As a vessel proceeded in the ship's channel, headed for south Gasparilla Island, the captain saw the front range light, a twenty-foot-tall steel structure with a flashing light on top. (Contrary to a common misconception, the Port Boca Grande Lighthouse never served as the front range light.) He lines up this range light with the tall rear range light on land. By so doing, he knew he was in the middle of the channel. A drift of fifty feet either way could run his ship aground.

In 1998, Florida Power and Light, the last remaining commercial user of Port Boca Grande, announced that by 2002 it will no longer need or use the oil terminal. The front range light was discontinued in 2003, and the rear range light was officially renamed Gasparilla Island Lighthouse. The Coast Guard discontinued the light in 2017.

That same year the Barrier Island Parks Society (BIPS) received a license to restore the badly rusting tower and open it for public access. BIPS rapidly raised the necessary $1.6 million through grants and donations, and visitors were able to climb the lighthouse for the first time on April 1, 2017. On February 9, 2019, the lighthouse was relighted as a private aid to navigation with a replica fourth-order Fresnel lens made by Artworks Florida.

SITE FACTS

Dates of Construction: 1881 (DE); 1927 (FL)
First Lighted: 1881 (DE); 1932 (FL)
Electrified: 1932 (when relighted in FL)
Automated: 1956
Discontinued: 1918–1932 and April 7, 2017–February 9, 2019
Tower Height: 105 feet
Focal Height: 105 feet
Designer/Manufacturer: Phoenix Iron Company, Trenton, NJ
Builder/Supervisor: unknown
Type of Tower: hexagonal skeletal
Foundation Materials: concrete
Construction Materials: iron
Number of Steps: 134
Daymark: white tower, black lantern
Status: active—private aid to navigation
Original Optic (DE): third-order fixed Fresnel lens (1881–1918)
Original Optic (FL): fourth-order fixed Fresnel lens (1932–1943)
Original Optic Manufacturers: unknown
Other Optics Used: FA-251 rotating beacon (?–2014)
Current Optic: replica fourth-order fixed Fresnel lens (2019–present)
Current Optic Manufacturer: Artworks Florida (2018)
Characteristic: fixed red, visible in range only (1932–1950s), occulting white and red (1950s–1970s), isophase white and red (1970s–2014), one white flash every six seconds (2018–present)
Station Auxiliary Structures: none
National Register of Historic Places: eligible, but not yet listed
Owner: US Coast Guard

Operating Entity: Barrier Island Parks Society
Grounds Open to the Public: yes—daily
Tower Open to the Public: limited schedule
Lighthouse Museum: yes—at Port Boca Grande Lighthouse & Museum
Gift Shop: yes—at Port Boca Grande Lighthouse & Museum
Lighthouse Passport Stamp: yes—at Port Boca Grande Lighthouse & Museum
Hours: check with BIPS for schedule
Handicapped Access: yes—to base
Contact: Barrier Island Parks Society, PO Box 637, Boca Grande, FL 33921
Phone: (941) 964-0060
Email: infoatbips@gmail.com
Website: www.barrierislandparkssociety.org

DIRECTIONS

From Bokeelia, retrace your route to return to the mainland via the Matlacha Pass Bridge. On the mainland, turn left (north) on Burnt Store Road (CR 765). Go about 18 miles to US Highway 41 and turn left (northwest). Pass through Punta Gorda and cross the Barron Collier Bridge to Port Charlotte. About five miles after the bridge, turn left (west) on El Jobean Road (SR 776). Cross the Myakka River bridge and the road becomes McCall Road. At the first traffic light after the bridge, turn left onto Gasparilla Road (SR 771). After about nine miles the road will cross a bridge and curve right. At the traffic light immediately after this curve, turn left onto Boca Grande Causeway and stop at the tollbooth ($6/car, SunPass not accepted). While on the causeway, off to your left you will be able to see the remains of an old wooden railroad bridge. After the causeway, the road becomes Gasparilla Road. Continue to downtown Boca Grande and turn right on 5th Street, then left on Gilchrist Avenue, which soon becomes Gulf Boulevard. The lighthouse is on the right side of the road and impossible to miss (220 Gulf Boulevard). Just before the lighthouse, also on the right, is a paved parking lot that is part of Gasparilla Island State Park and the nearest legal parking ($3 parking fee—also good for admission to the portion of the park containing Port Boca Grande Lighthouse). Do not park along Gulf Boulevard as it is both illegal (with signs posted) and inadvisable due to the sandy road shoulders.

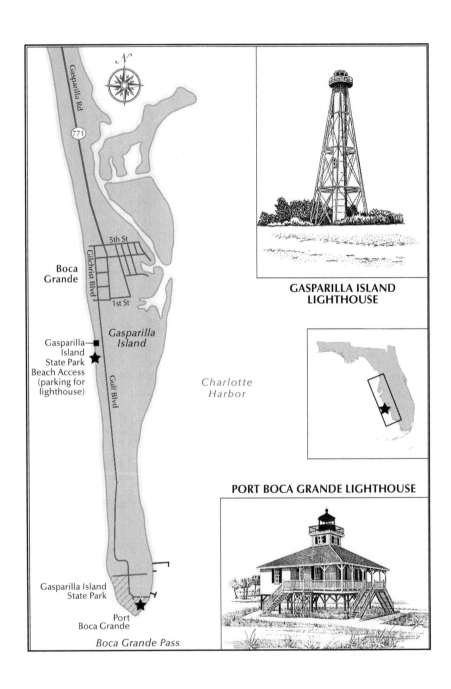

GASPARILLA ISLAND LIGHTHOUSE

PORT BOCA GRANDE LIGHTHOUSE

Gasparilla Rd

771

5th St

Boca Grande

Gilchrist Blvd

1st St

Gasparilla Island

Gasparilla Island State Park Beach Access (parking for lighthouse)

Gulf Blvd

Charlotte Harbor

Gasparilla Island State Park

Port Boca Grande

Boca Grande Pass

PORT BOCA GRANDE LIGHTHOUSE

GASPARILLA ISLAND, FLORIDA

Marilyn Hoecker

Congress allocated $35,000 for "a light or lights, and other aids to guide into Charlotte Harbor" on October 2, 1888. The Port Boca Grande Lighthouse was built in 1890 at the southern tip of Gasparilla Island to mark the entry into Charlotte Harbor from the Gulf of Mexico. It was originally called the Gasparilla Island Lighthouse—not be confused with the skeletal tower later built on the same island (covered in the preceding chapter). The lighthouse had one of the few third-and-a-half order Fresnel lenses used outside of the Great Lakes. The original characteristic was a fixed white light varied by a red flash every twenty seconds. Sometime in the early 1900s, the characteristic was altered, probably by replacing or covering the revolving flash panels with a blanking panel. The entire lens was replaced by a "clamshell" fourth-order lens prior to 1908. A brick oil house was added to the station in 1895.

A twenty-foot-tall square pyramid structure with a lens lantern was built fifty feet offshore to serve as a range with the lighthouse. Shifting sands washed the beacon away in 1892. It was replaced 475 feet from the lighthouse, this time as a range with the outer buoys of Boca Grande Pass.

The cottage-style lighthouse first saw service guiding cattle ships going from Charlotte Harbor to Cuba. In 1912, Port Boca Grande, served by a railroad from Polk County, opened as a state-of-the-art international shipping facility. For the next sixty-seven years, the lighthouse guided oceangoing ships from more than twenty countries traveling to the port to load phosphate, a valuable commodity worldwide for making fertilizer. Later, Florida Power & Light (FPL) used the port as an oil terminal.

The lighthouse, a one-story wooden dwelling on iron pilings with a black octagonal lantern on top, has survived numerous hurricanes, a fire that burned down a wash house just a few feet away, and severe beach erosion. In the early years, lighthouse keepers, living a lonely life on the isolated barrier island, played host to millionaires like John D. Rockefeller and John Jacob Astor, who came to Boca Grande Pass in their yachts to fish for the mighty tarpon. During World War II, the light guided hundreds of grateful cargo ships into safe harborage as they sought refuge from German submarines lurking in the Gulf.

The lighthouse was automated in 1956 and discontinued entirely in 1966, at which time the Coast Guard turned the building over to the General Services Administration for disposal. Thirteen acres of land and ownership of the dilapidated buildings were transferred to Lee County in 1972. At the time, the lighthouse was leaning at an angle, its stairs rotted away and the Gulf waters lapping at its base due to beach erosion. FPL helped the lighthouse survive by pumping sand around the structure and by building two rock groins along the new shoreline.

The lighthouse was placed on the National Register of Historic Places in 1980. The Gasparilla Island Conservation and Improvement Association and other local entities restored the lighthouse in 1985 to 1986 with help from the Florida Bureau of Historic Preservation. A fifth-order drum lens was installed, and the light was recommissioned by the Coast Guard on November 21, 1986, as Port Boca Grande Lighthouse.

The state of Florida took over ownership in 1988 and established Gasparilla Island State Park. Marnie Banks, founder of the *Boca Beacon* newspaper, formed the nonprofit Barrier Islands Park Society (BIPS) in 1989. The organization survived her untimely death two years later and in 1999 opened what was then called the Boca Grande Lighthouse Museum.

As of 2019, BIPS was serving as the citizen support organization for four state parks—Gasparilla Island, Don Pedro Island, Cayo Costa, and Stump Pass Beach—and operating not only the Port Boca Grande Lighthouse & Museum, but also the restored Gasparilla Island Lighthouse.

The Port Boca Grande Lighthouse came close to total destruction. It is open to the public today through the remarkable efforts of private citizens, businesses, and government working together to preserve an important piece of Florida's history. The lighthouse is the oldest building on Gasparilla Island. The assistant light keeper's house, of nearly identical style but without the lantern tower, remains next door and is the administrative office of Gasparilla Island State Park.

SITE FACTS

Dates of Construction: 1890
First Lighted: December 31, 1890
Electrified: 1931
Automated: 1956
Discontinued: 1966–1986
Tower Height: 44 feet
Focal Height: 41 feet
Designer/Architect: unknown
Builder/Supervisor: unknown
Type of Tower: cottage-style on pilings
Foundation Materials: iron pilings
Construction Materials: wood and iron
Number of Stairs: 60
Daymark: white building, green window shutters, black lantern
Status: active—public ATON
Original Optic: third-and-a-half order FVF Fresnel lens (1890–ca. 1907)
Original Optic Manufacturer: unknown
Other Optics Used: fourth-order bivalve lens (ca. 1907–1966)
Current Optic: fifth-order (375 mm) drum lens (1986–present)

Characteristic: fixed white, with one red flash every twenty seconds (1890–early 1900s); occulting white, seven-second eclipse every twenty seconds (early 1900s); one white flash every ten seconds (ca. 1907–1966); one flash every four seconds (1986–present)

Station Auxiliary Structures: assistant keeper's dwelling (1890)

National Register of Historic Places: yes (1980)

Owner: State of Florida

Operating Entity: Barrier Island Parks Society & Gasparilla Island State Park

Grounds Open to the Public: yes—daily

Tower Open to the Public: yes—building daily, lantern weekly

Lighthouse Museum: yes—in lighthouse

Gift Shop: yes

Park Hours: 8 AM–sunset daily

Lighthouse Hours—Climbing: Fridays 11 AM–3 PM

Lighthouse Hours—Museum: 10 AM–4 PM Monday–Saturday, Sunday 12 PM–4 PM.

Seasonal Hours: closed Monday/Tuesday in June–July and September–October, and the entire month of August

Lighthouse Passport Stamp: yes—in gift shop

Handicapped Access: yes—elevator to museum

Contact: Barrier Island Parks Society, PO Box 637, Boca Grande, FL 33921

Phone: (941) 964-0060

Email: infoatbips@gmail.com

Website: www.barrierislandparkssociety.org

DIRECTIONS

From the Gasparilla Island Lighthouse, continue south on Gulf Boulevard to the intersection with Belcher Road. The entrance to Gasparilla Island State Park is directly ahead ($3 per vehicle or annual pass). Continue past the main parking lot and the road will curve left to the parking lot for the lighthouse. Street address is 880 Belcher Road. See previous chapter for a map.

EGMONT KEY
LIGHTHOUSE

NEAR ST. PETERSBURG, FLORIDA

Richard Johnson and Josh Liller

EGMONT KEY   FLA.

Located at the mouth of Tampa Bay, Egmont Key was named in 1765 by George Gauld, a British surveyor, in honor of John Perceval, the second Earl of Egmont. After Spain ceded Florida to the United States in 1821, commerce along the Gulf Coast increased rapidly. Although Tampa Bay would not be a significant port for some years, a lighthouse was requested as early as 1833 to aid vessels running along the coast from Key West to Pensacola. Lt. Napoleon Coste in 1837 and Capt. Lawrence Rousseau in 1838 both recommended the construction of a lighthouse at Egmont Key during their surveys of aids to navigation in the Gulf.

On March 3, 1847, Congress appropriated $10,000 for a lighthouse on Egmont Key. Only $7,580 were used by contractor Francis A. Gibbons of Baltimore and Winslow Lewis, who supplied thirteen of his patented Lewis lamps with 21-inch reflectors. Mr. Walker, St. Marks Collector of Customs, supervised construction. Egmont Key Lighthouse was first lighted in May 1848, the first lighthouse ever constructed between St. Marks and the Florida Keys.

In September 1848, a severe hurricane damaged the tower and keeper's house. Despite various repairs, it was necessary to replace the original tower. Congress allocated $16,000 on August 18, 1856, for a new lighthouse and keeper dwelling, built to "withstand any storm." The replacement lighthouse was built ninety feet further inland and was twice as tall as the original. District Engineer William F. Raynolds designed the tower, which has numerous design similarities to his other lighthouses. The new lighthouse was first lighted in 1858 with a third-order Fresnel lens.

Early in the Civil War, keeper George Richards removed the lens and most of the lighthouse supplies to Tampa to keep them out of Union hands. Starting in July 1861, the island was occupied by Union forces and served as a base of operations for the East Gulf Blockading Squadron. Egmont was also a refuge for Unionists and escaped slaves. The lighthouse was relighted on June 2, 1866, with a fourth-order Fresnel lens.

In 1872, a buoy depot was established, and by 1889, all of the buoys used between Key West and St. Marks were repaired, serviced, and painted at Egmont Key. Between 1898 and 1923, the lighthouse keepers shared Egmont Key with Fort Dade, one of the army's primary coastal defense installations in the Gulf of Mexico. Extensive ruins of Fort Dade can still be observed on the island. The Tampa Bay Pilots Association established a station near the middle of Egmont Key in 1886, which remains active as of 2019. The pilots help guide ships through the bay channel to Port Tampa.

A red sector was added to the light in 1893. An oil house was completed in 1895 to store kerosene for the lamp. The optic was changed to a fixed third-order lens in 1896 due to the need for a brighter light; the change to an IOV lamp in 1912 further improved the light's visibility. After several years of requests for funding, a separate home was built in 1899 for the assistant keeper. In 1915, an automated acetylene light was built offshore to form a range with the lighthouse. Shortly thereafter the lighthouse's lens was modified to be an occulating light.

Until the construction of St. Johns Light in 1954, Egmont Key was the only coastal lighthouse in Florida to have been equipped with a fog signal. A fog horn was used at least as early as the 1880s to respond to fog signals from passing vessels. When the horn broke, the keepers blew a conch shell as a substitute. A fog bell was finally installed in 1916. This was supplemented by a radio beacon in 1930, the only one between the Dry Tortugas and Cape San Blas. The radio beacon transmitted the letter *P* in Morse code, changed to *H* in the late 1950s.

In 1944, because of water damage to the lantern room, the lantern was removed, the tower was shortened to seventy feet, and an aero beacon was placed atop the decapitated lighthouse. The historic keeper dwellings were later demolished and replaced by a single modern dwelling. Egmont Key became a National Wildlife Refuge in 1974 and was added to the National Register of Historic Places four years later. In 1989, the Egmont Key Lighthouse was the last lighthouse in Florida to be completely automated and unmanned, and the north end of the island became Egmont Key State Park. As of 2019, the Coast Guard still owns fifty-five acres surrounding the lighthouse, but changes are anticipated in the near future.

The nonprofit Egmont Key Alliance formed in 1991 from a coalition of lighthouse, military, and wildlife enthusiasts. The group has worked with the Coast Guard, state park, and wildlife refuge to restore the fog signal and radio beacon building as a small museum and gift shop, restore the Fort Dade guardhouse, and provide historical interpretation including the annual Discover the Island festival. The Alliance's long-term goal is to restore the lighthouse to its historic appearance (including a replica lantern), restore the surviving Fort Dade gun batteries, and preserve the island's history while providing public access.

SITE FACTS

Dates of Construction: 1847–1848; 1857–1858
First Lighted: May 1848; 1858
Electrified: 1930 (diesel generator)
Automated: 1989
Deactivated: never

Tower Height: 40 feet (1848); 81 feet (1858); 76 feet (1944)

Focal Height: 45 feet (1848); 85 feet (1858); 81 feet (1944)

Designer/Architect: Francis A. Gibbons (1848); William F. Raynolds (1858)

Builder/Supervisor: Mr. Walker (1848); unknown (1857–1858)

Type of Tower: conical brick

Foundation Materials: brick

Construction Materials: brick and iron

Number of Stairs: 99

Daymark: white tower without lantern (formerly white tower and black lantern)

Status: active—public ATON

Original Optic (old tower): 13 Lewis lamps with 21-inch reflectors

Original Optic (current tower): third-order fixed Fresnel lens (1858–1861)

Other Optics Used: fourth-order fixed Fresnel lens (1866–1896), third-order fixed Fresnel lens (1896–1944), DCB-236 (1944–1987), DCB-24 (1987–2010s)

Fresnel Lens Manufacturers: Henry-Lepaute (1858); unknown; L. Sautter et Cie (1860s?)

Current Optic: Vega VLB-44

Characteristic: fixed white (1848–1916); occulting—two eclipses every ten seconds (1916–1944); one flash every fifteen seconds (1944–present)

Station Auxiliary Structures: Coast Guard keeper's dwelling (1960s), oil house (1895), radio beacon and fog signal building (1916, expanded 1930)

National Register of Historic Places: yes—as part of Egmont Key (1978)

Owner: US Coast Guard

Operating Entity: US Coast Guard

Grounds Open to the Public: yes

Tower Open to the Public: no

Lighthouse Museum: yes

Gift Shop: yes—in former radio beacon room

Lighthouse Passport Stamp: yes—in gift shop or via mail to the Egmont Key Alliance

Hours: During special events and 10:30 AM–1:30 PM, third Saturday of every month, site open daily.

Adult Admission: free

Handicapped Access: no

Contact: Egmont Key Alliance, PO Box 66238, St. Pete Beach, FL 33736

Phone: none

Email: info@egmontkey.info
Website: www.egmontkey.info

DIRECTIONS

From Gasparilla Island, return to the mainland via the Boca Grande Causeway then turn left on Placida Road (CR 775). Drive about 5 miles to Winchester Boulevard and turn right. Turn right on River Road (CR 777) and follow it to I-75. Go north to I-275 (Exit 228). Cross the Sunshine Skyway bridge ($1.50/vehicle toll). At the north end of the bridge, take the left lane exit (Exit 17) to the Pinellas Bayway / SR 682. Turn left at the traffic light onto the Bayway. Turn left at the traffic light on SR 679 (signs for Tierra Verde). Continue south to Fort Desoto Park. Along the way you will pass the Tierra Verde (faux) Lighthouse. There are two toll bridges ($0.50 and $0.35) plus an admission fee at the park ($5). Turn right on the main park road (Anderson Boulevard).

If you are taking the ferry to Egmont Key, turn left into the parking lot with signs for "BAY PIER" and "Egmont Key Ferry." The ferry runs daily, but times change seasonally. Contact Hubbard's Marina for details (www.hubbardsmarina.com/egmont-key-ferry-cruise/ or 727-398-6577). Roundtrip cost is $25 for adults.

For the best view from land, continue just past the ferry parking lot to signs for "Gulf Pier & Historic Fort" and turn left onto the paved road leading to Fort DeSoto (restored gun batteries and a small museum) and the Gulf Fishing Pier. The Egmont Key Lighthouse is clearly visible a few miles southwest of the pier. The lighthouse is at the north end of the island.

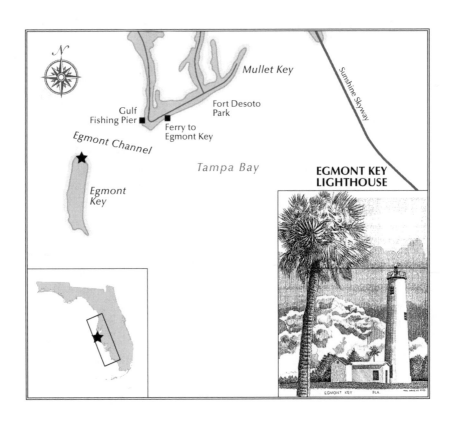

N

Mullet Key

Sunshine Skyway

Gulf
Fishing Pier

Fort Desoto
Park

Ferry to
Egmont Key

Egmont Channel

Tampa Bay

Egmont
Key

**EGMONT KEY
LIGHTHOUSE**

EGMONT KEY   FLA.

ANCLOTE KEYS LIGHTHOUSE

ANCLOTE KEY, OFF TARPON SPRINGS, FLORIDA

Janet and Scott Keeler and Josh Liller

PAUL BRADLEY '92

The City of Tarpon Springs was laid out in the early 1880s. Around the same time, the Lighthouse Board successfully sought $35,000 for a lighthouse on Anclote Key offshore of the burgeoning city. Work began in early 1887 near the south end of the island. The prefabricated iron tower arrived several months behind schedule, with the two keeper dwellings and the concrete foundation for the lighthouse finished months earlier. A kerosene lamp was first lighted in the third-order Fresnel lens on September 15, 1887. Originally, Anclote Keys Lighthouse was the official name, referring collectively to the main island and three smaller nearby islands. Today, the lighthouse is usually called Anclote Key (singular).

Incorporated a few months before completion of the lighthouse, Tarpon Springs began to build hotels to accommodate tourists. The lighthouse also facilitated the growth of the city's sponge industry, for which Tarpon Springs is still known. Up until the Anclote Key Lighthouse was constructed, nearly all the sponges used in the United States were imported from the islands of the eastern Mediterranean. There had been a sponge industry in the Bahamas and in Key West since the 1840s. Schooners from Apalachicola harvesting just a few miles off Anclote Key were forced to haul their bounty south to Key West. The lighthouse changed that: once it lighted the way from the sea up the Anclote River to safe haven in Tarpon Springs, Greek divers and their families flocked to the new American city. From 1907 to 1972, the Tarpon Springs Sponge Exchange was the largest such market in the United States. Though the industry has slowed from its heyday, Tarpon Springs continues to draw tourists, who eat Greek food such as gyros and souvlaki and almost always return home with a sponge.

Originally, two families lived on the island to tend the light. During the Spanish-American War of 1898, one keeper procured a small cannon for self-defense. He never had to use it. Another keeper kept pigs on the island, letting them roam free. They were stolen by the crew of a passing boat.

The light station got a brick oil house in 1894. Brick pathways were laid in 1898 to connect the various buildings and a wharf that extended hundreds of feet offshore. A boathouse was added in 1904. The light was upgraded to an IOV lamp in 1912. The assistant keeper's position was discontinued in 1923 when the light was electrified. The lighthouse was automated in 1952.

In the years after the lighthouse keepers left, arsonists burned down both dwellings, gunfire shattered the lantern glass, and graffiti artists defaced the structure from top to bottom. The untended lighthouse was also ravaged by the elements, with the cast iron badly rusted. The Coast Guard transferred most of the island to the State of Florida in 1960 and deactivated the lighthouse in 1984.

Concerned Gulf Coast residents began lobbying for the restoration and preservation of the once-proud, now-tattered lighthouse. Through their efforts, Anclote Key was listed on the National Register of Historic Places, the Coast Guard transferred the lighthouse to the State of Florida, and Anclote Key Preserve State Park opened in 1997. (Despite the singular name, the park includes all four of the islands comprising the Anclote Keys for which the lighthouse had originally been named.) The combined efforts of the Gulf Islands Alliance Citizen Support Organization, Tampa Bay Harbour Lights Club, and the Tarpon Springs Historical Society raised over a million dollars, mostly through state grants. The lighthouse and oil house underwent a complete restoration in 2003. The project culminated in a relighting ceremony on September 13 of that year with a replica fourth-order lens.

Following the restoration, a modern park ranger residence was constructed just north of the lighthouse to help protect against vandalism. The soil around the lighthouse became a problem when tests found it contaminated by lead from over a century of using lead-based paint on the lighthouse and careless disposal of the batteries that powered the lighthouse during its three decades of automation. After a failed decontamination effort, a fence was erected to keep visitors off the problem areas.

Access to the lighthouse remains on a very limited schedule, the iron tower isn't getting the regular maintenance it needs, the keeper dwellings remain only ruins, and no lighthouse museum has been built. The Friends of Anclote Key, the official citizen support organization (CSO) for the park and lighthouse, is doing its best. Anclote Key is a success story, but also an example of the challenges of a twenty-first-century offshore lighthouse.

SITE FACTS

Dates of Construction: 1887
First Lighted: September 15, 1887
Electrified: 1923 (diesel generator)
Automated: 1952
Deactivated: November 9, 1984–September 13, 2003
Tower Height: 106 feet
Focal Height: 101 feet
Designer/Architect: unknown
Manufacturer: Colwell Iron Works, New York City
Builder/Supervisor: unknown

Type of Tower: square pyramidal skeletal
Foundation Materials: concrete
Construction Materials: iron
Number of Stairs: 138
Daymark: brown tower, black lantern
Status: active—private ATON
Original Optic: third-order revolving Fresnel lens (1887–1960s)
Optic Manufacturer: Henry-Lepaute (date unknown)
Other Optics Used: 250-watt electric lamp (1960s–1984)
Current Optic: fourth-order revolving Fresnel lens
Optic Manufacturer: Artworks Florida (2003)
Characteristic: one red flash every thirty seconds (1887–1912); one white
   flash every thirty seconds (1912–1923); one flash every five seconds
   (1923–1970s); three flashes every thirty seconds (1970s–1984); four
   white flashes every thirty seconds (2003–present)
Station Auxiliary Structures: oil house (1894); ruins of two keeper dwellings
   and brick cisterns (1887)
National Register of Historic Places: yes
Owner: State of Florida
Operating Entity: Anclote Key Preserve State Park, supported by the
   Friends of Anclote Key State Park & Lighthouse
Grounds Open to the Public: yes
Tower Open to the Public: yes, but only for special events
Minimum Height to Climb: none
Lighthouse Museum: no
Gift Shop: no
Lighthouse Passport Stamp: yes—at the lighthouse when open for special
   events or Tarpon Springs Chamber of Commerce Welcome Center, 100
   Dodecanese Blvd., Tarpon Springs, FL 34689
Hours: park open 8 AM–sunset every day; lighthouse open for special events
   only
Adult Admission: none
Handicapped Access: yes—dock to base of tower
Contact—Park: Anclote Key Preserve State Park, c/o Honeymoon Island
   State Park, 1 Causeway Blvd., Dunedin, FL 34698 (the lighthouse has
   no physical address)
Contact—CSO: Friends of Anclote Key State Park & Lighthouse, PO Box
   2622, Tarpon Springs, FL 34688
Phone: 727-638-4447 (park) or 727-938-1630 (CSO)

Email: president@anclotecso.org (CSO)

Website—Park: www.floridastateparks.org/parks-and-trails/anclote-key-preserve-state-park

Website—CSO: www.anclotecso.org

DIRECTIONS

From Fort DeSoto Park, retrace your route back to I-275 northbound. Take Exit 30 for westbound Roosevelt Boulevard (SR 686). Once on Roosevelt Boulevard, follow signs for Ulmerton Road (SR 688). Turn right on US Highway 19 and go north to Tarpon Springs.

Anclote Keys is located three miles offshore and only accessible by boat. The state park lists five ferry/charter services in Tarpon Springs offering trips to Anclote Key: Sponge-O-Rama (727-943-2164); Odyssey Cruises (727-934-0547); Private Island Charters (727-534-8818); Windsong Charters (727-859-0213); and Island Paradise Charters (877-774-0589). Most operate out of the old sponge docks in downtown Tarpon Springs.

The best observation point from the mainland is the beach at Fred Howard Park ($5 parking fee). Sunset Beach Park is a smaller alternative a little farther south. From Egmont Key, turn left from US 19 on Klosterman Road. Cross Alt US 19. Turn right on Carlton Road, left on Curlew Place, and right on Florida Ave. This last road will intersect Gulf Road (left to Sunset Beach Park) then Sunset Drive (left to Fred Howard Park).

If you are launching your own watercraft, use Anclote River Park. (Some charter boats also operate here.) Take Alt US 19 north of Anclote River. Turn left (west) on Anclote Boulevard, which turns north and becomes Ballies Bluff Road just before the park entrance on the left. While this park is near the mouth of the river and not much further from the lighthouse than Fred Howard Park, trees on intervening islands may obscure your view of the lighthouse.

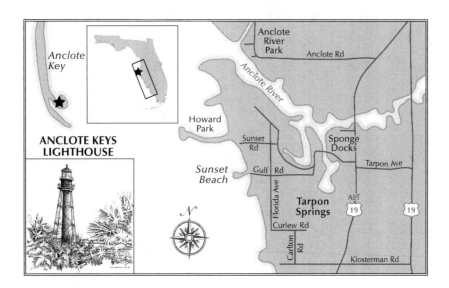

ANCLOTE KEYS LIGHTHOUSE

Anclote Key

Anclote River Park

Anclote Rd

Anclote River

Howard Park

Sunset Rd

Sponge Docks

Tarpon Ave

Sunset Beach

Gulf Rd

Florida Ave

Tarpon Springs

ALT 19

19

Curlew Rd

Carlton Rd

Klosterman Rd

CEDAR KEYS
LIGHTHOUSE

SEAHORSE KEY
(NEAR CEDAR KEY), FLORIDA

Elinor De Wire

Three miles from the town of Cedar Key, between the estuaries of the Suwannee and Waccasassa rivers, is Seahorse Key, a tiny green sequin on the dark blue dress of the vast Gulf of Mexico. Though small and remote, the Key has been important to navigation since 1854, when the government built the Cedar Keys Lighthouse as a beacon for freighters hauling the area's lumber and oysters. "Cedar Keys" refers collectively to Cedar Key, Seahorse Key, Atsena Otie Key, and other small islands in the area.

Congress originally appropriated funds for a lighthouse on Seahorse Key in 1850, with additional funds in 1852. Lt. George Meade selected the site on a fifty-two-foot sand hill and designed the lighthouse. Since it would serve as a local harbor light and benefited from natural elevation, he designed Florida's first cottage-style lighthouse. It is also the only cottage-style lighthouse in Florida made of brick rather than wood. Workers arrived in April 1853 and finished in July. Cedar Keys Lighthouse was first lighted August 1, 1853. At a cost of $12,000, this was one of Florida's least expensive lighthouses. Although Meade worked on seven Florida lighthouses, Cedar Keys represents the only one for which he selected the site, designed the structure, and saw it completed during his time as district engineer (although he did not personally supervise construction).

As with many other southern sentinels, the lighthouse saw travail and change during the Civil War. It was darkened in 1861 by Confederate troops, who stormed the islet, dismantled the lens, and occupied the station as quarters. A Union gunboat captured them a short time later and used the lighthouse as a prison until the end of the war. The beacon was relighted on August 23, 1866. A new detached kitchen was built in 1867; it was later connected to the main dwelling by a breezeway. A brick oil house was built in 1891. A hurricane damaged the lighthouse in September 1896 and devasted Cedar Key.

The lighthouse enjoyed several decades of vital service when Cedar Key was the western terminus of the only cross-Florida railroad. By the turn of the century, this railroad had plenty of competition from larger ports. The lumber and fishing industries in the area had begun to decline. Big freighters no longer plied the waters here, and fishermen in their small boats relied more on small beacons and post lights rather than the lighthouse. In addition, the Cedar Keys Lighthouse was becoming more difficult to see because of stands of trees on the key and its neighboring islets. The lighthouse was discontinued and abandoned in 1915.

The structure served as a private residence, whose owner added the wooden wings, until 1936, when the Cedar Keys National Wildlife Refuge was created, mainly to protect Florida's endangered nesting birds. Though the beacon was not relighted, the lighthouse became a staging point for various wildlife studies in the area. In 1953, the University of Florida established a marine laboratory in the lighthouse. Since that time, it has served as a beacon of learning for the many students and scientists whose projects add to our knowledge of Florida's natural environment.

Cedar Keys Lighthouse was relighted on July 5, 2019, with a replica fourth-order lens made by Artworks Florida. The lighthouse is only open to the public a few times each year when the Nature Coast Biological Station hosts open house events.

SITE FACTS

Dates of Construction: 1854
First Lighted: August 1, 1854
Electrified: 2019
Automated: never
Discontinued: 1915—July 5, 2019
Tower Height: 33 feet
Focal Height: 75 feet
Designer/Architect: George G. Meade
Builder/Supervisor: unknown
Type of Tower: brick cottage-style
Foundation Materials: brick
Construction Materials: brick, iron, and wood
Number of Stairs: 35
Daymark: white lantern on roof of white dwelling
Status: active—private ATON
Original Optic: fourth-order FVF Fresnel lens (Henry-Lepaute, 1854)
Other Optics Used: none
Current Optic: fourth-order FVF Fresnel lens (Artworks Florida, 2019)
Characteristic: fixed white light varied by one flash every sixty seconds
Station Auxiliary Structures: wood frame additions attached to original structure (1920s), oil house (1891), cistern, water tank
National Register of Historic Places: yes (part of Cedar Keys Historic & Archaeological District)
Owner: Cedar Keys National Wildlife Refuge
Operating Entity: University of Florida Nature Coast Biological Station
Grounds Open to the Public: open house events only
Tower Open to the Public: open house events only
Lighthouse Museum: none at lighthouse; permanent exhibit at Cedar Key Historical Society
Gift Shop: yes—at Cedar Key Historical Society
Hours: open house weekends only

Lighthouse Passport Stamp: yes—Cedar Keys Historical Society Museum or
  Cedar Keys NWR
Handicapped Access: no
Contact: Nature Coast Biological Station, PO Box 878, Cedar Key, FL
  32625 or Cedar Keys National Wildlife Refuge, 16450 NW 31st Place,
  Chiefland, FL 32626
Phone: 352-325-6078 (NCBS) or 352-493-0238 (NWR)
Email: ncbs@ifas.ufl.edu (NCBS) or lowersuwannee@fws.gov (NWR)
Websites: ncbs.ifas.ufl.edu/open-house and www.fws.gov/refuge/Cedar_
  Keys

DIRECTIONS

From Tarpon Springs, head north on Alt US 19, which will merge with US
Highway 19. Continue north to Otter Creek, merging with US Highway 98
along the way. Turn left (west) on State Road 24. After crossing a causeway,
you will reach Cedar Key where the road becomes D Street.

The lighthouse is on Seahorse Key, about 3 miles southwest of Cedar Key,
and only accessible by boat. Seahorse Key is visible from the Cedar Key Fishing
Pier, but the lighthouse is not normally visible. Boat ramps and charter boats
are available in Cedar Key, and ferry service is provided from Cedar Key to
Seahorse Key during NCBS open house events.

Cedar Keys Historical Society Museum has a permanent exhibit about the
lighthouse and the lighthouse passport stamp. They are located at the intersection of D Street (SR 24) and 2nd Street (609 2nd Street, Cedar Key, FL 32625;
(352) 543-5549; www.cedarkeyhistory.org; 11 AM–4 PM Saturday and 1
PM–4 PM Sunday–Friday).

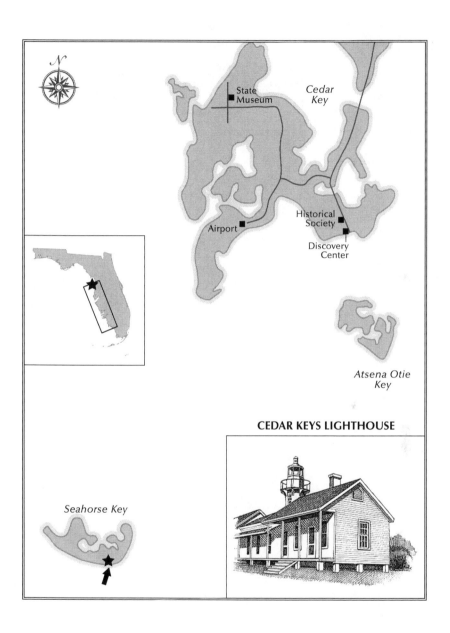

State
Museum

Cedar
Key

Airport

Historical
Society

Discovery
Center

Atsena Otie
Key

CEDAR KEYS LIGHTHOUSE

Seahorse Key

Section IV
THE FLORIDA NORTHWEST COAST

ST. MARKS
LIGHTHOUSE

NEAR ST. MARKS, FLORIDA

Josh Liller and Craig Kittendorf

The Spanish established Fort San Marcos de Apalachee in 1679 at the junction of the San Marcos (St. Marks) and Wakulla rivers. (The fort site is now a state park.) After the United States acquired Florida, the fort and river gave their name to a small port city established in 1823. It was the first of several such river ports serving Tallahassee, particularly for the export of cotton from the area.

Congress made three appropriations for a total of $20,000 to fund a lighthouse at the mouth of the St. Marks River. Winslow Lewis designed the tower and, typical for his projects, St. Marks came in well under budget. Shortly after construction began, builders Benjamin Beal and Jairus Thayer determined that the ground would not support the weight of the planned tower, so they used hollow walls instead of solid walls. The lighthouse was first lighted on January 29, 1830, but St. Marks Collector of Customs Jesse Willis refused to accept it and accused the builders of fraud. Calvin Knowlton was contracted to rebuild the lighthouse, with this second tower entering service in March 1831. Both lighthouses used the same fifteen Lewis lamps with 15-inch reflectors.

As the original builders predicted, the weight of the tower combined with erosion began to cause the tower to crack only a few months after it was completed. Metal bands were installed to hold the lighthouse together. In 1842, the government opted to demolish the existing lighthouse and build a new one at a better nearby location. Calvin Knowlton again supervised construction. The third and final St. Marks Lighthouse was first lighted April 21, 1842.

The hurricane of September 1843 devastated the nearby river towns of Port Leon, St. Marks, and Magnolia. St. Marks rebuilt, Magnolia moved to a better location and became Newport, and Port Leon was abandoned. Lighthouse keeper John T. Hungeford and his family rode out the hurricane in the lighthouse, but thirteen others who sought safety there drowned. A seawall was built in 1844 by Francis A. Gibbons of Baltimore (who did other lighthouse projects during this period) to protect the lighthouse, but it was badly damaged by another hurricane in 1851.

In 1854, a new permanent limestone keeper's dwelling was built on an elevated foundation that included a cistern under the kitchen (still extant). The dwelling walls were four feet thick, filled with shells and sand. The dwelling attached directly to the base of the tower. As part of the same project, a breakwater was built to protect the lighthouse. The wood piling foundation of the tower was found to be decayed, so a new grillage was built under the tower and the base of the tower reinforced with concrete. Underpinning a brick lighthouse is no easy feat, and no contractor would accept the job. However, it was accomplished without accident under the supervision of District Engineer Daniel Leadbetter. A fourth-order Fresnel lens was also installed in 1856.

As with most other Florida lighthouses, St. Marks was darkened during the Civil War. In 1862, Union ships shelled Confederate earthworks near the lighthouse. Union sailors burned the tower's wooden stairs in 1863 to prevent the lighthouse from being used as a lookout tower by the Confederates. In 1865, Union troops landed near the lighthouse and marched toward Tallahassee but were defeated at the Battle of Natural Bridge. At some point during the war, the keeper's dwelling was burned and the lighthouse damaged. The cause was suspected to be Confederates attempting to blow up the lighthouse. The lighthouse was repaired in the fall of 1866, and a new fourth-order fixed Fresnel lens was lighted on January 8, 1867. The keeper dwelling was rebuilt in 1871, but using essentially the same design as its 1854 predecessor.

The St. Marks National Wildlife Refuge was established in 1931 to protect local wildlife and migratory birds. The eight-acre lighthouse reservation was surrounded by a nature preserve that eventually grew to ninety thousand acres. As part of the construction at the refuge, the Civilian Conservation Corps built a road and electrical line to the lighthouse. Electricity allowed the light to be changed from fixed to occulting. The light was automated in 1960. The Fresnel lens was discontinued in 2000 but left in place. Its replacement was a solar-powered modern beacon attached to the gallery deck railing.

Transfer of the lighthouse from the Coast Guard to the Refuge was approved in 2006 but was delayed until 2013 because of the need to remove lead-contaminated soil around the tower. The lighthouse and dwelling were restored in 2016 to 2018, mostly funded by a $550,000 appropriation by the State of Florida. The Fresnel lens was removed from the tower, restored at Ponce Inlet Light Station, and placed on display in the Refuge's visitor center. A functional replica of the lens, manufactured by Artworks Florida, was installed in 2019 and first lighted on October 31 of that year to celebrate the eighty-eighth anniversary of the Refuge. The keeper's dwelling museum is open on a limited schedule, but the tower itself is not open for climbing.

SITE FACTS

Dates of Construction: 1829–1830; 1830–1831; 1841–1842
First Lighted: January 29, 1830; March 1831; April 21, 1842
Electrified: May 1939
Automated: 1960

Discontinued: 2016–2019

Tower Height: 88 feet

Focal Height: 82 feet

Designer/Architect: Winslow Lewis

Builder/Supervisor: Benjamin Beal and Jairus Thayer (1829–1830); Calvin Knowlton (1830–1831 and 1842)

Type of Tower: conical brick

Foundation Materials: wood (pilings and grillage), limestone, concrete

Construction Materials: brick and iron

Number of Stairs: 86

Daymark: white tower with black lantern and attached white dwelling

Status: active—private ATON

Original Optic: 15 Lewis lamps with 15-inch reflectors

Other Optics Used: fourth-order fixed Fresnel lens (1856–1861), fourth-order fixed Fresnel lens (1867–2000); solar-powered modern optic on gallery deck (2000–2016)

Current Optic: replica fourth-order fixed Fresnel lens (2019–present)

Fresnel Lens Manufacturers: unknown (1850s); Henry-Lepaute (1850s); Artworks Florida (2019)

Characteristic: fixed white light (1831–1938); occulting white, with a two-second eclipse every five seconds (1938–2016)

Station Auxiliary Structures: attached keeper dwelling (1854, rebuilt 1871)

National Register of Historic Places: yes

Owner: US Fish & Wildlife

Operating Entity: St. Marks National Wildlife Refuge

Tower Open to the Public: no

Grounds Open to the Public: yes—daily

Lighthouse Museum: yes—visitor center and keeper's dwelling

Gift Shop: yes—in visitor center

Lighthouse Passport Stamp: yes—in visitor center

Hours—NWR: daily sunrise–sunset

Hours—Visitor Center: 8 AM–4 PM Monday–Friday and 10 AM–5 PM Saturday–Sunday

Hours—Dwelling Museum: 10 AM–4 PM, first consecutive Friday and Saturday of every month. 11 AM–2 PM every Tuesday

Adult Admission: $5/car (refuge, including visitor center), $2/person (lighthouse museum)

Handicapped Access: yes—visitor center and keeper's dwelling museum

Contact: St. Marks National Wildlife Refuge, PO Box 68, St. Marks, FL
   32355
Phone: (850) 925-6121
Email: saintmarkslighthouse@fws.gov
Website: www.stmarkslighthouse.net and www.fws.gov/refuge/st_marks

DIRECTIONS

From Cedar Key, take SR 24 to Otter Creek. Turn left on North US Highway
19/98. Go almost 79 miles to Perry, turn left on West US Highway 98 (Hampton Springs Road). Go about 37 miles to Newport and turn left onto Lighthouse
Road (CR 59). Enter St. Marks National Wildlife Refuge and pay admission.
The Visitor Center will be on your right (1255 Lighthouse Road). The lighthouse is, appropriately, at the south end of Lighthouse Road.

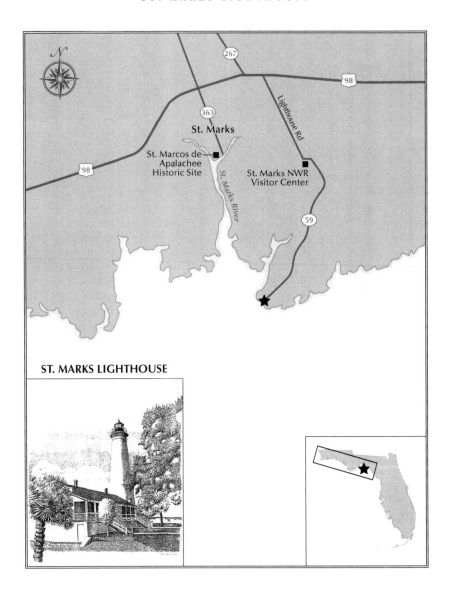

ST. MARKS LIGHTHOUSE

DOG ISLAND LIGHTHOUSE

NEAR CARRABELLE, FLORIDA
(Lighthouse Site Only)

Neil Hurley and Josh Liller

The merchants and mariners of St. Marks petitioned Congress for a light-house on South Cape Promontory (now known as Lighthouse Point) in 1834 to mark a shoal "on which disasters are of frequent occurrence." On March 3, 1837, Congress appropriated $10,000 for a lighthouse "at or near the east entrance . . . into Apalachicola Bay." Lighthouse authorities recommended the light be placed on the east end of St. George Island, and a compromise was eventually reached to build a lighthouse on the west end of Dog Island in 1838. As the Second Seminole War was then raging in Florida, three companies of the Sixth United States Infantry were stationed on the island to protect the lighthouse builders.

The contract called for a fifty-foot-tall conical brick tower with stone steps, a brick dwelling, a kitchen, and a privy. Winslow Lewis of Boston was the con-tractor, and Jacob D. Meyers, who became the first lighthouse keeper, was ap-pointed to superintend the lighthouse's construction. The white tower showed a flashing light from fourteen lamps with sixteen-inch reflectors.

An October 1842 hurricane destroyed the dwelling and badly damaged the top of the tower. A temporary wooden tower was erected until the lighthouse could be repaired. The Great Florida Panhandle Hurricane of 1851 collapsed the lighthouse and created a new channel through the island. The lighthouse was rebuilt the following year. In 1853, yet another hurricane struck, sweeping away the door at the base of the tower and breaking one of the windows and some of the lantern panes. In 1854, a new keeper's dwelling was built. In an ef-fort to make it resistant to storms, District Engineer Daniel Leadbetter designed the new octagonal house to stand eight feet off the ground on screwpiles that went eight feet into the sand. A fourth-order Fresnel lens replaced the old Lewis lamps in 1856.

During the Civil War, Confederate officials removed the lens to keep it out of Union hands. The island was used by Union blockade vessels to provide some rest for their crews. The keeper's dwelling and part of the lighthouse's wooden staircase were burned during the course of the war, and several holes were shot through the lantern. Everything was repaired in 1866.

In 1868, the Lighthouse Board forecast "the eventual destruction of the pres-ent tower" in a future hurricane due to its "dangerous exposure . . . on a low spit" of land. The Board recommended construction of a new iron screwpile tower on a nearby fifteen-foot sand hill. In the meantime, the base of the tower was reinforced with concrete. Beach erosion undermined the tower until, in 1872, it leaned one foot from the perpendicular. The lens was removed to a platform on the keeper's dwelling, which, because of its location farther back from the beach and its iron-pile foundation, was considered safer. Unfortunately, the Great Storm of 1873 destroyed both the tower and dwelling. The keeper and his assistant escaped unharmed and several years later were reimbursed by the government for private property lost to the storm.

Congress allocated $20,000 to rebuild the lighthouse. However, due to declining commerce in the area, the Lighthouse Board decided to indefinitely postpone building a new lighthouse. Two decades later, Crooked River Lighthouse was built on the nearby mainland and filled Dog Island's former role of guiding ships into East Pass.

Hurricanes and other natural forces have substantially reshaped Dog Island in the nearly century and a half since the destruction of the last lighthouse there. Numerous ships were washed ashore during a severe 1899 hurricane. The island was used for training in World War II by nearby Camp Gordon Johnston, located on the mainland near Carrabelle. Today, most of the island is owned by the Nature Conservancy, including the west part of the island closest to the former lighthouse site. Claims of brick rubble just offshore were proven true when Florida State University archaeologists located the submerged remains in 1999 and 2006.

SITE FACTS

Dates of Construction: 1838–1839; 1852
First Lighted: 1839; June 1, 1852
Electrified: N/A
Automated: N/A
Discontinued: 1873
Tower Height: 44 feet
Focal Height: 48 feet
Designer/Architect: Winslow Lewis
Builder/Supervisor: Jacob D. Meyers (1839); unknown (1852)
Type of Tower: conical brick
Foundation Materials: brick
Construction Materials: brick and iron
Number of Stairs: unknown
Daymark: white tower, black lantern
Status: destroyed
Original Optic: 14 Lewis lamps with 16-inch reflectors with revolving apparatus
Other Optics Used: fourth-order revolving Fresnel lens (1856–1861)

Optic Manufacturer: Henry-Lepaute (1855)

Current Optic: N/A

Characteristic: one flash every three minutes (1839–1856), one flash every minute (1856–1873)

Station Auxiliary Structures: none surviving

National Register of Historic Places: no

Owner: Nature Conservancy (site)

Operating Entity: N/A

Grounds Open to the Public: yes

Tower Open to the Public: N/A

Lighthouse Museum: yes—on the mainland at Crooked River Lighthouse

Gift Shop: none

Lighthouse Passport Stamp: no

Hours: daylight hours

Handicapped Access: no

Contact: none

DIRECTIONS

From the St. Marks Lighthouse, return to US Highway 98 and turn left (west). Follow the road to Carrabelle. The best place to observe the island from the mainland is from the top of the Crooked River Lighthouse (see next chapter).

Dog Island is three-and-a-half miles offshore and accessible only via boat or airplane (via the private airstrip). A boat ramp is located on Marine Street in Carrabelle. A passenger ferry service operates year-round between Carrabelle and Dog Island (Friday–Monday, once per day, reservations required). Carrabelle also has several marinas from which charter or rental boats may be available to take you to the island. Be aware that parts of the island are privately owned.

The former lighthouse site is in the Gulf just south of Dog Island near the east end of the island's western spit. Shifting sand may obscure the remains from divers. Nothing onshore marks the former site.

See next chapter for map.

CROOKED RIVER LIGHTHOUSE

CARRABELLE, FLORIDA

Barbara Revell

East Pass, between Dog and St. George islands, is one of the major entrances to St. George Sound and the port of Apalachicola. Originally, this pass was marked for navigation by the Dog Island Lighthouse, which was erected in 1839 and rebuilt in 1852. This last tower washed away in a hurricane in 1873. With commerce in the area diminished by the Civil War, the Lighthouse Board decided not to rebuild a lighthouse on Dog Island.

Depletion of northern forests ushered in a resurgence of the local economy in the late 1880s as a new lumber industry took hold. With increased trade now beginning to pour forth from the new booming port (named Carrabelle in 1897), a new lighthouse was needed. Petitions from local residents and reports from congressional committees favored the project. On July 31, 1888, Congress appropriated $40,000 for a lighthouse "on the main land to the westward of Crooked River."

Acquisition and proper surveying of twelve acres for the light station dragged on for several years, and some of the paperwork went up in flames during a courthouse fire. Work finally began in January 1895 and was completed in August of that year. The new skeletal iron tower had an unusual bivalve fourth-order Fresnel lens that rotated on possibly the first mercury float used in a US lighthouse. The tower was originally painted red with a black lantern. An oil house was completed early the next year, and a small beacon was built out in the bay to serve as a range with the lighthouse.

The station had a wharf over four hundred feet long with a boathouse. These structures had to be repeatedly rebuilt due to hurricanes and other storms. In 1901, to give the lighthouse better contrast against the darkness of the sur-rounding forest, it was painted with its present color pattern—its lower half white, its upper half dark red.

Although of great importance to area commerce, this lighthouse was con-sidered in need of only a principal keeper and one assistant. When one had to leave for an extended period—such as when the assistant keeper had to tend his seriously ill wife in Carrabelle in 1897—the other keeper had to assume all the duties.

Carrabelle was expected to develop into a major timber-exporting city, but the growth of Apalachicola to the west and a decline in the lumber industry slowed its planned growth, and only a relatively small city remained near the lighthouse. During World War II, when Camp Gordon Johnston was con-structed nearby to train recruits for amphibious assault landings, the impor-tance of the lighthouse as an aid to navigation increased. To avoid the German submarine threat off the coast of Florida, a gasoline pipeline and terminal were built in Franklin County to transport gasoline to Jacksonville. The lighthouse helped guide numerous gasoline barges into Carrabelle for the war effort. After the war, the pipeline and the training camp were dismantled, and the people of Carrabelle returned to fishing and some lumbering for survival.

The lighthouse remained to mark the east end of the north Gulf Coast's Intracoastal Waterway. Vessels coming west and north along Florida's west coast have to pass over two hundred miles of open Gulf waters from Tarpon Springs before reaching this shelter of an inland waterway. The Crooked River Lighthouse showed them the way.

The lighthouse was automated in 1952. The two keeper dwellings and outbuildings were auctioned off by the government in 1964 and moved offsite. One of the houses later burned down. In 1976, the Fresnel lens was replaced by a modern rotating beacon due to leakage from the lens' mercury float. The Coast Guard placed it on display in New Orleans at their Eighth District headquarters.

The Crooked River Lighthouse was decommissioned on August 23, 1995, and its future looked dismal. However, the Carrabelle Lighthouse Association formed in 1999 to preserve this important landmark of the area's maritime heritage. In 2000, the General Services Administration turned the lighthouse over to the City of Carrabelle, which leased the lighthouse to be restored and operated as a historic site by the Association.

With the aid of grants from the State of Florida and the Florida Communities Trust, the lighthouse was restored and relighted on December 8, 2007, with a replica of its original lens created by Dan Spinella's Artworks Florida. A replica of one of the keeper houses opened in 2009 to serve as a museum and gift shop. The Coast Guard has declined to return the original lens for display in the museum. Crooked River's wash house was found nearby, purchased, and returned to the station where it was restored in 2012. As of 2019, efforts were being made to acquire the surviving keeper dwelling and move it back to the light station where it too will be restored.

SITE FACTS

Dates of Construction: 1895
First Lighted: October 28, 1895
Electrified: 1933
Automated: 1952
Deactivated: August 23, 1995–December 8, 2007
Tower Height: 103 feet
Focal Height: 115 feet

Designer/Architect: unknown
Manufacturer: Tacony Iron and Metal Company, Philadelphia, PA
Builder/Supervisor: unknown
Type of Tower: square pyramidal skeletal iron
Foundation Materials: concrete
Construction Materials: iron
Number of Stairs: 138
Daymark: lower half white (since 1901), upper half dark red, black lantern
Status: active—private ATON
Original Optic: fourth-order open bivalve Fresnel lens (1895–1976)
Original Optic Manufacturer: Henry-Lepaute (1894)
Other Optics Used: 190 mm rotating beacon (1976–1995)
Current Optic: replica fourth-order open bivalve Fresnel lens (Artworks Florida, 2007)
Characteristic: two flashes every fifteen seconds
Station Auxiliary Structures: wash house (1895), replica keeper's dwelling (2009)
National Register of Historic Places: yes (1978)
Owner: City of Carrabelle
Operating Entity: Carrabelle Lighthouse Association (nonprofit)
Grounds Open to the Public: yes
Tower Open to the Public: yes
Minimum Height to Climb: 44 inches
Lighthouse Museum: yes
Gift Shop: yes
Lighthouse Passport Stamp: yes—in gift shop
Hours: 11 AM–4 PM Wednesday–Friday, 9 AM–4 PM Saturday, 1 PM–5 PM Sunday
Adult Admission: $5 lighthouse climb; museum free
Handicapped Access: yes—gift shop, museum, and base of tower
Contact: Carrabelle Lighthouse Association, 1975 W. Highway 98, Carrabelle, FL 32322
Phone: (850) 697-2732
Email: carrabellelighthouse@gmail.com
Website: www.crookedriverlighthouse.com

DIRECTIONS

From Carrabelle, continue west on US Highway 98 (Coastal Highway). The lighthouse will be on the right about 2 miles after the Carrabelle River bridge and one-half mile after the Camp Gordon Johnson Museum.

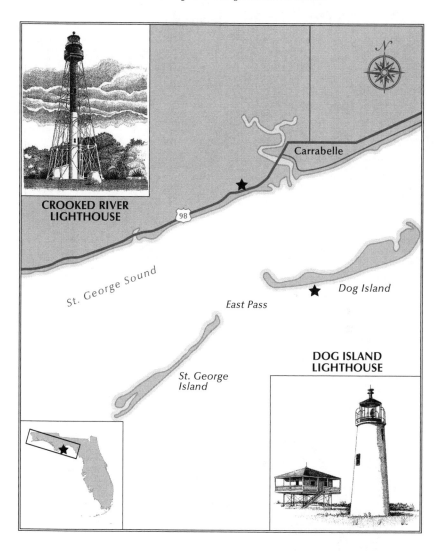

(NEW) CAPE
ST. GEORGE
LIGHTHOUSE

ST. GEORGE ISLAND, FLORIDA

Josh Liller

St. George Island is a twenty-eight-mile long barrier island in the Florida Panhandle, roughly parallel to the coast from Carrabelle to Apalachicola. It is no more than a mile wide and separated from the mainland by the four-mile-wide Apalachicola Bay (aka St. George Sound). It is separated from Dog Island by East Pass and Little St. George Island by the Bob Sikes Cut, aka Government Cut. Little St. George Island only became a separate island in 1954. The State of Florida acquired the eastern end of (Big) St. George Island in 1963 and opened it as Dr. Julian G. Bruce St. George Island State Park in 1980. The western end is occupied by St. George Plantation, a high-end residential community. The rest of the island is mostly vacation homes, with a small commercial district in the center. The St. George Island Bridge from Eastpoint was built in 1965 and replaced in 2004.

The nonprofit St. George Lighthouse Association (SGLA) formed in 2004. The organization initially planned to continue the work started by the Cape St. George Lighthouse Society to preserve the seriously endangered 1852 Cape St. George Lighthouse at its historic location on Little St. George Island. However, a series of storms culminated in the lighthouse being toppled on October 21, 2005, during heavy seas caused by Hurricane Wilma. An aerial photo taken the next day, showing the shattered lighthouse lying in the surf, galvanized support like nothing else could.

Six months later, a barge collected the broken pieces of the lighthouse and transported them to Eastpoint. The iron lens pedestal dating from the original 1857 Fresnel lens was recovered intact. Volunteers painstakingly cleaned the recovered bricks by hand. On December 1, 2006, the Association unveiled a full-size replica of the 1857 lantern in a beachfront park located at the south end of the causeway from the mainland.

Groundbreaking for a reconstruction of the 1852 lighthouse occurred on October 22, 2007. A special state legislative appropriation, several grants (some from the Florida Lighthouse Association), and funds raised by SGLA funded the project. Concrete pilings were driven forty feet deep to ensure maximum stability against any hurricane. The interior bricks of the lighthouse were mostly those salvaged from the destroyed lighthouse. The lantern was placed on the soapstone deck at the top of the tower on April 2, 2008. The lighthouse opened to visitors in November of that year. The formal dedication of the rebuilt lighthouse occurred April 4, 2009. The lighthouse received a VLB-44 LED beacon later that year. The light flashes only from November 1 through April 30; it is dark the rest of the year to avoid disturbing nesting sea turtles.

A gift shop and museum opened next to the lighthouse on August 21, 2011. The building was a near replica of the original brick keeper's dwelling, with some modifications to meet modern building codes as well as better hurricane resistance, ADA access, and air conditioning. The museum exhibits tell the story of the lighthouse and its keepers, including artifacts recovered from the wrecked lighthouse and a full-size replica of the lighthouse's third-order Fresnel lens. The fate of the lens removed in 1949 is uncertain, but it is suspected to be one displayed in the town hall in Berwick, Louisiana. (The Town of Berwick disagrees.)

Although sometimes called the St. George Island Lighthouse to distinguish it from its predecessors, SGLA decided to officially retain the name "Cape St. George Lighthouse" for the reconstructed tower even though it is no longer located at the cape. Whatever you call it, the lighthouse represents a remarkable accomplishment. Because it was built not only with the original drawings but also with much of the original material, the 2008 lighthouse is considered a reconstruction rather than a replica. Thus it is counted among the state's thirty surviving historic lighthouses. Lighthouse historian Neil Hurley sums it up nicely: "To go from a mass of rubble on an isolated beach to a vibrant local landmark, museum, and historic site—largely due to volunteers—is a model worthy of national recognition."

SITE FACTS

Dates of Construction: 2006–2008

First Lighted: October 31, 2009

Tower Height: 65 feet

Focal Height: 77 feet

Designer/Architect: unknown (duplicate of the 1852 Cape St. George Lighthouse)

Builder/Supervisor: Dennis Barnell

Type of Tower: conical brick

Foundation Materials: concrete pilings and cement

Construction Materials: brick (tower), wood (stairs), soapstone (deck), and steel (lantern)

Number of Stairs: 92

Daymark: white tower, black lantern

Status: active (seasonal)—private ATON

Original Optic: Vega VLB-44

Other Optics Used: none

Current Optic: original

Characteristic: one flash every six seconds
Station Auxiliary Structures: replica keeper's dwelling (2011)
National Register of Historic Places: yes
Owner: State of Florida Department of Environmental Protection
Operating Entity: St. George Lighthouse Association (nonprofit)
Grounds Open to the Public: yes
Tower Open to the Public: yes
Minimum Height for Climbing: 40 inches
Lighthouse Museum: yes
Gift Shop: yes
Lighthouse Passport Stamp: yes—in gift shop
Hours: 10 AM–5 PM Monday–Wednesday and Friday–Saturday (12 PM–5
  PM November–February); 12 PM–5 PM Sunday; closed Thursday
Adult Admission: $5 lighthouse climb; free museum.
Handicapped Access: yes—gift shop, first floor of museum, and to base of
  tower
Contact: Cape St. George Light Museum, 2B E. Gulf Beach Drive, St.
  George Island, FL 32328
Phone: (850) 927-7745
Email: info@stgeorgelight.org
Website: www.stgeorgelight.org

DIRECTIONS

From the Crooked River Lighthouse, head west on US Highway 98 to Eastpoint, turn left (south) on Island Drive (SR 300) and cross the St. George Island
Causeway. When the road ends at Gulf Beach Drive the lighthouse will be almost directly in front of you. Turn right, then take the first left where there is a
paved parking lot and adjacent sand lot (both free). Note that these parking lots
can be very busy on weekends due to beachgoers at the county park.

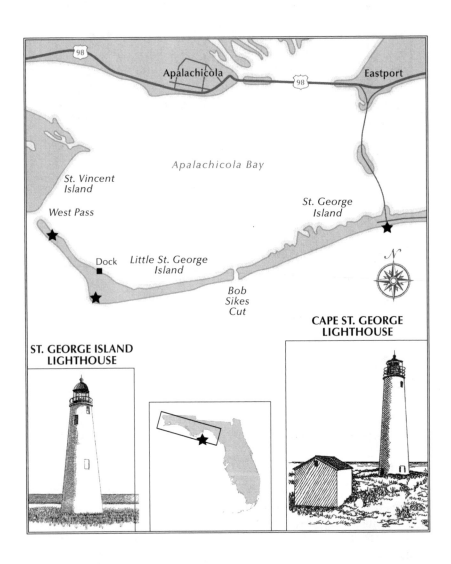

St. Vincent Island

West Pass

Apalachicola Bay

St. George Island

Apalachicola

Eastport

Dock

Little St. George Island

Bob Sikes Cut

CAPE ST. GEORGE LIGHTHOUSE

ST. GEORGE ISLAND LIGHTHOUSE

(OLD) CAPE ST. GEORGE LIGHTHOUSE

LITTLE ST. GEORGE ISLAND
OFF APALACHICOLA, FLORIDA
(Lighthouse Site Only)

Josh Liller and John Lee

While the original St. George Island Lighthouse was effective for marking West Pass, it was not in a good location for coastal shipping. The island angles southeast several miles to Cape St. George, thus vessels approaching from the east would not see the lighthouse until dangerously close to the cape. The simple solution was to move the lighthouse to this better location, and on March 3, 1847, Congress allocated $8,000 for that purpose. Later that year the existing lighthouse was taken down and rebuilt about three miles away. The illuminating apparatus from the old tower was lighted in the new tower on March 3, 1848.

The second lighthouse on St. George Island did not last long. A major hurricane made landfall in the Panhandle in August 1851 and caused the tower to fall over. This same hurricane also destroyed the lighthouses at Dog Island and Cape San Blas.

Edward Bowden of Franklin County built the 1852 lighthouse and was able to reuse two-thirds of the bricks from the 1847 lighthouse in his construction. The tower was sixty-five-feet tall from base to lantern deck with a base diameter of twenty feet and a top diameter of twelve feet. The walls were almost solid brick, with a header course every nine courses, and are uniformly graduated from four feet thick at the bottom to two feet thick at the top. The tower was capped with a five-inch-thick soapstone deck fourteen feet in diameter. This third lighthouse was first lighted on June 1, 1852. A third-order Fresnel lens was installed in 1857 and was visible from a distance of fourteen miles.

During the Civil War, the valuable lens and its components were removed for safekeeping and delivered to the Confederate Collector of Customs in Apalachicola. Federal troops occupied the light station for a short period during the Civil War. According to research by historian Neil Hurley, Cape St. George's lens was among the first batch sent back to France for repairs at the end of the war. The lighthouse was relighted with its old lens on August 1, 1866.

The light station originally had a brick keeper's dwelling. It may have been the same one as the original lighthouse at West Pass, taken apart and rebuilt at the new location much like the lighthouse. Another keeper's dwelling was added in 1877. A sandy trail led several miles across the island to a wharf on the bay side. A new 940-foot-long wharf was constructed in 1898, standing on iron pipe piles.

The lighthouse switched to kerosene lamps in 1882. In 1889, the lighthouse received a new lens of the same size that illuminated the entire horizon. The old lens had a "dark angle" of sixty degrees since the Civil War, and this drew complaints from mariners. An oil house was completed in December 1894. A rope handrail was added to the tower in 1903 to make climbing the stairs easier.

Electricity came to the station in the 1930s in the form of a diesel generator. Coast Guard lookouts were assigned to Cape St. George during World War II. Because the lighthouse lacked a traditional gallery deck, a lookout tower was built at the station. The assistant keeper's wooden house burned down during the 1940s. In 1949, the historic Fresnel lens was removed and replaced by a drum lens with a flashing light inside. The lighthouse was automated at this time. A modern beacon was installed in 1977 and, not long afterward, metal stairs replaced the wooden ones.

In 1954, the Army Corps of Engineers cut a channel through St. George Island to provide easier access to Apalachicola. This is known as Government Cut or Bob Sikes Cut (after the congressman who sponsored the project). The island between the new cut and West Pass became known as Little St. George Island (or sometimes Cape St. George Island).

Although originally built five hundred yards from the Gulf, erosion became a serious threat by the 1990s and the Coast Guard decommissioned the lighthouse in 1994. Hurricane Andrew washed away a large part of the surrounding beach in 1992, and Hurricane Opal left the tower with a serious lean in 1995. The tilt detached the staircase from the wall, and volunteers subsequently removed it as a safety concern. The Cape St. George Lighthouse Society formed to save the historic structure. By 1999 they had raised enough funds to hire a contractor, who removed sand to settle the tower back on an even keel and built a concrete foundation around the base. The Society disbanded in 2002.

Erosion continued, and within a few years the tower was standing in shallow water with the concrete foundation crumbling. By this time the brick keeper's house and oil house had also been destroyed. Hurricane Ivan in 2004 and Hurricane Dennis in 2005 accelerated the deterioration. Then on October 21, 2005, heavy seas caused by Hurricane Wilma sent the lighthouse toppling into the surf. Fortunately, the lighthouse would be reborn on nearby St. George Island in 2008 (see preceding chapter).

SITE FACTS

Dates of Construction: 1847–1848 and 1852
First Lighted: March 3, 1848, and June 1, 1852
Electrified: 1930s
Automated: 1949
Discontinued: May 19, 1994
Tower Height: 75 feet (1847); 72 feet (1852)

Focal Height: 70 feet (1847); 77 feet (1852)
Designer/Architect: Winslow Lewis (1847); unknown (1852)
Builder/Supervisor: Edward Bowden (1847); Charles Emerson and Edward Adams (1852)
Type of Tower: conical brick
Foundation Materials: brick (1848); pine pilings and brick (1852); brick and concrete (1999)
Construction Materials: brick, iron, soapstone, and wood
Number of Stairs: unknown
Daymark: white tower, black lantern
Status: destroyed
Original Optic: 15 Lewis Lamps with 16-inch reflectors (1847–1857)
Other Optics Used: third-order fixed Fresnel lens (1857–1889), third-order fixed Fresnel lens (1889–1949), fifth-order (375 mm) drum Fresnel lens (1949–1977), 300 mm lantern (1977–1994)
Fresnel Lens Manufacturers: Sautter et Cie (1850s), possibly Sautter et Cie (1860s?), unknown
Current Optic: N/A
Characteristic: fixed white (1847–1949); one white flash every ten seconds (1949–1977); one white flash every six seconds (1977–1994)
Station Auxiliary Structures: none surviving
National Register of Historic Places: yes
Owner: State of Florida (site)
Operating Entity: Apalachicola National Estuarine Research Reserve (site)
Grounds Open to the Public: yes
Tower Open to the Public: N/A
Lighthouse Museum: yes—offsite at the rebuilt lighthouse on St. George Island
Gift Shop: yes—offsite at the rebuilt lighthouse on St. George Island
Lighthouse Passport Stamp: no
Hours: daylight hours (site)
Adult Admission: none
Handicapped Access: no
Contact: none

DIRECTIONS

Cape St. George and the rest of Little St. George Island are accessible only by boat, and there is no regular ferry service to the island. The nearest boat ramps and potential charter service are in Apalachicola nine miles across the bay. There are two docks on the bay side of the island almost due north of the cape: Marshall Dock and Government Dock. From either dock, follow the Short Road trail nearly three-fourths of a mile across the island, then turn left on Lighthouse Road trail, which leads to the beach near the cape.

Cape St. George remains the southernmost point on the island, but the exact location has been shifted by hurricanes and barrier island dynamics. Nothing remains to indicate the former lighthouse site, which is now located just offshore.

From the cape it is five miles east to Sikes Cut and four miles west to West Pass. A few primitive campsites are available on the island at Government Dock and near both ends of the island. The few trails on the island are wide and sandy. The Marshall House is the only structure on the island and is not open to the public.

Map is located the end of the chapter about the rebuilt Cape St. George Lighthouse.

ST. GEORGE ISLAND (WEST PASS) LIGHTHOUSE

LITTLE ST. GEORGE ISLAND, OFF APALACHICOLA, FLORIDA
(Lighthouse Site Only)

Thomas W. Taylor

In the late 1820s, the new port of Apalachicola was growing rapidly, handling most of the commerce from several agricultural counties in Georgia, Alabama, and Florida. To help provide for the safe entrance of vessels into St. George Sound and Apalachicola Bay, the Florida territorial legislature, in 1829, passed a resolution requesting its congressional delegates to obtain an appropriation for the building of a lighthouse. In 1831, Congress finally authorized the building of a lighthouse on the west end of St. George Island for $11,400. This lighthouse would mark the West Pass that separated St. George Island from St. Vincent Island.

At first, there was some delay and confusion, as the fifth auditor of the treasury, the man who was responsible for building and maintaining America's lighthouses, had chosen the collector of customs from St. Marks to locate a site for and build the lighthouse. The fifth auditor had not known that Apalachicola now had its own collector of customs, who should have been in charge of the lighthouses in his area.

When the people of Apalachicola found out that a man from St. Marks would locate and oversee their lighthouse, they were indignant. The public pressure led the fifth auditor to appoint the Apalachicola collector to the task. Unfortunately, all of this delayed the construction of the new lighthouse.

Finally, in May 1833, Winslow Lewis received the contract for "building a light house and dwelling house on the west end of St. George's Island." Both structures were completed that fall. Like many of the lighthouses in this section of Florida, the new lighthouse on St. George Island was damaged in numerous storms and several major hurricanes. Because of this, this lighthouse was often "in bad order." After a major hurricane in 1842, the lighthouse was repaired and received fifteen new lamps with sixteen-inch reflectors. The local lighthouse superintendent could then report "everything in good repair and condition."

As commercial traffic in the Gulf increased, mariners needed a coastal aid to navigation on Cape St. George that would help them steer past the shoals, and the St. George Island Lighthouse on the west end of the island did not serve this purpose. A movement started to build a new lighthouse at the cape. Finally, in 1846, after Florida had become a state, Congress acceded to the demand for the new lighthouse. The contractor was permitted to tear down the St. George Island Lighthouse and use its materials to build the new lighthouse about three miles to the southeast. The lighting apparatus from the old tower was transferred to the new lighthouse. This new tower, the first Cape St. George

Lighthouse, was a near duplicate of the old St. George Island Lighthouse and was lighted on March 3, 1848.

Today, no major ruins of this lighthouse exist, but some brick rubble has been found on the west end of what is now Little St. George Island (sometimes called Cape St. George Island). The State of Florida acquired the island in 1977 for preservation, and today it is managed by Apalachicola National Estuarine Research Reserve.

SITE FACTS

Dates of Construction: 1833
First Lighted: late 1833
Electrified: N/A
Automated: N/A
Discontinued: 1847
Tower Height: 75 feet
Focal Height: 70 feet
Designer/Architect: Winslow Lewis
Builder/Supervisor: Winslow Lewis
Type of Tower: brick (tower), wood (stairs), soapstone (deck), and iron (lantern)
Foundation Materials: brick
Construction Materials: brick
Number of Stairs: unknown
Daymark: white tower, black lantern
Status: demolished
Original Optic: 13 Lewis lamps with 13-inch reflectors (1833–1842)
Other Optics Used: 15 Lewis lamps with 16-inch reflectors (1842–1847)
Characteristic: fixed white light
Station Auxiliary Structures: none surviving
National Register of Historic Places: no
Owner: State of Florida (site)
Operating Entity: Apalachicola National Estuarine Research Reserve (site)
Grounds Open to the Public: yes
Tower Open to the Public: N/A
Lighthouse Museum: yes—offsite at the rebuilt lighthouse on St. George Island
Gift Shop: yes—offsite at the rebuilt lighthouse on St. George Island

Lighthouse Passport Stamp: no
Hours: daylight hours (site)
Adult Admission: none
Handicapped Access: no
Contact: none

DIRECTIONS

Little St. George Island is accessible only by boat, and there is no regular ferry service to the island. The nearest boat ramps and potential charter service are in Apalachicola ten miles across the bay from West Pass. The Pass is now about four miles along the beach from Cape St. George, or about three miles from the Gulf end of the Short Road trail. The west end of the island has been reshaped and shifted further west in the 170-plus years since the original lighthouse was demolished and moved. Nothing remains to indicate the former lighthouse site.

Map is located the end of the chapter about the rebuilt Cape St. George Lighthouse.

ST. JOSEPH BAY LIGHTHOUSE

NEAR PORT ST. JOE, FLORIDA
(Site Only)

Thomas W. Taylor

In the 1830s, an important new boomtown sprang up on Florida's Gulf Coast. Located on the east shore of St. Joseph's Bay, the city of St. Joseph would later become a terminus of Florida's first railroad and site of the convention that drew up the first state constitution for the proposed state of Florida.

Because of the increasing commerce to this new port, the Legislative Council of the Territory of Florida passed a resolution in 1836 asking that a lighthouse be erected on one of the points at the entrance to St. Joseph's Bay. On March 3, 1837, Congress appropriated $10,000 for the construction of the lighthouse. It took more than a year to select the site and secure the title to the land, but finally, in the fall of 1838, the new lighthouse was under construction. It was completed on February 23, 1839, and the fourteen lamps of its light were lighted shortly thereafter.

For a couple of years, the St. Joseph's Bay Lighthouse was the best kept and most efficient of the lighthouses in the Apalachicola District. The lighthouse even weathered storms without any problem. However, in 1841, a ship carrying yellow fever entered the port of St. Joseph, and the town's population was soon decimated by an epidemic. Between the plague and a major hurricane in 1844, the town's economy was destroyed. Before long, the few remaining citizens of St. Joseph had had enough, and the town was completely abandoned. Commerce now bypassed the area to which it had formerly been attracted.

However, commerce to the town of Apalachicola to the east was increasing, and more and more, large oceanic vessels were coasting the shores of Florida on their way to the growing port. The commercial interests of Apalachicola realized that the larger, coastal commercial vessels needed a major landfall light at Cape San Blas rather than at the mouth of St. Joseph's Bay.

In 1842, the Apalachicola Chamber of Commerce declared in a Memorial to Congress that "in erecting a Light House at St. Joseph's Bay, the location has proved . . . unfortunate, being . . . a harbor light and in no degree useful to Commerce, as that port is entirely abandoned for commercial purposes." Ship captains also joined the fray to change the lighthouse to Cape San Blas.

In 1843, the Collector of Customs at Apalachicola declared that the St. Joseph's Bay Lighthouse was in poor condition, and the decision was made to abandon the lighthouse. In 1846, contracts were let to build the new Cape San Blas Lighthouse to the south, and the contractors were given the right "to use the materials of the old lighthouse . . . as far as they could." The old tower was torn down, and the bricks, lantern, and lighting apparatus were moved south to Cape San Blas.

Today, little is left of the St. Joseph's Bay Lighthouse. The Lighthouse Board thought the original site washed away in an 1851 hurricane. In the 1990s, the Florida Park Service unknowingly bulldozed what may have been the remains of the lighthouse's foundation. Hurricane Michael probably washed away whatever scant traces remained in 2018.

SITE FACTS

Dates of Construction: 1838–1839
First Lighted: March 1839
Electrified: never
Automated: never
Discontinued: 1843
Status: demolished (1846)
Tower Height: 55 feet
Focal Height: 50 feet
Designer/Architect: unknown—probably Winslow Lewis
Builder/Supervisor: unknown
Type of Tower: conical brick
Foundation Materials: brick
Construction Materials: brick, soapstone, and iron
Number of Stairs: unknown
Daymark: white tower, black lantern
Original Optic: 14 Lewis lamps with 16-inch reflectors
Other Optics Used: none
Current Optic: N/A
Characteristic: fixed white light
Station Auxiliary Structures: none surviving
National Register of Historic Places: no
Owner: State of Florida (site)
Operating Entity: T. H. Stone Memorial St. Joseph Peninsula State Park (site)
Grounds Open to the Public: yes
Tower Open to the Public: N/A
Lighthouse Museum: no
Gift Shop: no
Lighthouse Passport Stamp: no
Hours: 8 AM–sunset daily (park)

Handicapped Access: no
Contact: T. H. Stone Memorial St. Joseph Peninsula State Park, 8899 Cape
San Blas Rd., Port St. Joe, FL 32456
Phone: (850) 227-1327
Website: www.floridastateparks.org/parks-and-trails/t-h-stone-memorial-st-joseph-peninsula-state-park
NOTE: Contact information is for park information only. Few, if any, park
personnel are familiar with the lighthouse or its former location.

DIRECTIONS

From Apalachicola, head west on US Highway 98. Turn left on County Road
30A, then left again on County Road 30E (Cape San Blas Road). Just past an
USAF site the road will curve to the right. At the curve there will be a gate on
the left. This road leads one-third mile to the former Cape San Blas Light Station site. Unfortunately, there is no public access. Continue on the main road to
St. Joseph Peninsula State Park ($6/car admission). Follow the park road to its
northernmost point. Follow the park's trails to near the end of the peninsula on
the east shore, the approximate former location of the lighthouse. The hike is
upward of 5 miles one way over sandy ground with little shade and no shelter.

NOTE: In October 2018, Hurricane Michael's storm surge did massive
damage to St. Joseph Peninsula State Park, including washing out nearly a mile
of the park road and opening a pass through the narrowest section of the peninsula. At the time of this writing, only the southern end of the park is open, and
it could be years before the road and other park facilities are repaired enough for
public access. Until the park reopens, prospective visitors will need to use one
of the alternative access methods.

Besides a long hike, the site can be viewed from a distance from the top of
Cape San Blas Lighthouse in Port St. Joe. The St. Joseph Bay Lighthouse site
is a little over 6 miles away looking WNW.

There is a bayside boat ramp in the southern portion of the state park. It is
a little over 6 miles from the boat ramp to the former lighthouse site. It about
6.5 miles across the bay from the boat ramp in Port St. Joe at the end of 5th
Street. There are also several marinas in Port St. Joe that might provide charter
or rental boats.

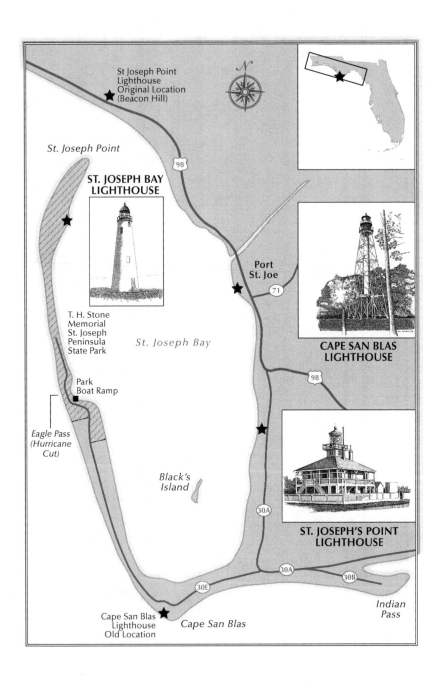

St Joseph Point
Lighthouse
Original Location
(Beacon Hill)

St. Joseph Point

98

**ST. JOSEPH BAY
LIGHTHOUSE**

Port
St. Joe

71

T. H. Stone
Memorial
St. Joseph
Peninsula
State Park

St. Joseph Bay

Park
Boat Ramp

98

**CAPE SAN BLAS
LIGHTHOUSE**

Eagle Pass
(Hurricane
Cut)

Black's
Island

**ST. JOSEPH'S POINT
LIGHTHOUSE**

30A

30A

30B

30E

Indian
Pass

Cape San Blas
Lighthouse
Old Location

Cape San Blas

ST. JOSEPH POINT LIGHTHOUSE

NEAR PORT ST. JOE, FLORIDA

Danny Raffield and Josh Liller

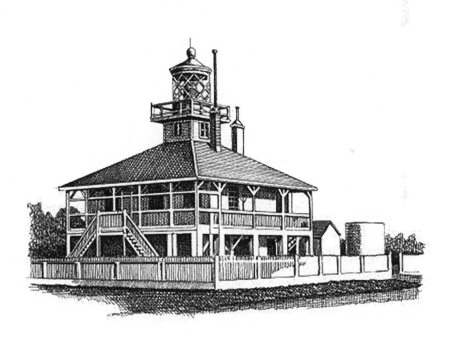

Although early Spanish and French explorers established a presence on the shores of St. Joseph's Bay, they did not stay, and the bay's sparsely populated shore stayed mostly unchanged until 1836, when the town of St. Joseph was founded. The town was a miracle of expansion, and with the increased commerce, a lighthouse was needed at the entrance to the bay. St. Joseph's Bay Lighthouse, located a short distance inside the peninsula marking the harbor's entrance, served this purpose from 1839 to 1846.

After the Civil War, the Lighthouse Board reconsidered the absence of a lighthouse on St. Joseph Point: "Though there is not, as yet, any important town on the bay, its merits as a harbor of refuge for ships of any size would justify the expense of a lighthouse of the fourth order." Congress took no action on this suggestion. The Board renewed its request in 1888, citing the large coastal fishing fleet, and estimated $25,000 would be sufficient for a lighthouse. After a decade of requests and a reduced cost estimate, Congress finally appropriated $15,000 on July 1, 1898, for a lighthouse "at or near" St. Joseph Point. A "thorough investigation" that included a survey of the whole peninsula found no suitable location for a lighthouse there, so a site was chosen on the mainland instead. Thus the lighthouse confusingly bears the name St. Joseph Point despite not being located on its namesake.

The new lighthouse was an elevated cottage-style structure reminiscent of the Port Boca Grande Lighthouse, with a different lantern style. The new station included a brick oil house and a wharf extending 245 feet into the bay. A beacon was placed offshore 660 feet from the lighthouse to form a range marking the main channel through the bar and into St. Joseph Bay. The front range light was a square, pyramidal, slatted wooden structure with a lens lantern that could be raised and lowered with a block-and-tackle. The lighthouse could be seen thirteen miles away and the front range light up to six miles away.

Due to a delay with the planned third-order lens, the lighthouse was first lighted on August 25, 1902, with a temporary lens lantern on the gallery deck. The third-order fixed Fresnel lens was first lighted on March 3, 1903. The lighthouse was electrified in 1936 with light that flashed on and off.

As St. Joseph's Bay is the only deep-water harbor between Tampa and Pensacola, during World War II most Allied ships navigating this section of Florida's coast tried to anchor there at night for safety from enemy submarines. At the lighthouse, the ground level section was enclosed to make living quarters for additional Coast Guard personnel. Their job was to keep a constant watch from the lantern gallery and patrol the beaches on horseback. They were not only looking for submarines and ships in distress, but also guarding against attempts to land German spies. The light served until 1955, when it was replaced by an automated light atop a seventy-five-foot metal tower. Five years later, the lighthouse was declared surplus and was sold at auction for $300. The Coast Guard had removed the lantern, leaving only the lantern gallery. Due to the height of the house, the lantern gallery and watch room had to be removed in preparation for the lighthouse's first move, six miles to the north. During this process, the lantern gallery was dropped, reducing it to scrap. Afterward, there was no effort toward restoration.

The lighthouse sat at ground level as a two-story dwelling for its first owner. A few years later, under its second owner, the house served as a hay barn for the numerous cows that were fed from its porches. In 1970, a third owner, Danny Raffield, purchased the house and started a restoration project involving a twenty-three-mile move south to the edge of St. Joseph's Bay in 1979.

A four-decade restoration project culminated in 2011 with the completion of a replica lantern room, although it remains unlit. Raffield received the FLA President's Award in recognition of his restoration work. In 2018, Hurricane Michael's storm surge badly damaged the lighthouse's ground floor, but the rest of the building was unharmed and repairs were soon underway. The lighthouse remains a privately owned residence, but it can be viewed from the highway.

The sand hill on which the lighthouse originally stood became known as Beacon Hill, a name it retains today. The former lighthouse reservation is now Beacon Park, home to sports fields and the Gulf County Veterans Memorial. Adjacent streets are named Lighthouse Avenue and Lightkeepers Drive.

SITE FACTS

Dates of Construction: 1901–1902
First Lighted: August 25, 1902
Electrified: 1936
Automated: 1952
Discontinued: 1955
Tower Height: 41 feet
Focal Height: 63 feet
Designer/Architect: unknown
Builder/Supervisor: unknown
Type of Tower: cottage-style
Foundation Materials: brick
Construction Materials: wood and iron
Number of Stairs: 40

Daymark: white dwelling, red roof, white tower, black lantern
Status: inactive
Original Optic: lens lantern (1902–1903)
Optic Manufacturer: unknown
Other Optics Used: third-order fixed Fresnel lens (1903–1955)
Optic Manufacturer: Barbier, Bénard, et Turenne (1901)
Current Optic: none
Characteristic: fixed white light (1902–1936); four-second white flash followed by six-second eclipse (1936–1955)
Station Auxiliary Structures: none
National Register of Historic Places: no
Owner: Danny Raffield (private owner)
Operating Entity: same
Grounds Open to the Public: no—private property
Tower Open to the Public: no—private residence
Lighthouse Museum: no
Gift Shop: no
Hours: roadside viewing during daylight hours
Lighthouse Passport Stamp: yes—contact John Kennedy of the Florida Lighthouse Association
Handicapped Access: no
Contact: none

DIRECTIONS

From Cape San Blas, follow Cape San Blas Road (CR 30E) back to County Road 30A and turn left. Go almost four-and-a-half miles and the St. Joseph Point Lighthouse will be on your left (2071 County Road 30A). Do NOT pull into the driveway; the lighthouse is on private property. There is also not enough space on the road shoulder. As of 2019, the lot immediately north of the lighthouse was being used for commercial purposes, and pulling in there was your best option to safely photograph the lighthouse. Be aware that use of this lot could change in the future.

The original location of the St. Joseph Point Lighthouse is now Beacon Hill Park, located thirteen-and-a-half miles north on US Highway 98 on the right (north) side of the road. You will pass Cape San Blas Lighthouse on the way.

See St. Joseph Bay chapter for map.

CAPE SAN BLAS LIGHTHOUSE

PORT ST. JOE, FLORIDA

Herman and Trip Jones and Josh Liller

Cape San Blas is sometimes referred to as the "Hatteras of the Gulf." A shoal juts out from the cape; fourteen miles into the Gulf the water is only sixty feet deep. Consequently, numerous wrecks lie buried beneath the shifting sands, along with the remains of three lighthouses. The cape holds the dubious honor of having the most towers constructed (four) and destroyed (three) of any Florida lighthouse site.

Despite its obvious geographic significance, there was originally little interest in establishing a lighthouse at the cape. In 1838, several naval officers agreed it would be "a useless expenditure." A mere five years later, the near-abandonment of Port St. Joseph and the increased coastal shipping, especially from Apalachicola, caused a reversal of public opinion. Congress appropriated $8,000 on March 3, 1847, to build the first Cape San Blas Lighthouse. As part of the project, the contractor demolished the St. Joseph Bay Lighthouse and reused the lantern, illuminating apparatus, and most of the bricks from the old lighthouse. The new sixty-five-feet-tall lighthouse was completed in April 1848. A hurricane destroyed it in August 1851.

Congress appropriated $12,000 to build a new lighthouse. The second brick tower was completed and lighted in November 1855. It was accompanied by an elevated keeper's dwelling of the same hurricane-resistant design as had been recently erected at Dog Island Lighthouse. The second Cape San Blas Lighthouse only lasted ten months. A hurricane in late August 1856 swept the site with a storm surge twenty-two-feet high. The keeper's house survived, but the tower was destroyed.

The third brick lighthouse, more substantial than its predecessors, was lighted on May 1, 1859, with a new third-order lens. Designed by Lt. George H. Derby, the ninety-six-foot-tall double-walled brick tower flared out at the top to support the lighthouse gallery. This was essentially a shorter version of the Pensacola Lighthouse, including the attached two-story oil house and dwelling. To give the tower further stability, the brick foundation went twelve feet into the sand and sat upon an extensive wood grillage. This lighthouse cost as much as the first two combined.

During the Civil War, the keeper's house and all wooden structures at the station were burned by the Confederates in order to deny use by the federals. The tower was also damaged. The Confederates also removed the lens and clockwork apparatus prior to the arrival of Union forces. It was relighted on July 23, 1866, with a new Fresnel lens. The keeper's dwelling was not rebuilt after the war, forcing the keeper to live in the lighthouse. Funds were finally appropriated for a new dwelling in 1870, with the structure placed several hundred yards inland for safety.

By 1870, the Gulf was washing the base of the tower during gales. Some $2,000 were finally allocated "for protecting the site" in 1877, but this amount was found to be inadequate and the Lighthouse Board determined a new lighthouse was necessary. At one point the tower stood in eight feet of water, and in calm seas the keepers rowed to the tower to light the lantern. Finally, on July 3, 1882, the "handsome" tower tumbled into the Gulf. Its position is now marked on nautical charts as an obstruction in twenty feet of water. Remarkably, the lens and lamps were saved. A temporary light was established using a sixth-order fixed lens atop a ninety-foot pole, visible eleven miles out into the Gulf. A few months after erosion claimed the tower, a hurricane destroyed the keeper's house.

In 1883, $35,000 was appropriated for a fourth lighthouse. On June 30, 1885, the new iron skeletal tower was lighted using the third-order lens from the previous tower. It was accompanied by two new keeper's dwellings on pilings, with all three structures being identical to their counterparts on Sanibel Island. Work had been delayed by an outbreak of malaria among the workmen, a severe drought, and the sinking of the ship transporting the materials. Luckily, the ship sank in shallow water near Sanibel Island, and all the material was salvaged.

The 1885 tower was built 1,500 feet from shore, but the cape's incessant erosion continued, and in only three years that distance was reduced to only 200 feet. In 1890, $20,000 was allocated for "reestablishment . . . on another and safer site." A plan was devised to disassemble the tower and rebuild it on Blacks Island, located one-and-a-half miles northeast inside St. Joseph Bay. Several years were spent trying to gain clear title to the island. A hurricane in October 1894 placed the tower in the surf and wrecked both keeper's dwellings. Temporary replacements were built.

Work on relocating the lighthouse and building two new dwellings began in early 1896, but funds ran out after only a couple of months. Another $4,500 was appropriated the following year. The tower was temporarily stabilized on its original site; the lens was brought out of storage and relighted in September 1897. The Lighthouse Board reconsidered the move to Blacks Island and decided a shell ridge a little over a mile north of the cape site was a better location. In 1900, Congress appropriated $15,000 for the move, but currents began to rebuild the shoreline so the light remained at its original location for another sixteen years. A pair of permanent two-story wood-frame dwellings were finally built in 1905, after the keepers had spent more than a decade living in temporary structures.

Hurricanes in 1915 and 1916 eroded the beaches once again, and the tower eventually stood 600 feet from shore. In 1918, the lighthouse was finally moved

1,857 feet and relighted on January 22, 1919. The station received electricity in 1938, and a radio beacon was established on January 1, 1939. This was the only radio beacon on the Gulf Coast between Egmont Key and Mobile Bay.

In 1949, the US Air Force acquired ownership of much of the area around the cape to support operations at Eglin Air Force Base. They also established a LORAN station southwest of the lighthouse. The LORAN station was transferred to the Coast Guard in 1955 and discontinued at the end of 1980. After the lighthouse was automated, the Air Force leased the light station property. The USAF remains active at Cape San Blas today, but erosion has destroyed the former LORAN station site.

The Coast Guard discontinued the light on January 18, 1996, and covered its exquisite bivalve Fresnel lens. In September 1998, Hurricane Earl undermined one of the two keeper's houses and left it sitting precariously on the beach and vulnerable to the surf. After nine months of being buffeted by waves, the house was finally moved, along with its sister cottage, to the base of the lighthouse and restored. It became clear that the historic lighthouse could not remain safely at the cape, a fact underscored when Hurricane Isaac brought the Gulf to within fifty feet of the keeper dwellings in August 2012. The City of Port St. Joe and Gulf County both applied for ownership of the light station buildings through the NHLPA process, with the city being awarded ownership in December 2012.

The Coast Guard removed the lens in January 2014. On July 15 of that year, three cranes lifted the lighthouse off its foundation and lowered it into a flatbed truck. Along with the two keeper dwellings and the oil house, the tower moved to a new bayfront home in George Core Park. The 12.3-mile move set a world record for longest move of an intact lighthouse and is one of the most dramatic success stories of lighthouse preservation. Working with the city, the St. Joseph Historical Society reopened the lighthouse for climbing on September 12, 2014, and later opened a gift shop in one of the keeper dwellings. Plans were made for further restoration of the keeper's houses, restoration and exhibiting of the lighthouse's bivalve lens, and possibly relighting the lighthouse with the lens formerly used in the St. Joseph Point Lighthouse.

Those plans were upended on October 10, 2018, when Hurricane Michael made landfall nearby as a Category 5 storm. All four historic light station structures were damaged, although the lighthouse was able to reopen for climbing a few months later. More importantly, Port St. Joe suffered severe damage, and the nearby community of Mexico Beach was almost leveled. A month and half after the hurricane, long lines of lights were strung from the lighthouse, turning it into a giant Christmas tree and providing a symbol of hope for a devastated community facing a long rebuilding process.

SITE FACTS

Dates of Construction: 1848, 1855, 1859, 1885, 1918

First Lighted: 1848; 1855; May 1, 1859; June 30, 1885

Electrified: 1938

Automated: 1972

Discontinued: 1851–1855; 1861–1866; January 18, 1996–present

Tower Height: 65 feet (1848); unknown (1855); 104 feet (1859); 101 feet (1885)

Focal Height: approx. 70 feet (1848); unknown (1855); 96 feet (1859); 98 feet (1885)

Designer/Architect: unknown (1848 and 1855); George H. Darby (1859); Phoenix Ironworks, Camden, NJ (1885)

Builder/Supervisor: Edward Bowden (1848); others unknown

Type of Tower: conical brick (1848), conical brick (1855), conical brick with attached storage structure (1859), square pyramidal skeletal iron (1885)

Foundation Materials: brick (1848 and 1855); brick with wood grillage (1859); brick piles on wood grillage (1885); unknown (1918); concrete (2013)

Construction Materials: brick and iron (1848, 1855, and 1859); iron (1885)

Number of Stairs: 138 (current tower; unknown for previous towers)

Current Daymark: white tower, black lantern (since 1930s)

Past Daymarks: unknown (1848–1851 and 1855–1856); natural red brick tower, black lantern (1859–1882); brown tower and lantern (1885–1930s)

Status: destroyed August 1851 (1848); destroyed 1856 (1855); destroyed July 1882 (1859); moved to new locations in 1918 and 2014, inactive (1885)

Original Optic—First Tower: 10 Lewis lamps with 15-inch reflectors on revolving apparatus

Original Optic—Second Tower: unknown Fresnel lens (1855–1856)

Original Optic—Third Tower: third-order revolving Fresnel lens (1859–1861)

Original Optic—Current Tower: third-order revolving Fresnel lens (1885–1896 and 1897–1906; also used in previous tower, 1866–1882)

Other Optics Used: sixth-order Fresnel lantern lens (temporary spar light, 1882–1885 and 1896–1897); third-order bivalve Fresnel lens (1906–1996)

Optic Manufacturers: Barbier, Bénard et Turenne (1906); others unknown

Current Optic: none

Characteristic: white flash every 195 seconds (1848–1851); unknown flash (1855–1856); white flash every 90 seconds (1859–1861); unknown (1866–1882); fixed white light (1882–1885); two flashes per minute, alternating red and white (1885–1896 and 1900–1906); white flash every 20 seconds (1906–1996)

Station Auxiliary Structures: two keeper dwellings (1905), oil house (1918)

National Register of Historic Places: yes (2015)

Owner: City of Port St. Joe

Operating Entity: St. Joseph Historical Society (nonprofit)

Grounds Open to the Public: yes

Tower Open to the Public: yes

Minimum Height to Climb: 44 inches

Lighthouse Museum: yes

Gift Shop: yes

Lighthouse Passport Stamp: yes—in gift shop

Hours: 12 PM–5 PM Thursday–Saturday

Adult Admission: $5

Handicapped Access: yes

Contact: St. Joseph Historical Society, PO Box 231, Port St. Joe, FL 32457

Phone: (850) 229-1151

Email: none

Website: www.capesanblaslight.org

DIRECTIONS

From the St. Joseph Point Lighthouse, continue north on County Road 30A for 2 miles to US Highway 98 and turn left. Go about four-and-a-half miles, then turn left on Fourth Street, then right on Miss Zola's Drive. There are parking spaces on the left just past the light station. Alternative parking lots are at the adjacent First Baptist Church and Gulf County Welcome Center.

See St. Joseph Bay chapter for map.

OLD PENSACOLA LIGHTHOUSE

PENSACOLA, FLORIDA
(Lighthouse Site Only)
Thomas W. Taylor

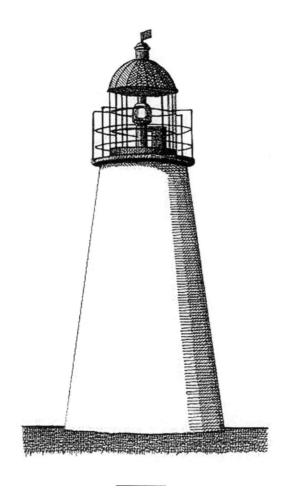

In the 1820s, Pensacola became the most important harbor of the Territory of Florida on the Gulf Coast. The city had already had a long and distinguished history as a major Spanish settlement and as the capital of British West Florida, a designation the Spanish retained when they returned in 1784. It was here that Gen. Andrew Jackson, the first US governor of Florida, received the transfer of the province from Spain.

To better direct the vastly expanding Gulf coastal trade into the excellent harbor and port of Pensacola, the Florida Territorial Legislature sent a petition to President James Monroe in September 1822, declaring the "necessity of erecting" a lighthouse at Pensacola. On March 3, 1823, Congress passed an act appropriating $6,000 to build the lighthouse. While the lighthouse was under construction, the lightship *Aurora Borealis* was assigned to the Pensacola station. She was the second lightship ever used in the United States.

In April 1824, Winslow Lewis was awarded the contract to build the thirty-foot brick tower with a seven-foot lantern, outfit the tower with his patented lamps, and build the one-story, two-room, brick keeper's dwelling. Lewis did the work for $5,735. Originally, the lighthouse was to be outfitted with a fixed light, but for $400 more, Lewis included a revolving light. Work began in October 1824 and was completed in mid-December. The lighthouse was first lighted on December 20, 1824, the first lighthouse completed on Florida's Gulf Coast. The *Pensacola Gazette* announced: "The new Light-House at the entrance of our harbor . . . equals our most sanguine expectations."

Not everyone was satisfied with the lighthouse's location. In 1838, Capt. Lawrence Rousseau recommended moving the lighthouse to the west bastion of the recently completed Fort Pickens and placing a lightship in the bay. Such an arrangement would make it safe for Navy ships "to leave or enter port at any time of night."

But all did not work perfectly. Keeper Jeremiah Ingraham found that the lamp's rotation mechanism was so poorly made that it continually failed. It was finally taken to the naval base, where it was completely rebuilt with successful results. Other problems appeared. The whitewash on the bricks began to wash off. The mortar between the bricks was too soft; it began to dissolve in the rain and water penetrated the walls of the tower. The tower was coated with Roman cement to waterproof it. Additionally, the glass of the lantern was of such poor quality that it began to become cloudy and discolored in the intense Florida sunlight, eventually obscuring the light and causing mariners to complain of its dim quality. Other mariners complained that the light was blocked by trees. The lighthouse was refitted in 1847 with a new lantern, new lantern glass, larger reflectors, and other improvements.

However, a new problem arose. In the years since the lighthouse was built, the entrance channel into Pensacola Bay had begun to shift westward, and by the 1850s the lighthouse was no longer effective for guiding ships into the bay. The new Lighthouse Board decided to build an entirely new lighthouse about one-half mile to the west on another bluff. This new 151-foot lighthouse, which still stands today, was completed and first lighted on January 1, 1859. The old tower was discontinued and abandoned. It was eventually torn down, but it is not absolutely known when this occurred. There are references to it during the Civil War, but within a few years after that, it was gone. The Fort Barrancas Range Lights would eventually be built on or near the site of the first Pensacola Lighthouse.

The former lighthouse site is now next to the Navy Lodge. In 1998, an archaeological survey prior to a construction project found numerous artifacts related to the original Pensacola Lighthouse. These artifacts are on display at Pensacola Lighthouse & Maritime Museum.

SITE FACTS

Dates of Construction: 1824
First Lighted: December 20, 1824
Electrified: never
Automated: never
Deactivated: January 1, 1859
Tower Height: 37 feet
Focal Height: 80 feet
Designer/Architect: Winslow Lewis
Builder/Supervisor: Benjamin Beall
Type of Tower: conical brick
Foundation Materials: brick
Construction Materials: brick and iron
Number of Steps: unknown
Daymark: white tower, black lantern
Status: destroyed
Original Optic: 10 revolving Lewis lamps with 14-inch reflectors (later 16 inch) in a revolving apparatus
Current Optic: N/A
Characteristic: one white flash every thirty-five seconds
Station Auxiliary Structures: none surviving

National Register of Historic Places: no
Owner: US Navy (site)
Operating Entity: N/A
Grounds Open to the Public: no—military base
Tower Open to the Public: N/A
Lighthouse Museum: yes—at New Pensacola Lighthouse
Gift Shop: yes—at New Pensacola Lighthouse
Lighthouse Passport Stamp: no
Handicapped Access: no

DIRECTIONS

To get from Port St. Joe to Pensacola, you have two options: US 98 and I-10. US 98 is the shorter and follows the coast, but passes through several urban areas.

For the first option, follow US Highway 98 west through Panama City, Destin, and Fort Walton Beach. Cross the Pensacola Bay Bridge, pass through the traffic light, and keep left at the fork onto Bayfront Parkway, which becomes Main Street. Turn left on Barrancas Avenue (SR 292). Do NOT turn at Navy Boulevard as there is no longer public access to NAS Pensacola at that entrance. Continue west to Blue Angel Parkway (SR 173) and turn left.

For the second option, from Port St. Joe go north on SR 71 (Cecil G. Costin Boulevard), toward Marianna. Get on I-10 westbound toward and through Pensacola to Exit 7 (Pine Forest Road / SR 297). From the offramp, turn left (south). Turn right (west) at Longleaf Drive (SR 173). This road curves south and becomes Blue Angel Parkway. Follow it to NAS Pensacola.

At the NAS Pensacola West Gate, the driver and all passengers eighteen or older will need to present ID. Registration and proof of insurance for the vehicle is also required. Gate hours for the public are 9 AM–4 PM. After the gate, continue on Blue Angel Parkway. Just past Sherman Cove Marina the road curves north along the bayfront and you will see the modern Caucus Cut Rear Range Light in the water on your right. (No parking available) Continue past the current Pensacola Lighthouse and the Naval Aviation Museum. Keep right onto Radford Boulevard. The first right is Lighthouse Road and the entrance to the Navy Lodge.

IMPORTANT: There is currently NO public access to the lodge grounds or the bluff behind it where the lighthouse was located. Also, you may NOT continue any further down Radford Boulevard.

FORT BARRANCAS RANGE LIGHTS

PENSACOLA, FLORIDA
(Light Station Site Only)

Neil Hurley

To better mark the entrance channel into Pensacola Bay, the Fort Barrancas range lights were constructed in 1859 "as ranges for crossing the bar and making a safe anchorage at night." It is not clear if there was a dwelling associated with these early lights; the keeper may have reused the house associated with the old Pensacola Lighthouse.

The lights were extinguished only two years later at the start of the Civil War. The range was rebuilt in late 1866 with prefabricated wooden structures topped with steamer lenses. The Barrancas Range was relighted on February 4, 1867, after a delay "being caused by the failure of the keeper to report for duty." Again, the lights did not last for very long, being discontinued on January 1, 1868, because it was felt they were no longer necessary for commerce in Pensacola.

The Fort Barrancas Range Lights were reestablished on February 15, 1888, near the site of the first Pensacola Lighthouse. The front light was on the beach about 150 feet from the water. The rear light was located on a twenty-five-foot bluff about four hundred feet back from the front light. Both lights were wooden frame towers with post lanterns and a storage shed at the base for oil and spare lanterns. A small two-room house for the keeper was located near the rear range light. A kitchen and dining room were added in 1897. New lens lanterns were installed on both lights in 1900. Both lights were destroyed by a hurricane in 1906 and rebuilt the following year.

Few details of the life of the keepers at this station are known. Keeper William J. Doyle was one of twenty Gulf Coast lighthouse keepers commended for "performing their duties under hazardous and unusual conditions" during the hurricane of 1917. Their duties consisted mainly of maintaining the lights at full intensity under trying circumstances, recovering property that had been washed away, giving refuge to people in the area, and making temporary repairs after the storm.

The Fort Barrancas Range Lights were automated before 1920 and discontinued in 1930, replaced by a new range closer to the Pensacola Lighthouse. The lights were removed, the dwelling and cistern auctioned off by the government, and the site repurposed a decade later for NAS Pensacola. Other than a few chunks of granite on the bluff and perhaps some of the artifacts recovered during a 1998 archaeological survey (see preceding chapter), nothing remains of this light station.

SITE FACTS

Dates of Construction: 1859, 1866, 1888, 1907
First Lighted: January 1, 1859
Electrified: never
Automated: 1920s
Deactivated: 1861–1867, 1868–1888, 1930–present
Front Range—Tower Height: 30 feet (1888)
Front Range—Focal Height: 36 feet (1888)

Rear Range—Tower Height: 50 feet (1888), 30 feet (1907)
Rear Range—Focal Height: 75 feet (1888), 55 feet (1907)
Designer/Architect: unknown
Builder/Supervisor: unknown
Type of Tower: square pyramidal slat tower
Foundation Materials: brick piles
Construction Materials: wood
Number of Stairs: N/A (ladder)
Daymark—Front: white
Daymark—Rear: white (1866–1868), red (1888–1900), white (1900–1950s)
Status: replaced by new range (1930)
Original Optics: lens lantern (1859–1961)
Other Optics Used: steamer lantern (1867–1868), post lantern (1888–1900), lens lantern (1900–1930)
Current Optic: N/A
Characteristic—Front: fixed white (1888–1900), fixed red (1900–1930)
Characteristic—Rear: fixed red (1888–1900), fixed white (1900–1930)
Station Auxiliary Structures: none surviving
National Register of Historic Places: no
Owner: US Navy (site)
Operating Entity: N/A
Grounds Open to the Public: no—military base
Tower Open to the Public: N/A
Lighthouse Museum: yes—at Pensacola Lighthouse
Gift Shop: yes—at Pensacola Lighthouse
Lighthouse Passport Stamp: no
Handicapped Access: no
Contact: none

DIRECTIONS

The location of the Fort Barrancas Range is very close to the location of the original Pensacola Lighthouse, with the rear range light and keeper's house on the bluff near where the Navy Lodge is today and the front range on the beach below. As noted in the previous chapter, this area is off limits to the public.

To visit the range's namesake fortification, take Lighthouse Road a few hundred feet to Taylor Road and turn right. Fort Barrancas, operated by the NPS as part of Gulf Islands National Seashore, is your first right. The fort has a small visitor center and the restored Civil War era fortifications. Open 9 AM–4 PM, Thursday–Monday.

See (New) Pensacola Lighthouse chapter for map.

(NEW) PENSACOLA LIGHTHOUSE

PENSACOLA, FLORIDA

Thomas M. Garner and Josh Liller

Although the harbor at Pensacola had been known by French and Spanish explorers as one of the finest on the Gulf Coast, it was the United States that first erected a lighthouse here in 1824. That first lighthouse was soon deemed ineffective because of insufficient height, the inadequate lighting devices used, and because the channel's shift to the west. In 1852, the new Lighthouse Board began a concerted campaign to modernize and improve the lighthouses of the United States. They planned a new, taller tower for Pensacola.

In August 1854, Congress appropriated $25,000 to start work on the new lighthouse and fit it with a new first-order Fresnel lens. Two years later, an additional $30,000 was appropriated to complete the lighthouse and also build appropriate range lights nearby. The new 151-foot-tall lighthouse was built on a forty-foot bluff approximately one-half mile west of the original Pensacola Lighthouse. Construction began in 1856 and was completed in late 1858. The lighthouse included a small attached two-story building. The lighthouse was first lighted on January 1, 1859, with a first-order lens.

Two days after Florida seceded from the Union on January 10, 1861, troops from Florida and Alabama seized all federal property on the mainland, including the lighthouse. Union troops withdrew to Fort Pickens. The Pensacola Lighthouse was the first on the Gulf Coast to be extinguished by Confederate order, and in May the new Confederate-appointed keeper removed the Fresnel lens from the tower for safekeeping.

During 1861, federal forces on the islands bombarded the Confederate works on the mainland, including the targets of the "Light House Batteries." A number of Union cannon shot hit and bounced off the lighthouse during these bombardments. By May 1862, the Confederates had withdrawn from Pensacola, and on December 20, 1862, the Pensacola Lighthouse was lighted once again with a temporary fourth-order lens.

After the war, the original first-order lens was discovered in the Pensacola Navy Yard. The lens was sent to the Staten Island Depot for further shipment to France for repairs. It remains uncertain whether this lens was the same one installed in the tower and lighted on April 1, 1869. Also in 1869, a new two-story keeper's dwelling was built and the white tower was given a more distinctive daymark: the lower third was repainted white and the upper two-thirds were painted black to stand out better against the blue sky.

Pensacola Bar Beacon, an enclosed square wooden tower, was placed in front of the lighthouse to serve as a front range light. The beacon had a sixth-order lens and stood twenty-six feet tall with a focal plane of fifty-five feet. The front was painted white and the sides black. The distinctive structure, reminiscent of an unusually tall shed or outhouse, appears in several early postcards. A strong hurricane destroyed the original beacon in 1906.

In the late 1870s, severe cracking was noted in the tower. Considered a result of the Civil War bombardment and two severe lightning strikes in 1874 caused by a defective lightning rod, the cracks were repaired during a major renovation completed in 1879. Repairs were also made to the lantern, including the installation of new glass. The tower received a fresh coat of paint, and the keeper's dwelling was repaired and painted. The lighthouse switched to a kerosene lamp in 1886, and a free-standing oil house was added six years later to safely store this fuel.

Pensacola Lighthouse was originally built on part of Fort Barrancas Military Reservation. On October 5, 1927, President Calvin Coolidge signed an Executive Order creating a separate seventy-five-acre Pensacola Lighthouse Reservation.

The lighthouse was electrified in 1938 and the keeper's dwelling fitted with all the modern conveniences. A year later, the lighthouse was taken over, as were all lighthouses, by the Coast Guard. The Pensacola Lighthouse was automated in 1965. Plans were developed to demolish the dwelling, but preservationists won out. The creation of Gulf Island National Seashore in 1971 included long-term plans to eventually assume ownership of the lighthouse when it was relinquished by the Coast Guard.

The Coast Guard Auxiliary began conducting weekly lighthouse tours in 1991, but stopped in 2007 due to liability concerns. The NAS Pensacola Historical Society began giving tours of the keeper's dwelling in 1995. The nonprofit Pensacola Lighthouse Association (PLA) formed in 2006 and secured a long-term lease with the Coast Guard for the light station. The tower reopened to the public in June 2008, with Gov. Charlie Crist on hand. In 2012, the PLA restored the station's carriage house back to its original 1892 configuration and adapted it for use as a gift shop and visitors center. From 2013 to 2018, Pensacola Lighthouse underwent an extensive phased restoration. The PLA's great success means the eventual transfer to the National Park Service no longer seems necessary or beneficial, and will likely never occur.

The lighthouse remains a public aid to navigation with an active first-order Fresnel lens. The keeper's dwelling has numerous exhibits, including a replica of the fourth-order Fresnel lens used at the lighthouse in the 1860s. Just south of the keeper's dwelling is a modern ATON, the Pensacola Rear Range Light.

SITE FACTS

Dates of Construction: 1856–1858
First Lighted: January 1, 1859
Electrified: 1938
Automated: 1965
Deactivated: N/A
Tower Height: 151 feet
Focal Height: 191 feet
Designer/Architect: George H. Derby
Builder/Supervisor: John Newton
Type of Tower: conical brick with attached storage structure
Foundation Materials: brick
Construction Materials: brick, granite, and iron
Number of Stairs: 177
Daymark: white lower third of tower, black upper two-thirds of tower (including lantern)
Status: active—public ATON
Original Optic: first-order revolving Fresnel lens
Original Optic Manufacturer: Henry-Lepaute (1858)
Other Optics Used: fourth-order fixed Fresnel lens (1862–1869)
Current Optic: first-order revolving Fresnel lens (also Henry-Lepaute, possibly the original lens)
Characteristic: white flash every twenty seconds
Station Auxiliary Structures: two-story keeper dwelling (1869), oil house (1892), carriage house (1892)
National Register of Historic Places: yes
Owner: US Coast Guard
Operating Entity: Pensacola Lighthouse Association (nonprofit)
Grounds Open to the Public: yes
Tower Open to the Public: yes
Minimum Height to Climb: 44 inches
Lighthouse Museum: yes
Gift Shop: yes
Lighthouse Passport Stamp: yes—in gift shop
Hours: 9 AM–5 PM daily
Adult Admission: $7 (lighthouse and museum)
Handicapped Access: yes

Contact: Pensacola Lighthouse & Maritime Museum, 2081 Radford Blvd.,
   Pensacola, FL 32508
Phone: (850) 393-1561
Email: info@PensacolaLighthouse.org
Website: www.pensacolalighthouse.org

DIRECTIONS

From Fort Barrancas or the Navy Lodge, go west on Blue Angel Parkway. The lighthouse is the first left after the Naval Aviation Museum (you passed it on your way in).

As noted in the previous chapter about the old Pensacola Lighthouse, the West Gate is the only public access to NAS Pensacola. Gate hours for the public are 9 AM–4 PM. The driver and all passengers 18 or older will need to present ID. Registration and proof of insurance for the vehicle are also required.

NOTE: The only public parking for the lighthouse is accessed from Blue Angel Parkway. GPS directions may erroneously send you onto nearby Lighthouse Road or Shell Road.

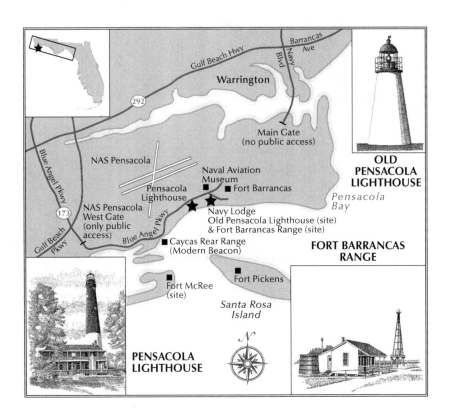

Warrington

Gulf Beach Hwy

Barrancas Ave

Navy Blvd

292

Main Gate
(no public access)

NAS Pensacola

Blue Angel Pkwy

173

Gulf Beach Pkwy

NAS Pensacola
West Gate
(only public
access)

Naval Aviation
Museum

Pensacola
Lighthouse

Fort Barrancas

Blue Angel Pkwy

Navy Lodge
Old Pensacola Lighthouse (site)
& Fort Barrancas Range (site)

Caycas Rear Range
(Modern Beacon)

Fort McRee
(site)

Fort Pickens

Santa Rosa
Island

Pensacola
Bay

FORT BARRANCAS
RANGE

OLD
PENSACOLA
LIGHTHOUSE

PENSACOLA
LIGHTHOUSE

FORT McREE
AND CAUCUS
RANGE LIGHTS

PERDIDO KEY, FLORIDA
(Light Station Site Only)

Neil Hurley and Josh Liller

Three forts guarded the entrance to Pensacola Bay shortly before the Civil War: Fort McRee (often misspelled McRae) on the west side was a wing-shaped brick fort started in 1834; Fort Barrancas was further north on the mainland; and Fort Pickens was located on Santa Rosa Island on the east side of the channel entrance.

Appropriations were made for a set of range lights at Fort McRee in 1854 and 1856 as part of an overall plan to light Pensacola Bay. As with the other beacons, the Fort McRee Range was completed in 1858 and lighted the same day as the new Pensacola Lighthouse. This range helped guide ships through the deepest part of the channel into the harbor. Although it is not clear if a full-time keeper maintained the lights, an 1861 drawing of Fort McRee shows two small houses almost in range at the location of the lights.

When the Civil War started, Union troops abandoned Forts McRee and Barrancas and fled to Fort Pickens, which they held throughout the war. In November 1861, Union forces opened up a furious bombardment on Confederate positions that turned Fort McRee into a pile of rubble. The range lights did not survive the war, probably having been destroyed by Confederates to prevent their use by Union ships.

In late 1866, a new Caycas Range was constructed and lighted on December 22. As with the Barrancas Range, this range was discontinued on January 1, 1868, "being no longer deemed necessary for the commerce of Pensacola."

A new Fort McRee Range was established on February 15, 1888. The front range was 800 feet from the water. The rear range was in shallow water 850 feet from the front range. Both beacons were wood frame structures with access ladders and a small shed near the base to store oil and spare lanterns. A one-story, three-room frame dwelling was built near the front range for the keeper, along with an outhouse and large cistern.

A storm in May 1890 badly damaged the front range light. It was moved one hundred feet and repaired. The beacons were upgraded to five-day lens lanterns in 1900, their colors swapped, the front range moved nine feet west, and the rear range raised seven feet. A 200-foot wharf was added to the station in 1898 and a brick oil house in 1902.

In December 1900, a new Caucus Cut Range was established nearby to mark a channel through the Caucus Shoal (formerly Caycas Shoal) that extends south from the east end of Perdido Key. The new range consisted of two triangular wooden beacons with lens lanterns, one near the Fort McRee Breakwater and the other on the beach. The Fort McRee keepers were also responsible for this new range.

In 1905, the Fort McRee Range was discontinued and both range lights were taken down. However, at the same time a new beacon, called the Fort McRee Cut-Off Rear Range Light, was established in Pensacola Bay. The Caucus Cut Rear Range Light doubled as the front light for this new range. Combined with other beacons in the bay, ships could follow the main channel by passing from one range to the next.

These exposed stations suffered from major storms. Repairs or replacement of beacons was required because of hurricanes or tropical storms in 1901, 1904, 1906, 1916, and 1917. The Caucus and Fort McRee Cut-Off Ranges were automated in 1918. They and the other Pensacola Bay beacons have all since been replaced by modern beacon lights.

Nothing is known to remain of the towers or keeper's dwelling today. The ruins of Fort McRee were visible until the 1930s, when the last bit of the old fort washed into the channel. The remains of two small concrete gun batteries, Slemmer and Center, are the only historic structures left in the area. They were built around the time of the Spanish-American War and used through World War I.

SITE FACTS

(for Fort McRee Range only)
Dates of Construction: 1859, 1866, 1888
First Lighted: January 1, 1859
Electrified: N/A
Automated: N/A
Deactivated: 1861–1866, 1868–1888, 1905
Front Range—Tower Height: unknown
Front Range—Focal Height: 36 feet (1888)
Rear Range—Tower Height: unknown
Rear Range—Focal Height: 49 feet (1888), 56 feet (1900)
Designer/Architect: unknown
Builder/Supervisor: unknown
Type of Tower: square pyramidal slat tower
Foundation Materials: brick piles (front range); pine piles and cement in cast iron pipes (rear range)
Construction Materials: wood
Number of Stairs: N/A—ladder used
Daymark—Front Range: white (1888–1900), red (1900–1905)
Daymark—Rear Range: red (1888–1900), white (1900–1905)
Status: removed
Original Optics: small lens lantern (1859–1961)
Other Optics Used: steamer lantern (1866–1868), post lantern (1888–1900), lens lantern (1900–1905)
Current Optic: N/A
Characteristic—Front: fixed white (1888–1900), fixed red (1900–1905)
Characteristic—Rear: fixed red (1888–1900), fixed white (1900–1905)
Station Auxiliary Structures: none surviving

National Register of Historic Places: no
Owner: National Park Service (site)
Operating Entity: Gulf Islands National Seashore (site)
Grounds Open to the Public: yes
Tower Open to the Public: N/A
Lighthouse Museum: no
Gift Shop: no
Hours: 5 AM–6 PM, November–February; 5 AM–9 PM, March–October
  (park entrance)
Lighthouse Passport Stamp: no
Handicapped Access: no
Contact: none

DIRECTIONS

The site of this light station is just off the eastern end of Perdido Key. It is accessible only by boat or a long hike. You can view the area from a distance atop Fort Pickens (1.25 miles east) or the Pensacola Lighthouse (1.5 miles NNE).

From the Pensacola Lighthouse, head west on Blue Angel Parkway and leave NAS Pensacola. Turn left on Gulf Beach Highway (CR 292A). Turn left on Perdido Key Drive (SR 292). Turn left on Johnson Beach Road, which will bring you to the Johnson's Beach entrance of Gulf Islands National Seashore, operated by the National Parks Service ($10/person or $20/car; admission pass is good for a week at Perdido Key, Fort Barrancas, and Fort Pickens). Follow the park road all the way to its end at a cul-de-sac. The road may not be accessible during stormy weather. There is also no shelter during the hike in case of inclement weather. Walk along the beach east then a little north to the easternmost point on the island where you will find a modern range light. This is the general area of Fort McRee and the Fort McRee Range. The remains of Battery Center and Battery Slemmer are a short distance west just past a small pond.

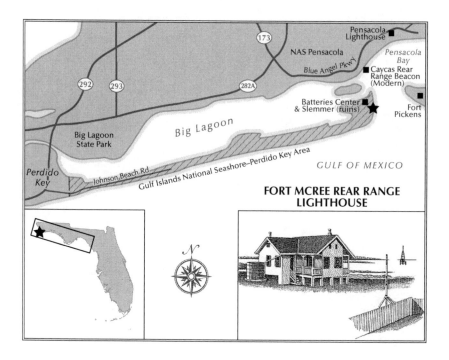

APPENDIXES

GLOSSARY

Acetylene: a colorless gas used during the 1900s as a fuel for the illuminating apparatus in some lighthouses. Combined with a timer to turn the gas on and off, it could be used to create a flashing light with a fixed Fresnel lens. However, the gas was stored in pressurized tanks that were an explosion risk, thus it was almost exclusively used as method to automate a lighthouse.

Active: a lighthouse or other aid to navigation that is still in operation.

Aerobeacon: a directional electric beacon designed as an aid to navigation for aircraft. Some were used in lighthouses to replace Fresnel lenses.

AGA: AB Gasaccumulator Company, a Swedish company that made Fresnel lenses in the early 1900s. They mostly produced drum lenses for lightships, buoys, and post lights. AGA also produced various acetylene-related lighting equipment.

Aid to Navigation (ATON): a natural landmark or man-made structure or object, such as a lighthouse, that serves to help mariners navigate.

Anodes, Sacrificial: anodes are metal objects affixed to other metal objects to reduce corrosion from being submerged in saltwater or other wet conditions. The anodes are made of materials such as aluminum, zinc, and/or magnesium, and the resulting electro-chemical reaction causes them to corrode instead of what they are attached to. Sacrificial anodes are an important method of protecting the iron pilings of offshore lighthouses.

Argand lamp: type of oil lamp invented in 1780 by Aimé Argand using a concentric wick and a glass chimney to improve airflow and thus brightness. Argand lamps were a significant improvement over all earlier oil lamps used in lighthouses. Winslow Lewis incorporated a version of the Argand lamp into his Lewis lamp. The oil lamps used in Fresnel lenses used the same principles as an Argand lamp.

Artworks Florida: Florida company owned and operated by Dan Spinella that makes functional, full-size Fresnel lenses replicating historic lenses for use as private aids to navigation and museum displays. Artworks Florida usually makes the lenses out of acrylic plastic. He can also make individual glass prisms to replace damaged or destroyed prisms in historic lenses.

Astragal: the metal frame that holds the lantern glass in place.

ATON: Aid to Navigation.

Aids to Navigation Team (ANT): A Coast Guard team responsible for all public aids to navigation within a particular area. ANT replaced a smaller system of Light Attendant Stations, and are also responsible for automated lighthouses.

Automated: to make changes to a lighted aid to navigation so that it can operate without human involvement. For lighthouses, this involves timers or sensors to turn the light on and off automatically.

Bar: a sandbar, especially one that naturally forms across the mouth of a river.

Barbier: In 1862, Frederic Barbier (bar-be-yea) and Stanislaw Fenestre (fu-nea-tra) formed a business partnership in Paris, France, called Barbier et Fenestre in 1862. This became the third Fresnel lens manufacturer. The company became F. Barbier et Cie after Fenestre's death in 1887 and Barbier et Bernard (Beh-nar) in 1894. It finally became Barbier, Bernard, et Turenne in 1901 (BBT—no relation to the bank). The name changes aid in dating the company's Fresnel lenses, but far fewer of these lenses were used in the United States than Sautter or Henry-Lepaute.

Barrel Panel (Barrel Lens): a catoptric section of Fresnel lens producing a fixed light, with a horizontal band across the center. A fixed lens consists entirely of barrel panels while a fixed-varied-by-flashes lens has a mix of barrel panels and bull's-eye panels.

Beacon: a lighted, unlighted, or electronic aid to navigation.

Beacon Light: A structure that serves as a lighted aid to navigation, but is not a lighthouse. Beacons are usually much smaller and less sturdy than lighthouses (both in height and diameter) and lack an enclosed tower or staircase. They are often placed in the water. Range lights, especially front range lights, are usually beacons lights.

Beehive Lens: the classic style of Fresnel lens that is cylindrical in its lower two-thirds and conical in its upper third. The central panels were catoptric (some combination of barrel panels and bull's-eye panels), while the upper and lower panels consisted of catodioptric prisms. Nearly all nineteenth-century Fresnel lenses are of a beehive design.

Bivalve Lens: a newer style of Fresnel lens introduced around 1900. It consisted of a large circular arrangement of prisms in a shape similar to a clamshell. Bivalve lenses were only made practical by new rotational mechanisms like mercury floats.

Blanking Panels: metal panels (usually copper) placed to obscure parts of a Fresnel lens and eclipse part of the light, thus changing its characteristic.

Bull's-Eye Panel (Bull's-Eye Lens): a catoptric panel consisting of a circular lens in the middle surrounded by catoptric rings. Each bull's-eye lens bends light into a beam, like a spotlight. These panels create the appearance of a flash when seen at a distance.

Bureau of Lighthouses: official name for the federal government agency in the Department of Commerce responsible for the US Lighthouse Service from 1910 to 1939.

Catodioptric Apparatus: an illuminating device, such as a Fresnel lens, that both reflects (catoptric) and refracts (dioptric) light.

Catoptric Apparatus: an illuminating device that reflects light (but does not refract it), such as the lenses used in a Lewis lamp or in many aerobeacons.

Chance Brothers: the largest manufacturer of Fresnel lenses outside of France. They mostly produced lenses for Trinity House (which managed British and Commonwealth lighthouses) and Scotland's Northern Lighthouse Board, so very few were used in the United States.

Characteristic: the audible, visual, or electronic signal displayed by an aid to navigation.

Cistern: a structure for storing rainwater, usually collected via gutters from the roof of an adjacent building. These may be in-ground or above-ground vaults, or large barrels. Most lighthouses had cisterns connected with their keeper's dwelling(s).

Coast Guard: a branch of the US armed forces formed in 1915 by the merger of the Revenue Cutter Service and Life Saving Service. The Lighthouse Service merged with the Coast Guard in 1939. The Coast Guard remains responsible for all public aids to navigation.

Conical Tower: a lighthouse tower built with a wide base that tapers to a narrow top, like a cone.

Cottage-Style: a lighthouse in which the keeper's dwelling forms the main part of the structure and the lantern is either directly attached to the dwelling roof or on a very short tower projecting from the roof.

CSO: Citizen Support Organization (aka a Friends group), a nonprofit organization that supports a national park, national wildlife refuge, state park, or similar public lands with fundraising and volunteer work. In contrast, a nonprofit that *operates* a lighthouse has a signed lease or other formal agreement to be responsible for the lighthouse *instead* of its government owner.

Daybeacon: an unlighted aid to navigation.

Dayboard: the daytime identifier (*daymark*) of a channel marker or minor aid to navigation in one of several standard shapes (square, triangle, or rectangle) and colors (red, green, white, orange, yellow, or black).

Daymark: a daytime identifier of an aid to navigation to distinguish it from other similar aids to navigation. Lighthouses use different paint schemes as daymarks—usually some combination of white, black, red, and brown and possibly including stripes or other geometric patterns.

DCB: Directional Code Beacon, a type of aerobeacon resembling a searchlight designed by Carlisle & Finch Company. The Lighthouse Service first introduced DCBs in the 1930s as a successor to Fresnel lenses. They had become widespread in the 1950s, especially for automated lighthouses, but by the 1990s were slowly being phased out in favor of newer optics.

Deactivate (Decommission, Discontinue): to remove an aid to navigation from operation. For lighthouses, this usually means ceasing to exhibit a light or maintain the structure, but not necessarily removal of the structure.

Drum Lens: A smaller style of fixed Fresnel lens consisting of a cylindrical catoptric lens, without upper or lower sections. Drum lenses were commonly used on lightships and smaller aids to navigation such as small range lights, post lights, channel markers, and dock lights. Because they have a consistent diameter, their size is often given as their diameter in millimeters rather than their order.

Eclipse: the period of darkness in the flashing characteristic of a signal.

Electrified: when an aid to navigation first begins operating with electricity, either commercial power or a constantly running generator.

Establish: to place an authorized aid to navigation in operation for the first time.

Fifth-Order: a small Fresnel lens measured just over twenty-one inches tall and 375 mm (almost fifteen inches) in diameter. This size of lens was primarily used for major channel lights or other small lighthouses.

First-Order: the largest standard-sized Fresnel lens measuring about eight-and-a-half feet tall and over six feet in diameter. This size of lens was used for most major seacoast lighthouses.

Fixed and Flashing Light (FFL): see Fixed-Varied-by-Flashing Light.

Fixed Light: a light characteristic that is steady; that is, does not flash.

Fixed-Varied-by-Flashing Light (FVF): a light that is steady with some flashes. This is normally accomplished by using a mixture of barrel panels and bull's-eye panels.

FLA: The Florida Lighthouse Association, a nonprofit organization formed in 1996. Its mission is to safeguard Florida's remaining historic lighthouses for future generations by supporting community-based restoration, preservation, and education efforts.

Flashing Light: A light that shines intermittently with a longer period of darkness than light. Fresnel lenses originally accomplished this with bull's-eye panels rotating around a constant light source. Later, acetylene gas burners with timers and electric flashers could be used to produce the same effect.

Flash Pattern: nickname for the characteristic of a lighted aid to navigation.

Flash Tube Array: an experimental optic used on the Florida Reef Lights in the early 1980s that provided brief but intense flashes, like a strobe light. They were found to be unreliable, and the short duration of the flash made it difficult to take a bearing on the light. They were all soon replaced by more traditional modern beacons.

Focal Plane: the height of the light above sea level.

Fog Signal: an aid to navigation that emits a loud sound during periods of foggy weather when visibility is reduced—usually a bell or horn. Some light stations included a fog signal. The Lighthouse Service also considered radio beacons to be a form of fog signal.

Fourth-Order: a small Fresnel lens measuring about two-and-a-half feet tall and one-and-a-half feet in diameter. This size of lens was primarily used for lighthouses marking the entrance to harbors or other local hazards. It is the most widely used of the six main orders of Fresnel lenses, both in the United States and worldwide.

Fresnel, Augustin Jean: French physicist and engineer who invented the Fresnel lens. Pronounced "frey-nel."

Fresnel Lens: the lens developed by Augustin Jean Fresnel for improving lighthouses. It consists of a series of prisms arranged so that they make a light source appear much brighter than normal. Although the verbs *focus* and *magnify* are often used to describe what a Fresnel lens does, these are not technically correct. The light goes out from the lens in a beam toward the horizon rather than being aimed at one spot like a magnifying glass.

Gallery Deck (Main Gallery, Lantern Gallery): a platform with a railing encircling a lighthouse at the height of the lantern room or watch room used for observation of the surrounding area and access to the exterior of the lantern.

Some older (pre-1850s) lighthouses do not have a gallery deck. Lantern gallery sometimes specifically refers to a second smaller deck around the lantern glass used for maintenance purposes.

Geographic Range: the distance a light (or other object) can be seen due to the curvature of the Earth. This is a function of the height of the light and the height of the observer. A lookout in a ship's mast or a pilot in an airplane can see farther away than someone at sea level. A light cannot be seen beyond its Geographic Range, no matter the clarity of the sky nor the intensity of the light.

GPS: Global Positioning System, a network of satellites that can be used to triangulate location using the same principles as radio beacons and LORAN, but with greater accuracy and coverage.

Grillage: a heavy framework of cross-timbering beams used as part of the foundation of a building (such as a lighthouse) to help stabilize it on soft, wet ground such as a low-lying sandy island near the beach.

Groins: low rock walls built on beaches to trap sand and decrease erosion.

Group Flashing: a light characteristic in which a specific number of flashes is regularly repeated.

Henry-Lepaute: the second company to manufacture Fresnel lens was owned by Augustin Michel Henry-Lepaute (on-ree lua-po-teh) in Paris, France.

HOR: House of Refuge. A station operated by the US Life Saving Service as a refuge for shipwreck survivors. Unlike LSS/LBS, a HOR had no crew and usually no rescue equipment.

Hyper-Radial Lens: the largest size of Fresnel lens, developed in the late 1800s and even bigger than a first-order. It measures over 12 feet tall and 1330 mm (8 2/3 feet wide). Only twenty-nine were ever made, and only one was ever used in the United States. It was originally intended for the Mosquito Inlet (Ponce de Leon Inlet) Lighthouse but instead was eventually installed at the Makapu'u Point Lighthouse, Hawaii.

Illuminating Apparatus: a device used to create light in a lighthouse, especially one that uses lenses. The term has not been used consistently through history. Today it would specifically refer to the light source, such as a lamp or bulb, but in the nineteenth century the term was also sometimes used in reference to Fresnel lenses.

IOV Lamp: a lamp using incandescent oil vapor (i.e., pressurized kerosene) and a mantle to create the flame, rather than a wick, resulting in a much brighter light. Similar to a modern Coleman camping lantern. The Lighthouse Service introduced IOV lamps to most lighthouses in the 1910s.

Keeper: a person assigned to operate and maintain a light station. Some light stations had a single keeper, while others had several. In the latter case, one was the principal or head keeper and the others were assistant keepers.

Keeper's Dwelling: the structure that serves as the home for a lighthouse keeper. The dwelling may be part of the lighthouse, attached to the lighthouse, or a completely separate building.

Landfall Light: see Seacoast Light.

Lantern: the top section of a lighthouse consisting of a lantern room, internal and external catwalks for accessing the lens and lantern glass, a lightning rod, usually a gallery deck, and sometimes a watch room.

Lantern Gallery: see Gallery Deck.

Lantern Glass (Storm Panes): the large glass windows that enclosed the sides of the lantern room and protected the optic.

Lantern Room: the enclosed area at the top of a lighthouse inside the lantern and containing the optic.

LBS: Life Boat Station. This name was used by the Coast Guard to refer to what had been Life Saving Stations. The modern Coast Guard equivalent is a Small Boat Station.

LED: Light-Emitting Diode, a modern light source. LEDs are longer lasting than light bulbs and use less power.

Lens: a transparent object with curved sides, such as a collection of prisms in a frame, that bend light rays in a way to make the light appear brighter.

Lens Lantern: a lighting apparatus used for some beacon lights and other minor aids to navigation. It consists of a drum lens enclosed in a metal lantern.

Lepaute: see Henry-Lepaute.

Lewis Lamp: an oil lamp with a catoptric lens and parabolic reflector developed and patented by Winslow Lewis around 1810 for use in American lighthouses. Lewis lamps were used until the 1850s when they were phased out in favor of Fresnel lenses. While an improvement on most of its predecessors, Lewis lamps were inferior to many similar lamps used in Europe during this period and vastly inferior to the Fresnel lens.

Light: a term commonly used to refer to the illuminating apparatus or optic of a lighthouse or the signal emitted by a lighted aid to navigation; sometimes used to refer to the lighthouse itself.

Lighthouse: an enclosed structure consisting of a tower, lantern, and optic built as an aid to navigation for mariners.

Light House: until the late 1800s, "lighthouse" was often written as two words. The meaning is the same.

Lighthouse Board: a committee consisting of the secretary of the treasury (secretary of commerce after 1903), army engineers, Navy officers, and civilian scientists who oversaw the operation of the US Lighthouse Establishment from 1852 until 1910.

Lighthouse Establishment: see USLHE.

Lighthouse Service: an unofficial but widely used name for the Lighthouse Establishment, Lighthouse Board, and Bureau of Lighthouses.

Lighting Apparatus: see Illuminating Apparatus.

Light List: an annual publication of the Coast Guard (formerly by the Lighthouse Service) that lists all aids to navigation as a guide to mariners.

Lightship: a ship serving as a floating aid to navigation. A lightship is normally moored in one place and displays one or more lights.

Light Station: A lighthouse, auxiliary structures, and grounds. A group of beacons to navigation maintained by a keeper was also considered a single light station by the Lighthouse Service and Coast Guard. The location of a lightship was also considered a light station as the vessel might be replaced (temporarily or permanently) by another without changing the location.

LORAN: Long Range Aid to Navigation, a navigation system operated by the Coast Guard that preceded GPS. A system of special radio stations operating together would transmit pulsed signals, and the difference in timing between the signals could be used to determine location.

LSS: Life Saving Station. A rescue station operated by the US Life Saving Service, a civilian predecessor to the Coast Guard.

Luminous Range: the greatest distance a light is expected to be seen based on the intensity of the light in typical clear weather conditions. For maritime aids to navigation, luminous range is usually listed in nautical miles.

Mercury float: a circular trough containing the liquid form of the element mercury. This provided nearly frictionless rotation of Fresnel lenses, especially bivalve lenses. Most revolving Fresnel lenses from the late 1800s and early 1900s used mercury floats. Due to problems with leakage and evaporation, as well as a modern understanding about the hazardous nature of this element, mercury floats were phased out in the later half of the twentieth century.

Modern Optic: any post-Fresnel lens optic. Modern optics often use plastic rather than glass. They are generally smaller and easier to maintain (or replace) than a Fresnel lens. Examples include aerobeacons, DCBs, VRBs, and VLBs.

National Historic Lighthouse Preservation Act (NHLPA): congressional act passed in 2000 creating an official process for relinquishment of US lighthouses. When the Coast Guard deems a lighthouse excess, it is first offered to any other federal agency that owns the surrounding land or water, such as a National Park or Wildlife Refuge. Then it is offered to local government agencies (municipal or county). Then nonprofit organizations may apply for ownership, with the applications reviewed by the National Park Service. If no government agency wants the lighthouse and no nonprofit applicant qualifies, the lighthouse is auctioned off by the General Services Administration (GSA).

Nautical Miles: unit of measurement typically used to describe distances at sea. One nautical mile equals 2,000 yards or 1,852 meters. (A statute mile, used for land distances, is 1,760 yards.)

Occulting: A light characteristic that shines intermittently with a longer period of light than darkness. (The opposite of a flashing light.)

Oil House: a common auxiliary building used to store fuel for a lighthouse. Oil houses became widely used after kerosene replaced lard oil as the primary lamp fuel in the 1880s.

Operating Entity: The organization responsible for the operation, maintenance, and public access of a lighthouse.

Optic: a device used to send out the light in a lighthouse, such as a Fresnel lens.

Pile (Piling): a long, heavy post driven into the seabed or riverbed to serve as support for a lighthouse or other aid to navigation, or a dock/wharf. Maritime piles are usually made from wood, concrete, iron, or steel.

Private Aid to Navigation: A maritime aid to navigation maintained by someone other than the federal government. In the United States, these require permits from the Coast Guard.

Public Aid to Navigation: An aid to navigation maintained by the federal government; that is, Lighthouse Service or Coast Guard.

RACON: radar beacon. When triggered by a vessel's radar pulses, a RACON transmits a coded reply, visible on a radar screen, that identifies the particular station.

Radio Beacon: A type of radio signal broadcast as an aid to navigation. A navigator could use a radio direction finder to take bearings on multiple radio beacon signals and thus triangulate the vessel's location. Radio beacons were introduced in the 1920s and became an important aid to navigation around the country, especially in foggy or stormy weather, until after the introduction of LORAN and later GPS. The radio beacon system in the United States was phased out by 1995.

Range: The maximum distance at which an aid to navigation can be seen or received. Also, a channel with a pair of structures that, when aligned, indicate the center of a navigable channel. Ranges can be either lit (using range lights) or unlit (using a pair of daybeacons).

Range Lights: A pair of lighted aids to navigation used together to indicate a channel, with the rear light higher than the front light. If the two lights appear lined up, the viewer is in the channel. In the nineteenth century, most range lights had a lighthouse as the rear range and a beacon as the front range.

Red Sector: an arc or section of a lighted aid to navigation that shows a red light to indicate a danger area. A red sector is created by placing red-colored glass inside part of the lens or lantern.

Reef Lights: the six offshore lighthouses marking the Florida reef.

Replica: An exact duplicate of a historic structure or artifact. A replica looks the same and functions the same as what it is replicating, but may use modern materials and does not have the historical value of the original.

Sautter: Louis Sautter's company, located in Paris, was the first to manufacture Fresnel lenses, originally under the ownership of Francois Soleil. Sautter (so-tay) purchased the company in 1852 and renamed it L. Sautter et Cie after himself (*et Cie* is French for "and company"). From 1870 to 1890 it was Sautter, Lemonnier, et Cie because of partner Paul Lemonnier (le-mon-yea).

Screwpile: a specially designed pile that can be screwed into the bottom of a seabed for better support of a lighthouse or other aid to navigation. Screwpipes were typically used when the seafloor consisted primarily of sand or soft mud. Not all lighthouses with pile foundations used screwpipers.

Seacoast Light (Landfall Light): A major lighthouse that guides ships traveling along a coast or making landfall (i.e., sighting the coast after traveling across open ocean). In contrast, other lighthouses guide ships into a harbor or around a local hazard. Many seacoast lights are located at an inlet or bay as an additional benefit.

Second-Order: a large Fresnel lens measuring nearly seven feet tall and more than four-and-a-half feet in diameter. Typically used on seacoast lights. The largest bivalve lenses are considered second-order lenses because of their diameter, but they are actually taller and brighter than a normal first-order lens.

Sixth-Order: the smallest size of Fresnel lens, measuring one-and-a-half-feet tall and one foot in diameter. Typically used on range lights and other minor aids to navigation.

Skeletal Tower: a lighthouse or other lighted aid to navigation in which the lantern or modern optic is held up by an open metal framework and built on piles. Skeletal lighthouses include an enclosed central column (containing the staircase), and a dwelling. Skeletal towers are less expensive than their brick counterparts in a marine environment, are considered more resistant to wind and wave action, and were prefabricated in a foundry. Most were intended to be capable of disassembly should they no longer be needed or if they had to be moved. However, because they are entirely made of metal, they require much more maintenance than other lighthouses and are also much hotter inside. Many modern ATONs are steel skeletal designs.

Steamer Lens: a lens of sixth-order or smaller that only shines in one direction. Used for some early range lights as well as the front lamps on locomotives and steamships.

Third-and-a-Half-Order: a medium-sized Fresnel lens a little over three-and-a-half feet tall and two feet in diameter. These were specifically designed for use in the Great Lakes, although a few were used elsewhere. Only twenty-five were ever produced.

Third-Order: a medium-sized Fresnel lens measuring a little more than five feet tall and more than three feet in diameter. Most often used for harbor lights that doubled as minor seacoast lights.

Tower: The part of a lighthouse that elevates the lantern.

Tower Height: The height of a lighthouse from its base (or the ocean floor, for offshore lights) to the top of the lantern (excluding cupolas, vents ball, lightning rods, antennas, etc.).

USLHE: United States Light House Establishment, the federal agency responsible for all US lighthouses from 1789 until 1910. The USLHE was part of the Department of the Treasury until 1903, when it was transferred to the new Department of Commerce. From 1852 to 1910, the USLHE was managed by the Lighthouse Board.

USLHS: United States Lighthouse Service or United States Lighthouse Society. The former was never an official name, although the acronym was sometimes used as an official mark, especially by the Bureau of Lighthouses. The latter is a nonprofit organization, founded in 1984, that publishes *Keeper's Log* magazine and supports lighthouse research, education, and preservation nationwide.

Vega: Vega Industries is a New Zealand company founded in 1972 that specialized in navigation and signal lights, including the VRB and VLB. Vega produced the first LED beacons for lighthouse use.

Ventilator Ball (Vent Ball): A round object found on the roof of many lighthouses. It allowed smoke from the lighthouse oil lamps to exit through the roof while preventing rain or snow from getting in.

VLB: Vega LED Beacon. A type of modern flashing optic made of LED lights in one or more plastic rings.

VRB: Vega Rotating Beacon. A type of modern rotating optic with plastic lenses and capable of running off solar power. VRBs began replacing DCBs in the 1990s. Early VRBs used halogen or incandescent bulbs, but are now switching to LEDs or being replaced by VLBs.

Watch Room: the area directly below the lantern room in which keepers stood watch, monitoring the quality of their light. Supplies for the light, such as spare lamps, glass chimneys, and cleaning items, were also typically kept in the watch room. Most pre-1860s lighthouses did not have a watch room, so the lantern room served this purpose as well.

LIGHTHOUSE
PASSPORT STAMPS

The US Lighthouse Society introduced the Lighthouse Passport program in the early 2000s. Participants purchase a USLHS passport booklet and get it ink stamped each time they visit a new lighthouse. Each booklet holds sixty stamps, and they can be purchased at most lighthouse gift shops or directly from the USLHS. All thirty surviving historic Florida lighthouses have a passport stamp, as do two lost lights (Volusia Bar and Rebecca Shoal), two faux lighthouses (Boca Chita and Terre Verde), two of the Keys beacons (Pacific Reef and Tennessee Reef), and the Gilbert's Bar House of Refuge. In most cases, the stamps are available at the lighthouse's gift shop and are always available at the lighthouse when a FLA event occurs there.

If you forget your stamp book at the time of your visit (or hadn't purchased one yet), most lighthouse organizations will respond to mail-in requests as long as you provide a self-addressed stamped return envelope (a donation of at least $1 is also customary). Stamp information for each lighthouse is listed in the Site Info section of each lighthouse chapter of this book.

For lighthouses lacking gift shops, there are two main contact points:

Contact: Eric Martin (Florida Keys Reef Lights Foundation)
Address: 1067 Drift Creek Cove, Orlando, FL 32828
Phone: (407) 341-7374
Email: ericlighthouse@yahoo.com
Lighthouse Stamps: Fowey Rocks, Pacific Reef, Carysfort Reef, Alligator Reef, Tennessee Reef, Sombrero Key, American Shoal, Sand Key, and Rebecca Shoal.

Contact: John Kennedy (Florida Lighthouse Association)
Mailing Address: 1634 S. Hermitage Road, Fort Myers FL, 33919
Phone: (239) 482-3838
Email: jktigre2@aol.com
Lighthouse Stamps: St. Johns River, St. Johns, Volusia Bar, and St. Joseph
  Point

More information about the Lighthouse Passport Stamp program can be found
on the USLHS website: www.uslhs.org/fun/passport-club.

THE UNMANNED
BEACON LIGHTS OF
THE FLORIDA KEYS

A series of large beacon lights in the Florida Keys are not true lighthouses, although they are sometimes referred to as such by the media. They were never manned and are not enclosed except for their lantern. However, they do resemble small lighthouses, used Fresnel lenses, and date from the civilian Lighthouse Service era, so they have some historical significance and interest to lighthouse buffs. The seven lights were built between 1921 and 1935 to mark local hazards, in some cases replacing older wooden beacons without lanterns. The lights are listed below in geographical order, from the upper Keys to the Dry Tortugas.

Lighthouse passport stamps are available for two of the seven lights, Pacific Reef and Tennessee Reef, through the Florida Keys Reef Lights Foundation.

Pacific Reef

Location: 3 miles SE of Elliott Key
First Lighted: 1921
Design: square pyramidal skeletal tower
Tower Height: 45 feet
Original Optic: fourth-order Fresnel lens
Daymark: brown
Characteristic: flashing
Status: active with a modern optic, plus an automated weather station; lantern removed
Notes: Lantern on display in Islamorada's Founder's Park since 2000.

Molasses Reef
Location: 8 miles SE of Key Largo
First Lighted: 1921
Design: square pyramidal skeletal tower
Tower Height: 45 feet
Original Optic: fourth-order Fresnel lens
Daymark: white
Characteristic: flashing
Status: active with a modern optic, plus an automated weather station; lantern removed

Hen & Chickens Shoal
Location: 2 miles SE of Plantation Key in Hawks Channel
First Lighted: 1929
Design: triangular skeletal tower
Tower Height: 35 feet
Original Optic: drum lens
Daymark: red
Characteristic: flashing red
Status: inactive—daymark (lantern removed)

Tennessee Reef
Location: 4 miles SSE of Long Key on the Florida Reef
First Lighted: 1933
Design: hexagonal pyramidal skeletal tower
Tower Height: 49 feet
Original Optic: fourth-order Fresnel lens
Daymark: black
Characteristic: flashing white
Status: active—still has lantern

Smith Shoal
Location: 11 miles NNW of Key West
First Lighted: 1933
Design: hexagonal pyramidal skeletal tower
Tower Height: 49 feet
Original Optic: fourth-order Fresnel lens
Daymark: white
Characteristic: flashing white

Status: replaced by new structure with a modern optic, plus an automated weather station

Cosgrove Shoal
Location: 10 miles WSW of Key West, S of the Marquesas Keys
First Lighted: 1935
Deactivated: unknown
Design: hexagonal pyramidal skeletal tower
Tower Height: 49 feet
Original Optic: 200 mm drum lens
Daymark: white
Characteristic: flashing white
Status: replaced by new structure

Pulaski Shoal
Location: 30 miles NW of Key West, N of the Dry Tortugas
First Lighted: 1935
Deactivated: unknown
Design: hexagonal pyramidal skeletal tower
Tower Height: 49 feet
Original Optic: fourth-order (500 mm) drum Fresnel lens
Daymark: black
Characteristic: flashing white
Status: lantern removed and replaced by an automated weather station

FLORIDA LIGHTSHIPS

Josh Liller and Neil Hurley

No lightships remain in Florida, but at least eight different vessels served as lightships in Florida waters between the 1820s and 1950s.

AURORA BOREALIS

The *Aurora Borealis* was the second lightship ever built by the US Lighthouse Service and the only one to serve at multiple stations in Florida. The wooden vessel was just under sixty feet long with a lantern suspended between her two masts, plus a fog bell. She was originally stationed at the mouth of the Mississippi River (1821–1823). She then moved to Florida where she was stationed at Pensacola Bay (1823–1825) and the Dry Tortugas (1825–1826). After completion of the first lighthouse on Garden Key, *Aurora Borealis* was sent to Norfolk for repairs. The vessel is thought to have remained in service as a relief lightship at least as late as 1837.

CARYSFORT REEF LIGHTSHIPS

Before the construction of a lighthouse at Carysfort Reef, the site was marked by a lightship anchored inside the reef. Built in New York for $20,000, the wooden lightship *Caesar* wrecked in a storm off Key Biscayne before reaching her station. Repaired in Key West, she served from 1825 to 1830 when severe dry rot required her replacement, making her "the shortest-lived lightship in Lighthouse Service history" according to LighthouseFriends.com. The Lighthouse Service spent another $20,000 on another wooden lightship, *Florida*, which served until 1847 when the lighthouse was completed. Sailing north from her former station, the *Florida* wrecked in the Bahamas because of a storm.

DAMES POINT LIGHTBOAT

While the term *light boat* was often used for lightships in the early 1800s, in the case of Dames Point it may have been a very accurate description. The little vessel was towed to Jacksonville by a steamer rather than sailing under her own power. The light boat only had a crew of three with a small fixed white light, fog horn, and fog bell. The vessel was apparently so inconsequential that, after being towed upriver early in the Civil War, she was never mentioned again.

KEY WEST LIGHTSHIPS

For nearly two decades, the end of the Northwest Passage to Key West was marked with the 145-ton lightship *Key West*. In 1853, the wooden vessel was condemned and removed. It would be another two years before the completion of the lighthouse at the same location. During World War II, Key West was an important naval base and also an anchorage for merchant shipping, protected by an extensive minefield. The Gulf Sea Frontier War Diary indicates that the USS *Seven Seas* (IX-68) served as lightship at Key West from early 1942 to early 1944, presumably marking the entrance to the minefield and anchorage. She was not a traditional lightship, but a converted Swedish navy three-masted training ship, *Abraham Rydberg*, built in 1912. *Seven Seas* was 168 feet long, displaced 430 tons, and almost certainly was the last wooden lightship used by the United States.

SAND KEY LIGHTSHIP

After the destruction of the original Sand Key Lighthouse in 1846, the 140-ton wooden lightship *Honey* was stationed near the island in 1847. The lightship was expected to remain on station until completion of the new lighthouse. However, by the summer of 1852, the vessel was in such poor condition that it was condemned by the Key West Collector of Customs, dismantled, and sold at auction.

ST. JOHNS LIGHTSHIP (LV-84/WAL-509)

When the Brunswick (Georgia) Lightship station was discontinued in 1929, the vessel moved down the coast to a new station five miles off the mouth of the St. Johns River. The steel-hulled lightship had been built in 1907 and was the only metal lightship to serve in Florida. She was 135 feet long, displaced 683 tons, and had two masts with lanterns. As part of the change in stations, the lightship received upgrades including electric lens lanterns and a radio beacon. In 1935, an air horn replaced the lightship's old fog signal—a steam chime whistle. The lightship remained on station during World War II. Having replaced the St. Johns River Lighthouse in 1929, the St. Johns Lightship was in turn replaced by the new St. Johns Lighthouse in 1954. The vessel served on relief duties until 1965 when she was decommissioned. The lightship was sold into private hands for several decades before being scrapped in the 1990s.

DREAM LIGHTS

PROPOSED FLORIDA
LIGHTHOUSES THAT WERE
NEVER BUILT

Josh Liller

Not everything planned comes to fruition. The following are Florida light-houses that never broke ground despite being proposed on multiple oc-casions, and in some cases even at least partly funded. The sites are listed in clockwise order around the Florida coast.

MOUNT CORNELIA LIGHTHOUSE

In 1889, the Lighthouse Board proposed construction of a 150-foot tall light-house on Mount Cornelia. The sixty-five-foot hill is the highest point in Duval County and is near the mouth of the St. Johns River. The proposed lighthouse would be a significant improvement from the St. Johns River Lighthouse and have enough range to allow for the discontinuing of the Amelia Island Light-houses. The estimated cost of the proposed light station was $175,000.

The Annual Report of the Lighthouse Board repeated the funding request for the Mount Cornelia Lighthouse every year through 1894. Requests resumed again in 1902 and continued for several years thereafter. In 1912, the Jackson-ville Board of Trade unsuccessfully appealed for a lighthouse at Mount Cornelia on the St. Johns River North Jetty. Congress never appropriated funds for the project.

Mount Cornelia is now part of Fort George Island State Park. A park hiking trail going north from the Ribault Club passes over the hill.

INDIAN RIVER LIGHTHOUSE

On February 8, 1847, the Florida Legislature issued a resolution requesting the construction of a lighthouse at "Indian River Bar" (i.e., Old Indian River Inlet). In the nineteenth century, Old Indian River Inlet (a few miles north of the modern Fort Pierce Inlet) was the only reliable inlet on the Indian River Lagoon, and a lighthouse on the north side of the inlet would seem a fairly typical placement.

The 1852 Report of the Lighthouse Board listed the seventeen most important lighthouses needed on the entire Atlantic and Gulf coasts. Five of the top seven were in Florida. Two would be built promptly (Jupiter and Dry Banks; i.e., Sombrero Key), and two would be built decades later (Hillsboro Inlet and Mosquito Inlet; i.e., Ponce Inlet). The recommendation for a lighthouse "15 miles north of Indian River Inlet" was never acted upon. The distance given would have put the lighthouse in the vicinity of the Indian River Shores neighborhood (between Vero Beach and Wabasso).

In later years, members of the Lighthouse Service would occasionally note the distance of over one hundred miles between Cape Canaveral and Jupiter and suggest it as one of the unlighted gaps that should be closed. However, there was never sufficient local or national interest to prompt the Lighthouse Board to request funding for such a project.

CAPE ROMANO LIGHTHOUSE

Not to be confused with Cape Romain (in South Carolina), Cape Romano is the southernmost point of an island of the same name in southwest Florida. Just south of Marco Island, Cape Romano is one of the westernmost of the Ten Thousand Islands and the point where the Florida Gulf Coast turns southeast. A shoal extends outward from the cape. Since it is also almost due north of Key West, a lighthouse at Cape Romano would serve as a useful aid to navigation for shipping between Key West and Fort Myers. Those two ports are over one hundred miles apart without a lighthouse between them.

Executive Orders on January 9, 1878, and April 13, 1898, reserved Cape Romano Island as a lighthouse reservation. In 1901, the secretary of the treasury formally requested a $35,000 appropriation from Congress for construction of a lighthouse with a second-order Fresnel lens. In 1906, increases in material costs raised the request to $45,000. Congress never provided the funds. In 1919, the

Department of Commerce sought to lease the lighthouse reservation, and the island was eventually sold into private ownership.

Although Marco Island has been heavily developed, Cape Romano and its nearby islands remain in a natural state. The cape gained fame in the 1980s when six unusual concrete dome-shaped houses were built there. The western shore of the island has been eroding significantly in the twenty-first century, especially from hurricanes Wilma and Irma. Built on dry land, the Cape Romano Dome Homes are now a couple hundred feet offshore and slowly sinking. Had Cape Romano Island Lighthouse been built it would probably no longer be standing.

ST. ANDREW BAY LIGHTHOUSE

More than a hundred straight-line miles separate the Pensacola Lighthouse from Beacon Hill, former site of the St. Joseph Point Lighthouse. This is one of the longest stretches of the Florida coast never to have a lighthouse. St. Andrews Bay is the body of water adjacent to Panama City, but that city was not incorporated until 1909. However, although sparsely settled in the nineteenth century, it was a significant fishing and salt-producing area during the Civil War, and the bay looked promising for future commercial development.

In September 1856, Congress appropriated $15,000 "for a lighthouse to mark the entrance to St. Andrew's Bay" plus an additional $4,000 for buoys and stakes to mark the bar and channel. The funds allocated suggest a cottage-style lighthouse. Later, state legislature resolutions for a lighthouse at the bay entrance also amounted to nothing. St. Andrews Bay was finally marked with two lighted range beacons in 1900.

Had a lighthouse been built it presumably would have been located on the St. Andrews Sound Military Reservation on the west side of the inlet. This military reservation had been created by an executive orders in 1849 and 1897. In 1947, the property became St. Andrews State Park.

Panama City almost got a lighthouse in the twenty-first century. The location would have been the Panama City Marina, directly across St. Andrews Bay from the inlet. The idea started as a way to honor the local fishing community and serve as a tourist attraction, but it grew in size and scope to be a private aid to navigation with an elevator. The idea was not without merit; not only was Panama City predominately a tourist town but also a similar attraction had been built on Hilton Head Island, South Carolina, in 1970. A nonprofit organization,

Panama City Lighthouse, Inc., formed to build and operate the attraction and even collected some donations. The Panama City Commission was initially supportive but bailed on the idea when the price tag spiraled to $1.6 million. The project was abandoned in 2016, and the nonprofit dissolved.

PROMINENT FLORIDA FAUX LIGHTHOUSES

Josh Liller

F *aux lighthouse* is a broad term referring to any nonhistoric lighthouse. This includes: structures intentionally built to resemble lighthouses, but which have never served as an aid to navigation; privately built aids to navigation that resemble a lighthouse; and large miniature versions of real lighthouses. Some are free-standing; others are attached to the sides of other buildings including churches, restaurants, marinas, and parking garages. Faux lighthouses are not eligible for Florida Lighthouse Association support. However, they are often of interest to lighthouse buffs, so a list of the more notable examples is included here, in clockwise order around the state.

BOCA CHITA LIGHTHOUSE

Located on Boca Chita Key in Biscayne Bay, this sixty-five-foot tall private lighthouse was built around 1940 by Mark Honeywell, heir to the Honeywell Instruments Corporation and then owner of the island. It was only briefly lighted as the project had not been approved by the Coast Guard. The island is only accessible by boat and is now part of Biscayne National Park.

> Passport Stamp: yes—Dante Fascell Visitor Center (9 AM–5 PM every day)
> Contact: Biscayne National Park, 9700 SW 328th Street, Homestead, FL 33033
> Phone: (305) 230-1144
> Email: bisc_information@nps.gov
> Website: www.nps.gov/bisc/planyourvisit/bocachita.htm

KEY LARGO LIGHTHOUSE

Privately built in 1959, this little lighthouse stands in the back yard of a private residence on the south side of Key Largo next to a canal leading to the Pilot House Marina. What makes it particularly notable is the lantern is from the Rebecca Shoal Lighthouse, removed when that lighthouse was demolished in 1953 and purchased intact from an Ocala scrap dealer. The short, square tower has a white lower half and a red-and-white checkered upper half. Due to surrounding buildings and trees, it is only visible by boat.

Passport Stamp: no
Contact: none—privately owned

FARO BLANCO LIGHTHOUSE

This fifty-foot-tall concrete lighthouse at Marathon in the Florida Keys was built by a marina around 1950. It remains an active private aid to navigation with a rotating aerobeacon. The name is Spanish for "white lighthouse." The tower is clearly visible on the marina dock, but not normally open for climbing.

Passport Stamp: no
Contact: Faro Blanco Resort & Yacht Club, 1996 Overseas Highway, Marathon, FL 33050
Phone: (305) 743-1234
Email: info@faroblancoresort.com
Website: www.faroblancoresort.com

TIERRA VERDE LIGHTHOUSE

This faux light is located in Tierra Verde on Cunningham Key. It was built as an educational center in 2005 by Tampa Bay Watch, a nonprofit environmental organization. The building exterior resembles a larger version of the Port Boca Grande Lighthouse. Although the building is a public aid to navigation with a light maintained by the Coast Guard, the building lacks a true lantern room. The "lantern" is actually an atrium, without any stairs.

Passport Stamp: yes
Contact: Tampa Bay Watch, 3000 Pinellas Bayway South, Tierra Verde, FL 33715
Phone: (727) 867-8166
Website: www.tampabaywatch.org

MOUNT DORA LIGHTHOUSE

Located in Grantham Point Park on the east shore of Lake Dora, this faux lighthouse is the only registered inland private aid to navigation in Florida. Although it resembles a miniature lighthouse, it is more accurately a large beacon light since there is no staircase and the lantern is miniature. Standing thirty-five feet tall with red and white stripes, it was built in 1988 by local civic groups.

Passport Stamp: no
Contact: none

NEW CANAL LIGHTHOUSE

SuEllyn and Brian McCabe built an oversize replica of Louisiana's New Canal Lighthouse in 1998 to serve as a vacation rental home. It is located in Santa Rosa Beach, in the Florida panhandle between Destin and Panama City. Street Address: 512 Old Beach Road, Santa Rosa Beach.

Passport Stamp: no
Contact: various rental agencies

For additional Florida faux lighthouses see: https://www.floridalighthouses. org/page-1096080.

CHRONOLOGICAL LIST
OF ALL FLORIDA
LIGHTHOUSES

Built	Name	Status
1824	St. Augustine 1	destroyed by erosion (1880)
1824	Pensacola I	demolished after replacement (1860s)
1825	Cape Florida I	demolished to rebuild (1846)
1826	Key West I	destroyed by hurricane (1846)
1826	Dry Tortugas I Garden Key I	demolished due to deterioration (1877)
1827	Sand Key I	destroyed by hurricane (1846)
1829	St. Marks I	demolished—faulty construction (1830)
1830	St. Johns River I	destroyed by erosion (1833)
1831	St. Marks II	demolished due to replacement (1842)
1833	St. George Island (West Pass)	demolished to move & rebuild (1847)
1835	Mosquito Inlet I	destroyed by erosion (1836)
1835	St. Johns River II	destroyed by erosion (early 1900s?)
1839	Dog Island I	destroyed by hurricane (1842)
1839	St. Joseph Bay	demolished to move & rebuild (1847)
1839	**Amelia Island**	**extant (newer lantern)—active**
1842	**St. Marks III**	**extant—active**
1843	Dog Island II	destroyed by hurricane (1851)
1846	**Cape Florida II**	**extant (replica lantern)—active**
1847	Cape St. George I	destroyed by hurricane (1851)
1847	**Key West II**	**extant (newer lantern)—active**
1847	Cape San Blas I	destroyed by hurricane (1851)
1847	Cape Canaveral I	demolished to use material (1894)

Built	Name	Status
1848	Egmont Key I	demolished to replace (1858)
1852	Cape St. George II	destroyed by hurricane & erosion (2005)
1852	Dog Island III	destroyed by hurricane (1873)
1852	**Carysfort Reef**	**extant—inactive**
1853	**Sand Key II**	**extant (without cylinder)—inactive**
1854	**Cedar Keys**	**extant—active**
1855	Northwest Passage I	demolished & rebuilt (1879)
1855	Cape San Blas II	destroyed by hurricane (1856)
1858	**Egmont Key II**	**extant (without lantern)—active**
1858	**Sombrero Key**	**extant—inactive**
1858	**Dry Tortugas II Loggerhead Key**	**extant—inactive**
1858	Amelia Island North Rear Range I	destroyed (Civil War)
1859	**St. Johns River III**	**extant—inactive**
1859	Cape San Blas III	destroyed by erosion (1882)
1859	**Pensacola II**	**extant—active**
1860	**Jupiter Inlet**	**extant—active**
1868	**Cape Canaveral II**	**extant—active (moved 1894)**
1872	Amelia Island North Rear Range II	destroyed (unknown)
1872	Dames Point	destroyed by fire (1913)
1873	**Alligator Reef**	**extant—inactive**
1874	**St. Augustine II**	**extant—active**
1876	**Tortugas Harbor Garden Key II**	**extant—inactive**
1878	**Fowey Rocks**	**extant—active**
1878	Northwest Passage II	destroyed by fire (1971)
1880	**American Shoal**	**extant—inactive**
1884	**Sanibel Island**	**extant—active**
1885	**Cape San Blas IV**	**extant—inactive (moved 1919 & 2014)**
1886	Volusia Bar	destroyed by fire (1972)
1886	Rebecca Shoal	removed (1953)
1887	**Anclote Key**	**extant—active**
1887	**Mosquito Inlet II Ponce Inlet**	**extant—active**
1890	**Port Boca Grande**	**extant—active**
1890	Charlotte Harbor	demolished (1943)
1895	**Crooked River**	**extant—active**

Built	Name	Status
1907	Hillsboro Inlet	extant—active
1927	Gasparilla Island	extant—active
1954	St. Johns IV	extant—active
2008	Cape St. George III	extant—active

VISITING STATUS
FOR FLORIDA
LIGHTHOUSES

LIGHTHOUSES FULLY OPEN TO THE PUBLIC

Daily/Weekly Access with Tower Climbing

1. St. Augustine
2. Ponce de Leon Inlet
3. Jupiter
4. Cape Florida
5. Key West
6. Crooked River
7. St. George Island
8. Cape San Blas
9. Pensacola

LIGHTHOUSES PARTLY OPEN TO THE PUBLIC

Monthly Access with Tower Climbing

1. Hillsboro Inlet
2. Gasparilla Island

LIGHTHOUSES PARTLY OPEN TO THE PUBLIC

Daily/Weekly/Monthly Access *Without Tower Climbing*

1. Amelia Island
2. Cape Canaveral

3. Port Boca Grande (climbing one day per week)
4. St. Marks

LIGHTHOUSES OCCASIONALLY OPEN TO THE PUBLIC

Special Events Only with Climbing

1. Anclote Keys (ferry service from Tarpon Springs)
2. Cedar Keys (ferry service from Cedar Key)

LIGHTHOUSES CLOSED, GROUNDS OPEN

Accessible by Car

1. Sanibel Island

Only Accessible by Boat

1. Tortugas Harbor / Garden Key (ferry service from Key West)
2. Dry Tortugas / Loggerhead Key (no ferry service)
3. Egmont Key (ferry service from Fort DeSoto Park)

LIGHTHOUSES CLOSED, LOCATED OFFSHORE

Only Accessible by Boat

1. Fowey Rocks
2. Carysfort Reef
3. Alligator Reef
4. Sombrero Key
5. American Shoal
6. Sand Key

LIGHTHOUSES WITH NO ACCESS

1. St. Johns River (military base, no support organization)
2. St. Johns (military base, no support organization)
3. St. Joseph Point (private residence)

OWNERSHIP STATUS
FOR FLORIDA
LIGHTHOUSES

OWNED AND OPERATED BY A NONPROFIT

1. St. Augustine
2. Key West

OWNED BY THE GOVERMENT, OPERATED BY A NONPROFIT

1. Ponce de Leon Inlet
2. Cape Canaveral
3. Jupiter Inlet
4. Hillsboro Inlet
5. Port Boca Grande
6. Gasparilla Island
7. Crooked River
8. Cape St. George
9. Cape San Blas
10. Pensacola

OWNED AND OPERATED BY THE GOVERNMENT

1. Amelia Island
2. St. Johns River

3. St. Johns
4. Cape Florida
5. Fowey Rocks
6. Tortugas Harbor (Garden Key)
7. Dry Tortugas (Loggerhead Key)
8. Sanibel Island
9. Egmont Key
10. Cedar Keys
11. Anclote Key
12. St. Marks

PRIVATELY OWNED

1. St. Joseph Point

TO BE DETERMINED

1. Carysfort Reef
2. Alligator Reef
3. Sombrero Key
4. American Shoal
5. Sand Key

LIGHTING STATUS OF SURVIVING HISTORIC FLORIDA LIGHTHOUSES

PUBLIC AID TO NAVIGATION

1. Amelia Island
2. St. Johns
3. Cape Canaveral
4. Jupiter Inlet
5. Hillsboro Inlet
6. Fowey Rocks
7. Sanibel Island
8. Port Boca Grande
9. Egmont Key
10. Pensacola

PRIVATE AID TO NAVIGATION

1. St. Augustine
2. Ponce de Leon Inlet
3. Cape Florida
4. Gasparilla Island
5. Anclote Key

6. Cedar Key
7. St. Marks
8. Crooked River
9. Cape St. George

INACTIVE

1. St. Johns River
2. Carysfort Reef
3. Alligator Reef
4. Sombrero Key
5. American Shoal
6. Key West
7. Sand Key
8. Tortugas Harbor (Garden Key)
9. Dry Tortugas (Loggerhead Key)
10. Cape San Blas
11. St. Joseph Point

FLORIDA'S
FRESNEL LENSES

This is a list of all historic and replica Fresnel lenses (sixth-order or larger) used in, intended for, and/or exhibited at a Florida lighthouse or other lighted aid to navigation. It does not include lens lanterns, steamer lenses, or other small lenses. Manufacturer and year of manufacture are listed in parenthesis. Stations not included are not known to have any associated Fresnel lenses. Note that a lens being "exhibited" means on display in some way, but not necessarily in a location accessible to the general public (ex.: on a military base). The current whereabouts of each lens is unknown unless otherwise stated.

AMELIA ISLAND LIGHTHOUSE

- Third-order revolving lens (unknown). Active 1856–1861. Removed during the Civil War.
- Third-order revolving lens (Henry-Lepaute, 1860s?). Active 1865–1903. Replaced by a new lens. Sent to the Staten Island Depot in 1906.
- Fourth-order revolving lens (unknown). Active 1881 on a temporary structure while the lighthouse received a new lantern.
- Third-order revolving lens. (Barbier & Bénard, 1894–1901). Active 1903–present. Public ATON.

AMELIA ISLAND NORTH RANGE FRONT LIGHT

- Sixth-order fixed lens (unknown). Active 1858–1861. Removed or destroyed during the Civil War.

AMELIA ISLAND NORTH RANGE REAR LIGHT

- Sixth-order fixed lens (unknown). Active 1858–1861. Removed or destroyed during the Civil War.
- Sixth-order fixed lens (unknown). Active 1872–1893. Moved from the lighthouse to a beacon on a tramway in 1880. Removed when the permanent beacons were discontinued in 1893.

DAMES POINT LIGHTHOUSE

- Fifth-order fixed lens (unknown). Active 1872–1893. Removed when the lighthouse was deactivated.

ST. JOHNS RIVER LIGHTHOUSE

- Fourth-order fixed lens (unknown, 1850s). Active before 1858 in the second lighthouse at this station, per 1858 Light List. Removed when the third (current) lighthouse was lighted.
- Third-order fixed lens (probably Henry-Lepaute, 1859). Active 1859–1861. Damaged during the Civil War, apparently removed in 1867.
- Third-order fixed lens (Henry-Lepaute, 1860s?) 1867–1929. Described as a "new lens" in the Annual Report of the Lighthouse Board. Removed after the lighthouse was deactivated.

ST. AUGUSTINE LIGHTHOUSE

- Fourth-order FVF lens (unknown). Active 1856?–1861. Removed during the Civil War.
- Fourth-order FVF lens (unknown). Active 1867–1874. Possibly the repaired prewar lens. Removed after the new lighthouse was lighted.

- First-order FVF lens (Sautter, Lemonnier, et Cie., 1874). Active 1874–present. Fixed lens with three rotating bull's-eye panels. Restored in 1993 after gunshot damage from 1986.
- Fourth-order fixed lens (Barbier et Bernard, between 1894 and 1901). Exhibited in museum. Past use unknown.

VOLUSIA BAR LIGHTHOUSE

- Fourth-order fixed lens (unknown). Active 1886–1899. Replaced by smaller lens.
- Fifth-order fixed lens (unknown). Active 1899–1908. Removed some time after light was discontinued.

PONCE DE LEON LIGHTHOUSE

- Hyper-radiant fixed lens (F. Barbier et Cie., 1887). Purchased for this lighthouse, but never installed there. Displayed at various major exhibitions and fairs. Installed at Makapu'u Point Lighthouse in 1909 where it remains active as a public ATON.
- First-order fixed lens (Barbier et Fenestre, 1867). Active 1887–1933. Replaced by revolving lens in 1933. Stored at Mystic Seaport (1946–1977). On exhibit since 2003.
- Third-order revolving Fresnel lens (Barbier, Bernard, et Turenne, 1904). Active 1933–1970 and 2004–present. Private ATON. Previously active in the Sapelo Island Lighthouse, GA (1905–1933).
- Sixth-order revolving lens (Artworks Florida, 2004). On exhibit. Never active.

PONCE DE LEON LIGHTHOUSE—LENS COLLECTION FROM FOREIGN LIGHTHOUSES

- Third-order drum lens (Barbier, Bernard, et Turenne, between 1901 and 1915). On exhibit. Provenance unknown, but not used in the United States.
- Third-order middle fixed lens (Chance Brothers, ca. 1917). On exhibit. Used in the Hannibal Islands Lighthouse, Queensland, Australia.

- Fourth-order fixed lens (Chance Brothers, 1859). On exhibit. Used in Spit Bank Lighthouse, County Cork, Ireland.
- Fourth-order fixed red lens (Chance Brothers, 1869). On exhibit. Used in the Granton Harbor Lighthouse, Scotland.
- Fourth-order fixed lens (Barbier, Bernard, et Turenne, 1914). On exhibit. Used in Madagascar. Port light in lantern.
- Fourth-order drum lens (AGA, early 1900s). In collection, but not on exhibit. Used in Peru. Two identical lenses.
- Fourth-order bivalve lens (Barbier, Bernard, et Turenne, ca. 1930). On exhibit. Used at Halong Bay Lighthouse, Vietnam.
- Fifth-order fixed lens (Chance Brothers, between 1890 and 1918). On exhibit. Used in Australia. Harbor light lens covering 180 degrees.
- Sixth-order fixed lens (Barbier et Fenestre, ca. 1882). On exhibit. Used in France.
- Sixth-order revolving lens (Barbier, Bernard, et Turenne, aft. 1901). On exhibit. Used in France. Flashing green and white.
- Sixth-order fixed harbor light lenses (Barbier, Bernard, et Turenne, 1913). On exhibit. Used in Normandy, France.

CAPE CANAVERAL LIGHTHOUSE

- Fourth-order fixed lens (unknown). Active 1867–1868. Removed after completion of the replacement lighthouse.
- First-order revolving lens (Henry-Lepaute, 1860). Active 1868–1993. On exhibit at Ponce de Leon Inlet Lighthouse & Museum since 1995.
- Fourth-order revolving lens (unknown). Active 1893–1894 on a temporary wooden structure while the lighthouse was being disassembled, moved, and rebuilt.

JUPITER INLET LIGHTHOUSE

- First-order revolving Fresnel lens (L. Sautter et Cie, 1854). Active 1860–1861. Removed 1866. Repaired 1868 and stored in the Staten Island Lighthouse Depot at least as late as 1906.
- First-order revolving Fresnel lens (Henry-Lepaute, 1852?). Ordered for Cape Disappointment, but reassigned to Montauk. Shipped to Florida due to delays with the Sautter lens, but never installed. Shipped back

north and installed (for the first time anywhere) at Montauk Point Lighthouse, New York, in 1858. Active until 1903. Removed and sent to the Staten Island Lighthouse Depot where it remained as late as 1906.
- First-order revolving Fresnel lens (Henry-Lepaute, 1863). Active 1866–present. Originally VRN. Panels reconfigured and blanking panels added in 1928. Public ATON.

HILLSBORO INLET LIGHTHOUSE

- Second-order bivalve lens (Barbier, Bernard, et Turenne, 1906). Active 1907–present. Public ATON.

CAPE FLORIDA LIGHTHOUSE

- Second-order fixed lens (Henry-Lepaute, 1855?). Active 1856–1861. Partly destroyed by Confederate sympathizers. Removed 1866. Alleged to have been repaired and installed in the Grosse Point Lighthouse (Evanston, IL) in 1872, but this is unconfirmed. If correct then the lens is still active.
- Second-order fixed lens (Henry-Lepaute, 1863?). Active 1866–1878. Lens removed when the lighthouse was deactivated, but the pedestal was left in the lantern. Shipped to the Staten Island Depot in 1879 where it remained at least as late as 1906.
- Fifth-order (375 mm) drum lens (probably AGA, 1930s). Active 1978–1988. Previous use and disposition unknown.

FOWEY ROCKS LIGHTHOUSE

- First-order fixed lens (Henry-Lepaute, 1876). Active 1878–1982. On exhibit at the USCG Aids to Navigation School Museum, Yorktown, VA.

PACIFIC REEF BEACON

- Fourth-order fixed lens (unknown). Active 1921–unknown. Replaced with a modern optic.

CARYSFORT REEF LIGHTHOUSE

- First-order revolving lens (Henry-Lepaute, 1850). Mistakenly held by the New York Customs Office, then auctioned off. Reclaimed by the federal government through legal action. Disposition unknown; installed at another lighthouse in the 1850s or 1860s.
- First-order revolving lens (Henry-Lepaute, 1857). Active 1858–1962. Prominently exhibited at the History Miami museum (formerly Historical Society of South Florida).
- Third-order fixed lens (Henry-Lepaute, unknown). Active 1962–1982. Formerly exhibited at CG Station Islamorda. Currently exhibited at CG Base Miami.

MOLASSES REEF BEACON

- Fourth-order fixed lens (unknown). Active 1921–unknown. Replaced with a modern optic.

ALLIGATOR REEF LIGHTHOUSE

- First-order revolving lens (unknown). Active 1873–1935. Destroyed by the Labor Day Hurricane of 1935.
- First-order revolving lens (Henry-Lepaute, 1928). Active 1935–1982. Replaced with a modern optic.

TENNESSEE REEF BEACON

- Fourth-order fixed lens (unknown). Active 1933–unknown. Replaced with a modern optic.

SOMBRERO KEY LIGHTHOUSE

- First-order fixed lens (Henry-Lepaute, 1857). Active 1858–1982. On exhibit in the Visitor Center at the Key West Lighthouse Museum.

AMERICAN SHOAL LIGHTHOUSE

- First-order FVF lens (Henry-Lepaute, 1880). Purchased with the appropriation for this lighthouse, but never installed there. Stored in the Staten Island Depot at least as late as 1906.
- First-order revolving lens (Henry-Lepaute, 1874). Active 1880–1980. Removed to install a modern optic. Possibly in storage at the USCG Exhibit Center in Forrestville, MD.

KEY WEST LIGHTHOUSE

- Third-order fixed lens (Henry-Lepaute, 1858). Active 1858–1969. Still in lantern, but no longer an aid to navigation.

SAND KEY LIGHTHOUSE

- First-order revolving lens (Henry-Lepaute, 1853). Active 1853–1982. Replaced by modern optic.

NORTHWEST PASSAGE LIGHTHOUSE

- Fifth-order fixed lens (L. Sautter, 1855). Active 1855–1879. Replaced by larger lens.
- Fourth-order fixed lens (unknown). Active 1879–1921. Removed when the lighthouse was discontinued.

SMITH SHOAL BEACON

- Fourth-order fixed lens (unknown). Active 1933–unknown. Replaced with a modern optic.

REBECCA SHOAL LIGHTHOUSE

- Fourth-order revolving lens (unknown). Active 1886–1925. Alternated red and white flashes. Replaced with a fixed lens with an acetylene flasher.

- Fourth-order fixed lens (unknown) Active 1925–1953. Removed when the lighthouse was replaced with a modern ATON.

GARDEN KEY / TORTUGAS HARBOR LIGHTHOUSE

- Fourth-order fixed lens (Henry-Lepaute, 1858). Active 1858–1921 in the original brick Garden Key Lighthouse then the iron Tortugas Harbor Lighthouse. Moved when the new lighthouse was built in 1876 and removed when it was discontinued in 1921.

LOGGERHEAD KEY / DRY TORTUGAS LIGHTHOUSE

- First-order fixed lens (Sautter et Cie, 1858). Active 1858–1911. Removed due to storm damage and replaced with new lens.
- Second-order bivalve lens (Barbier, Bernard, et Turenne, 1910). Active 1911–1986. Removed due to problems with the mercury float. On exhibit at the USCG Aids to Navigation School Museum, Yorktown, VA.

PULASKI SHOAL BEACON

- Fourth-order (500 mm) drum lens (unknown). Active 1935–unknown. Replaced with a modern optic.

SANIBEL ISLAND LIGHTHOUSE

- Third-order FVF lens (unknown). Active 1884–1923. Replaced.
- Third-order fixed lens (unknown). Active 1923–1962. Replaced.
- Fourth-order (500 mm) drum lens (AGA, 1920s). Active 1962–1982. Replaced by modern optic and placed in USCG warehouse storage in St. Petersburg, FL. On exhibit at the Sanibel Historical Museum & Village since 1998.

CHARLOTTE HARBOR LIGHTHOUSE

- Fifth-order fixed lens (unknown). Active 1890–1932? Removed when lighthouse deactivated.

PORT BOCA GRANDE LIGHTHOUSE

- Third-and-a-half-order FVF lens (unknown). Active 1890—ca. 1907. Originally a fixed white light with a red flash. Changed in the early 1900s to occulting, probably by replacing the revolving red panels with blanking panels. Replaced by a new lens.
- Fourth-order bivalve lens (unknown). Active ca. 1907–1966. Removed when lighthouse deactivated.
- Fifth-order (375 mm) drum lens (unknown). Active 1986–present. Public ATON.

GASPARILLA ISLAND LIGHTHOUSE (FORMERLY BOCA GRANDE REAR RANGE LIGHT)

- Third-order fixed lens (unknown, 1881). Active 1881–1918 (in Delaware). Removed when the lighthouse was disassembled and sent to San Francisco. Presumably installed in a Pacific Coast lighthouse.
- Fourth-order fixed lens (unknown). Active 1932–1943. Replaced by a modern optic.
- Fourth-order fixed lens (Artworks Florida, 2018). Active 2018–present. Private ATON.

EGMONT KEY LIGHTHOUSE

- Third-order fixed lens (Henry-Lepaute, 1858). Active 1858–1861. Removed during the Civil War.
- Fourth-order fixed lens (unknown). Active 1866–1896. Replaced with a larger lens.
- Third-order fixed lens (L. Sautter et Cie, 1860s). Active 1896–1944. Converted from fixed to occulting in 1916, presumably using rotating blanking panels. Lens removed when the lantern was removed.

ANCLOTE KEY LIGHTHOUSE

- Third-order revolving lens (Henry-Lepaute, 1884). Active 1887–1960s. Replaced with modern optic.
- Fourth-order revolving lens (Artworks Florida, 2003). Active 2003–present. Private ATON.

CEDAR KEYS LIGHTHOUSE

- Fourth-order FVF lens (Henry-Lepaute, 1854). Active 1854–1861. Removed during the Civil War. Active 1866–1915. Removed after lighthouse deactivated. Probably the same lens was reinstalled after the war.
- Fourth-order FVF lens (Artworks Florida, 2019). Active 2019–present. Fixed lens with two revolving bull's-eye panels. Private ATON.

ST. MARKS LIGHTHOUSE

- Fourth-order fixed lens (unknown, 1850s). Active 1856–1861. Removed during Civil War.
- Fourth-order fixed lens (Henry-Lepaute, 1850s). Active 1866–2000. Removed in 2014 for restoration at Ponce de Leon Inlet Lighthouse Museum. On exhibit in the St. Marks NWR Visitor Center.
- Fourth-order fixed lens (Artworks Florida, 2019). Active 2019–present. Private ATON.

DOG ISLAND LIGHTHOUSE

- Fourth-order revolving lens (Henry-Lepaute, 1856). Active 1856–1861. Removed during the Civil War.
- Fourth-order revolving lens (unknown). Active 1866–1873. Destroyed along with the lighthouse during an 1873 hurricane.

CROOKED RIVER LIGHTHOUSE

- Fourth-order open bivalve lens (Henry-Lepaute, 1894). Active 1895–1976. Replaced with a modern optic. On exhibit at the 8th Coast Guard District Headquarters, New Orleans, LA.

- Fourth-order open bivalve lens (Artworks Florida, 2007). Active 2007–present. Replica of original lens.

CAPE ST. GEORGE LIGHTHOUSE

- Third-order fixed lens (Sautter et Cie, 1857). Active 1857–1861 and 1866–1889. Removed during the Civil War. Reinstalled after postwar repairs in France. Replaced with a new lens and shipped to the Staten Island Depot where it remained at least as late as 1906.
- Third-order fixed lens (unknown). Active 1889–1949. Replaced with a drum lens. Possibly the lens (Sautter et Cie) on exhibit in the Berwick, Louisiana, town hall since the 1990s.
- Fifth-order (375 mm) drum lens (probably AGA, date unknown). Active 1949–1977. Replaced with a modern optic.
- Third-order fixed lens (Artworks Florida, 2016). Replica of 1889–1849 lens on exhibit in the Cape St. George Lighthouse Museum.

CAPE SAN BLAS LIGHTHOUSE

- Third-order revolving lens (unknown). Active 1855–1856. Presumably destroyed during a hurricane along with the lighthouse.
- Third-order revolving lens (unknown). Active 1859–1861. Removed during the Civil War.
- Third-order revolving lens (unknown). Active 1866–1906. Replaced with new lens.
- Third-and-a-half-order bivalve lens (Barbier, Bénard, et Turenne, 1906). Active 1906–1996. Removed 2014 prior to the lighthouse being moved. In USCG storage pending adequate facilities to place on exhibit at the Cape San Blas Lighthouse Museum. The clockwork and weight remain in the tower, the only ones in Florida.

ST. JOSEPH POINT LIGHTHOUSE

- Third-order fixed lens (Barbier, Benard, et Turenne, 1901). Active 1903–1955. Removed when the lighthouse was deactivated. Currently in USCG storage in Panama City, FL. Might be loaned to Cape San Blas Lighthouse Museum in the future.

PENSACOLA LIGHTHOUSE

- First-order revolving lens (Henry-Lepaute, 1858). Active 1859–1861. Removed during Civil War. Repaired in France after the war. Believed to be the same lens installed in 1869 and still active. Public ATON.
- Fourth-order fixed lens (unknown). Active 1862–1869. Temporary lens replaced by permanent lens.
- Fourth-order fixed lens (Artworks Florida, 2016). Never active. On exhibit in the Pensacola Lighthouse Museum to show what the 1860s lens looked like.

FLORIDA FRESNEL LENSES BY THE NUMBERS

*T*hese statistics only account for the seventy-nine Fresnel lenses known to have been active in a Florida lighthouse at some point. There is some uncertainty with this list as it is not clear how many lenses removed during the Civil War were reinstalled after the war in the same tower, or in another Florida lighthouse. Some of the unknowns likely represent such a situation. Furthermore, lenses of fourth-order or smaller were considered almost completely interchangeable. The Lighthouse Service only belatedly assigned numbers to its lenses, and then only to those in the Staten Island Depot.

FRESNEL LENSES BY ORDER

First-order: 13
Second-order: 5
Third-order: 20
Third-and-a-half order: 2
Fourth-order: 28
Fifth-order: 7
Sixth-order: 4

FRESNEL LENSES BY TYPE

Fixed: 43 (including 5 Drum)
Revolving, Fixed Varied by Flashes: 8
Revolving, Flashing: 28 (including 7 Bivalve)

FRESNEL LENSES BY MANUFACTURER

Henry-Lepaute: 22
Sautter: 6 (L. Sautter et Cie or Sauttier, Lemmonnier, et Cie)
Barbier: 7 (includes Barbier et Fenestre; Barbier et Bénard; and Barbier, Bénard, et Turenne)
Chance Brothers: 0
AGA: 3
Artworks Florida: 4
Unknown: 37

FRESNEL LENSES BY CURRENT STATUS

In Tower: 13
On Exhibit: 9
In Storage: 4
Destroyed: 3
Unknown: 50

THE HISTORY OF THE FLORIDA LIGHTHOUSE ASSOCIATION, 1996–2019

Harry Pettit

> *Never doubt that a small group of thoughtful committed citizens can change the world; indeed, it's the only thing that ever has.*
>
> —Margaret Mead

Our executive vice president, Jon Hill, uses this inspirational quote in his emails, and it is a fitting reference as we consider the history of the FLA. It was indeed a small group of thoughtful, committed citizens whose vision and dedication to the preservation of our historic lighthouses led them to organize the FLA. Here are some key facts:

- The Florida Lighthouse Association was formed at an organizational meeting at the Key Biscayne Community Church on July 27, 1996. Tom Taylor chaired that first meeting with twenty-six in attendance.
- FLA incorporated in 1996 as a not-for-profit corporation under Chapter 617, Florida Statutes, and was recognized as exempt under section 501(c)(3) of the Internal Revenue Code in a determination letter issued in August 1997. The initial voting members, and the initial board members, were Ann Caneer, Joseph Pais, Kathy Fleming, George Blanck, Larry McSparren, Hibbard Casselberry, and Richard Johnson. Thomas W. Taylor was the initial registered agent, and the initial principal office was at Ponce Inlet Lighthouse and Museum. The initial officers were Ann Caneer, president; Rick Schulze, vice president; Arnold Shore, secretary; and Kathy Fleming, treasurer.

The founders included those who had walked the walk in historic preservation, participated in the rescue of endangered lighthouses, and in the maintenance, management, and protection of these historic structures for the education and enjoyment of future generations. Their vision was for a statewide association of lighthouse groups and enthusiasts that would provide for dissemination and sharing of information, for educational opportunities, and for popularizing interest in lighthouses generally, so as to provide the resources for preservation, restoration, and protection. As we approach FLA's twenty-fifth anniversary, the organization has grown into a thriving, strategically planned organization that remains true to the founders' vision.

Ann Caneer was the first president of the FLA, serving 1996 to 1998. She brought the passion and experience that she had applied to rescuing and restoring the Ponce Inlet Lighthouse. Issues in these formative years included securing 501(c)(3) status, developing by-laws, defining lighthouse districts, designing a logo (by Paul Bradley), the License Plate and Front Plate Projects, and advocating for lighthouse issues of the day, including the fate of the St. John's River Lighthouse, which as of the October 1997 issue of *FLASH* was expected to be opened to the public on a regular basis in 1998. Ann Caneer passed away in 2012.

Tom Taylor, a major visionary and driving force behind the organization of the FLA, was president 1998 to 2002. This period included the first ever FLA tour, which featured the Northwest Florida Lighthouses. Tom's tenure also included trips to the Reef Lights, Annual Appeal fundraising and advocacy for St. Marks and Crooked River, a successful campaign to save the keepers' houses at Cape San Blas, a successful campaign to defeat an attempt by commercial interests to convince the Navy to permit the move of the 1859 St. Johns River Lighthouse, state funding of special category grants, the first edition of *The Florida Lighthouse Trail* book, securing petition signatures for the license tag project, and fund raising for the required $60,000. Issues of *FLASH* included petition forms for the license plate project, an annual appeal letter for Crooked River, and a preprinted donation envelope. A call went out for letters of support for the transfer of the St. Augustine Lighthouse under the National Historic Lighthouse Preservation Act, and on July 20, 2002, the St. Augustine Lighthouse became the first of Florida's thirty lighthouses transferred under the NHLPA. The Condition Assessment Report of Florida's thirty lighthouses was completed during this period. Membership reached over 650. Tom Taylor was also the founder of the Florida Keys Reef Lights Foundation. He passed away in May 2004.

Wayne Hawes served as president from 2002 to 2004. He was a prime supporter of the restoration and relighting of the Anclote Key Lighthouse, in his capacity as president of the Tampa Bay Harbour Lights Collectors Society. Wayne brought the Harbour Lights' enthusiasm and his commitment to lighthouse preservation into the FLA and continued the work to secure a specialty license tag. His influence carried over into the following administration, when the Tampa Bay Harbour Lights' Collectors Society issued a critical $1,000 challenge donation to the license plate fund, sparking matching donations from groups and individuals. Florida Governor Jeb Bush proclaimed Florida Lighthouse Day on September 13, 2003, in conjunction with the relighting of the Anclote Key Lighthouse.

Gene Oakes was elected president at the October 2004 Annual Meeting, and served until his untimely death January 20, 2006. Gene introduced himself by bluntly stating (in his words) that he was not Tom Taylor, as he lacked Tom's education and knowledge, and he was not Wayne Hawes, as he did not have Wayne's personality and energy level. However, he said that he did have Tom's vision and Wayne's passion. He had "an intense desire to achieve positive results" and embraced the founders' vision and objectives. He focused on moving the Specialty License Tag project forward, and fundraising emphasis shifted to securing the large amount necessary for the project. Gene also achieved much administrative progress, especially regarding the use of the website for tracking membership and its use by the general membership. With personal testimony from his July 2005 visit to the Cape St. George lighthouse, the Board voted to designate it as "Florida's Most Endangered Lighthouse." An appeal went out for all concerned to support the St. George Lighthouse Association with donations toward their match for a state grant. Before the rescue plan could be implemented, the lighthouse collapsed into the Gulf of Mexico on October 21, 2005. Under Gene's leadership, the FLA supported the indefatigable St. George Lighthouse Association with a check for $15,000 for the recovery and salvage operation. This represented over 20 percent of the FLA's liquid assets at the time, a very significant contribution. Gene's tenure saw attendance increases at each meeting, a revitalized membership, and stronger ties to the Florida Trust for Historic Preservation.

Stan Farnham was elected president by the Board on January 27, 2006, and served through 2010. His background as a turnaround expert was excellent preparation for stepping into the leadership of FLA. He dedicated himself to building upon the vision set by Gene Oakes, and he focused on leading the organization in the development of clear strategic plans necessary to accomplish the vision. The number one goal was to achieve the long-standing dream of having an FLA Specialty License Tag to provide a sustainable source of funds for lighthouse restoration. Under Stan's leadership, the focus was sharpened. The tenth anniversary meeting of FLA was held at Sanibel on October 21, 2006, and featured the presentation of certificates of recognition to: Ann Caneer as first president and founder; one to the mother and sister of the late Tom Taylor as an organizer, founder, and past president; one to be delivered to Kathy Fleming as a founder and officer; and certificates to be delivered to founding members Bill and Frieda Trotter. Certificates were also presented to Paul Bradley, Hib Casselberry, Cindi Para, and Richard Johnson as founders.

The January 2007 meeting featured the planting of the Gene Oakes Memorial Tree at the St. Augustine Lighthouse. Another emphasis during this period was developing strategic alliances and partnerships such as *Visit Florida, Florida Trust for Historic Preservation,* and *Florida Association of Museums.* A report in March 2007 said "the Governor's recommended budget includes $5 million to be transferred to the Department of State for restoration of lighthouses statewide." Subsequently Governor Crist and the legislature approved some of the lighthouse restoration budget initiative totaling $1 million, split over Cape St. George, Crooked River, and Anclote Key. QuickBooks software for nonprofits was purchased to enhance financial professionalism.

A detailed plan for "FLA Specialty License Plate Success" was drawn up, and help from the membership was enlisted to secure legislative sponsorship for the 2008 session and to contact representatives for support. The April 2008 meeting was at Tallahassee (St. Marks Lighthouse), offering the opportunity for FLA members to speak with legislators about funding in the state budget and license plate approval.

The funds from the license plate, now renamed "The Gene Oaks Memorial License Plate Fund," were $13,480 in 2006 and an additional $60,000 by October 2007, and application was made for the "Visit Our Lights" tag. The application required a $60,000 (refundable if unsuccessful) fee to cover production of the tags and results of a $14,000 marketing survey. Gene Oakes's vision for the specialty tag was realized when the "Visit Our Lights" tag was approved by the Department of Highway Safety, passed by the Florida Legislature on April 29, 2008, and signed into law by Governor Crist effective October 1, 2008. The first tags went on sale in December 2008.

After approval of the license plate, strategic goals shifted to boosting its sales, increasing membership, continuing and forging new alliances, promoting increased public interest, and securing comprehensive funding (corporate, gifting, legacy).

Local volunteers accomplished amazing things during this period. The miraculously rebuilt Cape St. George Lighthouse opened November 29, 2008. Crooked River and Cape San Blas were restored, as were Cape Canaveral, Anclote Key, and Amelia Island.

Ken Smith served as president from 2010 to 2015, extending his term one additional year at the request of a grateful Board and membership. Ken began his term of office by listening to and responding to members' desires for more meeting content and more social time. Ken introduced the "Lighthouse Congress" meeting concept, extending the meeting plan to two-and-a-half days in some cases, and began adding "down time" with snacks, wine, soft drinks, and more to the meeting schedule. At the first Lighthouse Congress, which occurred in 2011, the board changed the name of the president's award to the Ann Caneer President's Award to honor our first president, and created a second grant program, the Tom Taylor Keepers Fund, to honor Tom for his passion. At that meeting, eleven grants were awarded; five were the first Tom Taylor grants.

A major upgrade to the website made for a much more valuable tool for both officers and members. It soon became clear that Ken's passion for the core mission of raising money and giving it to lighthouses for worthwhile projects would be the hallmark of his presidency. Every meeting featured a celebration of what we had been able to give to lighthouses, complete with four-foot-long (or longer!) ceremonial checks and photo ops. Each meeting also became an opportunity to encourage giving to the cause. This focus supported the consistent message that we must continue to expand our fund raising, and resulted in the formation of a Revenue Development committee, which Ken still chairs. Various giving "societies" were defined to reflect levels of support and to provide special events for supporters.

Ken recognized that FLA needed better administrative and governance support and sought expert consultants' input to help our all-volunteer organization take the next step toward a more professional organization structure and image. After consultation with the board and trusted advisers, he brought in support for administration, fundraising, and governance. FLA finally had an address and telephone number, and someone to answer the phone, route emails, keep financial records, prepare reports, and more. With the encouragement of our experienced consultant, we developed a well-defined organization, compliant with our legal responsibilities, and based on a committee structure designed to carry out strategic goals, which are established or reviewed at a board retreat each year. Officer job descriptions and committee commissions (committee job descriptions) were written. Development of a board orientation manual was begun.

This period saw the threatened destruction due to erosion and the subsequent move of the Cape San Blas Lighthouse and keeper's houses. FLA offered immediate timely support.

During Ken's administration, the small grants program grew into two significant programs. The Gene Oakes Lighthouse Fund channels money from the license plates to bricks and mortar preservation and restoration efforts. The Tom Taylor Keepers Fund is used for other projects like education and replication efforts. Together, in the period 2011 to 2015, FLA provided over $370,000 in grants to benefit over half of the thirty remaining historic lighthouses of Florida. Many of the local recipient preservation groups leveraged these funds to secure matching funds, effectively growing our impact into well over a million dollars.

Chris Belcher was elected FLA's sixth president in October 2015 and served until the end of 2019. During his tenure, FLA celebrated its twentieth anniversary. Chris brought a "back to basics" approach that "focused on the here and now of our association's purpose." This included a project to substantially clean up the organization's by-laws (a lengthy project spearheaded by Harry Pettit as governance chair) and successfully reducing FLA's operating expenses by nearly half.

The organization's income continued to increase due to an active membership increase of 38 percent and also the growing number of license plate sales. The five thousandth FLA plate sold during this time. Chris was especially proud that FLA awarded over $325,000 in grants during his four years as president, representing 40 percent of all FLA's lifetime grants. By the time Chris left office, the annual grant budget from license plate funds exceeded $150,000 annually. Major lighthouse projects during this time, all supported by FLA grants, included the restoration and opening of Gasparilla Island and St. Marks, and the completion of a phased restoration of the Pensacola Lighthouse.

While the original Visit Our Lights plate had proven successful, after a decade it was time for a redesign to a more appealing and eye-catching look. The multiyear project was led by Sharon McKenzie, FLA marketing chair. Jupiter Inlet Lighthouse was chosen to represent FLA on the new plate. The new plates debuted in August 2019.

Jon Hill became FLA's seventh president starting in 2020. The largest challenges for the foreseeable future will be supporting the restoration of the Reef Lights.

PAST RECIPIENTS
OF THE FLA
PRESIDENT'S AWARD

This award is given at most once per year by FLA for "outstanding service on behalf of lighthouse preservation." The award was first given in 2001. In 2005, it was renamed the Tom Taylor President's Award after Tom's passing. In 2013, the award was renamed the Ann Caneer President's Award after Ann's death, and the General Fund Grant program was renamed in Tom's honor.

2001   George Blanck, Tom Gardener, and Barbara Revell for their work with Jupiter, Pensacola, and Crooked River lighthouses, respectively.

2002   Hal Belcher, for his role in helping the Amelia Island Lighthouse be transferred to the City of Fernandina Beach and for his work as a lighthouse historian.

2003   None.

2004   Tom Taylor (posthumous), for lifetime achievement as a historian and FLA president.

2005   Gene Oakes, for his work on the FLA license plate and his leadership as FLA president supporting the Cape St. George Lighthouse.

2006   Hib Casselberry, for "distinguished service" in support of FLA, including being a founding member, district commissioner, and education committee chair.

2007   Paul Bradley, lighthouse artist.

2008   Dennis Barnell, for his leadership as president of the St. George Lighthouse Association in attempting to save the Cape St. George Lighthouse and in rebuilding the lighthouse after it collapsed.

2009   George W. Evans, for "outstanding and selfless contributions to the Florida Lighthouse Association and its goals."

2010   Fred Gaske, director of the Florida Division of Historical Resources.

2011   Danny Raffield, for completing a lifetime of work restoring the St. Joseph Point Lighthouse.

2012   None.

2013   Al King, for leadership as the first FLA Grants Chair.

2014   None.

2015   Mel C. Magidson Jr., former mayor of Port St. Joe, recognizing his leadership in leading the city to rescue the Cape San Blas Lighthouse.

2016   John Kennedy, for dedicated service as FLA treasurer (2006–2016)

2017   None.

2018   Hib Casselberry, for lifetime achievements in support of Florida's lighthouses, including being a founding member of FLA, the Hillsboro Lighthouse Preservation Society, and the Florida Keys Reef Lights.

2019   Ron and Chris Ecker, for a decade of service with FLA as Meetings Chair, Membership Chair, and Cope Canaveral Lighthous representatives

FLORIDA LIGHTHOUSE ASSOCIATION FOUNDERS FIRST MEETING ATTENDEES: JULY 1996

Name	Home	Affiliation	Status
George Blanck	Palm Beach Gardens	Jupiter	
Joan Gill Blank	Key Biscayne	Cape Florida	
Paul Bradley	Ft. Lauderdale	artist	RIP
Ann Caneer	Ponce Inlet	Ponce Inlet	RIP
Hib Casselberry	Ft. Lauderdale	Hillsboro Inlet	RIP
James Dunlap	Ponce Inlet	Ponce Inlet	
Don Ferguson	Miami		
Kathy Fleming	St. Augustine	St. Augustine	
Scott Keeler	St. Petersburg	Anclote Keys	
Merri Ketterer	St. Augustine	St. Augustine	
Roger McCormick	Cape Canaveral	Cape Canaveral	
Carmen McGarry	Hillsboro Beach	Hillsboro Inlet	
Larry McSparren	Tarpon Springs	Anclote Keys	
Joe Pais	Key West	Key West	
Cindi Para	St. Petersburg		
Larry J. Parker	Palm Beach Gardens	Jupiter	
Betty Rice	Key Biscayne	Cape Florida	
Don Sackieder	Key Biscayne	Cape Florida	
Rick Schulze	Plantation		
Arnold Shore	Jupiter	Jupiter	
Bernice Shore	Jupiter	Jupiter	
Tom Taylor	Allandale	Ponce Inlet	RIP
Frieda Trotter	Jacksonville Beach	St. Johns River	
William L. Trotter	Jacksonville Beach	St. Johns River	
Jean Yehle	Key Biscayne	Cape Florida	

THE U.S. LIFE SAVING
SERVICE IN FLORIDA

Josh Liller

The United States Life Saving Service (USLSS) traces its roots to a program started in 1848 by the Revenue Marine that established some rescue stations in the northeast with volunteer response crews. A review in 1871 found this system woefully inadequate, so the Revenue Marine began employing full-time crews and building more stations around the country. A separate Life Saving Service was formally established in 1878 as a civilian agency in the Department of the Treasury. In 1915, the Life Saving Service merged with the Revenue Marine to form the US Coast Guard—to be joined by the Lighthouse Service in 1939. Given these historical similarities and their similar purpose— altruistic aid to mariners—it should come as no surprise that the Life Saving Service and Lighthouse Service are considered "sister services."

A typical Life Saving Station (LSS)—later called LifeBoat Station under the Coast Guard—had a crew that would actively attempt to rescue those in distress with their surfboat and other equipment. Houses of Refuge (HOR) were operated by the Life Saving Service but lacked a crew or rescue equipment. Instead they had a lone keeper (often with his family) who provided aid and comfort for shipwreck survivors who made it ashore. Five Houses of Refuge were established in Florida in 1876 and five more in 1885, along with two traditional lifesaving stations. All ten Houses of Refuge had an identical design. After the creation of the Coast Guard, some of the Houses of Refuge transitioned into lifeboat stations.

GILBERT'S BAR HOUSE
OF REFUGE

STUART, FLORIDA

What is the only non-lighthouse in Florida to have a lighthouse passport stamp? What is the oldest building in Martin County? What is the only nineteenth-century station from the Life Saving Service remaining in Florida? The answer to all three: Gilbert's Bar House of Refuge.

Gilbert's Bar was among the first five Florida Houses of Refuge built in 1876. The station was located on Hutchinson Island at a place known as St. Lucie Rocks, referring to the remains of an ancient coral reef on the beach there. The namesake bar was a sporadically open inlet located several miles away, south of the modern St. Lucie Inlet. Several shipwrecks occurred nearby, most notably the barkentine *Georges Valentine* in 1904. The wreck is only one hundred feet offshore from the station and is on the National Register of Historic Places.

During World War II, Gilbert's Bar served as a beach patrol station and had a lookout tower to monitor passing ships and watch for German submarines. The station was decommissioned in 1945 at the end of the war. In 1953, Martin County purchased the station and sixteen-acre grounds. The Historical Society of Martin County formed two years later to restore and preserve the historic structure, the last surviving House of Refuge in Florida (the organization now also operates the nearby Elliott Museum). From 1963 to 1987 the station was also home to a sea turtle program run by Ross Witham, grandson of a Surf-man at Jupiter Inlet Life Saving Station. The adjacent beach is now named in Witham's honor.

SITE FACTS

Dates of Construction: 1876
Decommissioned: 1945
Designer/Architect: Francis W. Chandler
Builder/Supervisor: Albert Blaisdale
Foundation Materials: unknown
Construction Materials: wood
National Register of Historic Places: yes (1976)
Owner: Martin County
Operating Entity: Historical Society of Martin County (nonprofit)
Grounds Open to the Public: yes—daily
Station Open to the Public: yes—daily
LSS Museum: yes
Gift Shop: yes
Lighthouse Passport Stamp: yes—in gift shop
Hours: 10 AM–4 PM Monday–Saturday, 1 PM–4 PM Sunday
Handicapped Access: no
Adult Admission: $8
Contact: House of Refuge at Gilbert's Bar, 301 SE MacArthur Blvd., Stuart,
    FL 34996
Phone: (772) 225-1875
Email: none
Website: www.houseofrefugefl.org

OTHER HOUSES OF REFUGE IN FLORIDA

SMITH'S CREEK HOUSE OF REFUGE (1886-1918 AND 1924-1945)

AKA: Bulow House of Refuge, Flagler Beach Lifeboat Station
Location: Flagler Beach (20 miles south of Matanzas Inlet)
Notes: The station was used for beach patrol and aircraft lookout purposes during World War II. The former station reservation is now Gamble Rogers State Park.

MOSQUITO LAGOON HOUSE OF REFUGE / LIFEBOAT STATION (1885-1938)

Location: New Smyrna Beach, FL (near the south end of Atlantic Ave)
Notes: Replaced by a new Ponce Inlet LBS. Site now part of Canaveral National Seashore.

CHESTER SHOAL HOUSE OF REFUGE (1886-1945)

Location: 11 miles north of Cape Canaveral
Notes: Beach patrol station during World War II. Site is not publicly accessible because it is near the former space shuttle launch pad.

CAPE MALABAR HOUSE OF REFUGE (1886-1891)

Location: Melbourne Beach, FL (30 miles south of Cape Canaveral)
Notes: The namesake cape is located on the west side of the Indian River. The former station reservation was sold to Brevard County in 1950 and is now Spessard Holland Beach Park.

BETHEL CREEK HOUSE OF REFUGE (1876-1936)

AKA: Indian River House of Refuge
Location: Vero Beach, FL (16 miles north of the Old Indian River Inlet)
Notes: Name changed in 1885 to avoid confusion with the Indian River Inlet HOR. Station reservation transferred to the City of Vero Beach in 1950 and became Jaycee Park.

INDIAN RIVER INLET HOUSE OF REFUGE / LIFEBOAT STATION (1885-1937)

Location: Fort Pierce, FL (formerly south side of the Old Indian River Inlet)
Notes: Replaced by a new Fort Pierce LBS. Part of a Navy Underwater Demolition Team (UDT) training site during World War II. Site is now Pepper Park.

ORANGE GROVE HOUSE OF REFUGE (1876-1896)

Location: Delray Beach, FL
Notes: Building burned down in 1927. Historical marker located at the former site.

FORT LAUDERDALE HOUSE OF REFUGE (1876-1928)

AKA: New River House of Refuge
Location: Fort Lauderdale Beach, FL (7 miles north of New River Inlet)
Notes: Destroyed by a hurricane in 1928.

BISCAYNE BAY HOUSE OF REFUGE (1876–1926)

Location: Miami Beach (near 72nd Street)
Notes: Wrecked by a hurricane in 1926. Site now home to the North Shore Community Center.

SANTA ROSA ISLAND LIFE SAVING STATION

PENSACOLA BEACH, FLORIDA

In additional to the Houses of Refuge, the Life Saving Service also established three identical, traditional Life Saving Stations in 1885: Morris Island, near Charleston, SC; Jupiter Inlet, FL; and Santa Rosa Island, near Pensacola, FL. These stations kept busy aiding vessels entering and exiting Charleston Harbor, Jupiter Inlet, and Pensacola Bay.

The Morris Island station only lasted a decade before it was replaced by a new station on Sullivans Island on the opposite side of the harbor mouth. Morris Island has since been reduced from an island to a sandbar.

Jupiter Inlet, located just south of its namesake, served for a decade before being reduced to a House of Refuge, then being decommissioned entirely in 1899. The building was demolished around 1920. The former LSS reservation is now Carlin Park, named after the station's only keeper, Charles Carlin.

Santa Rosa lasted until 1906, when it was destroyed by a major hurricane. The station was rebuilt in 1907 with a completely different design. It remained in operation until 1979 when it was permanently put out of action by another hurricane. The building has undergone numerous expansions, renovations, and hurricane repairs. The former station now serves as the ranger station for Fort Pickens Campground in Gulf Islands National Seashore. The building is on the north side of the main park road just under four miles from the park entrance ranger station.

SITE FACTS

Dates of Construction: 1885 and 1906
Decommissioned: 1979
Designer/Architect: J. Lake Parkinson (1885); George R. Tolman (1906)
Builder/Supervisor: unknown
Foundation Materials: unknown
Construction Materials: wood
National Register of Historic Places: yes (2013) as part of a general listing for all surviving pre-1950 lifesaving/lifeboat stations
Owner: National Park Service
Operating Entity: Gulf Islands National Seashore
Grounds Open to the Public: yes—daily
Station Open to the Public: yes—daily, but very limited interior access
LSS Museum: no
Gift Shop: no
Lighthouse Passport Stamp: no
Hours: 9 AM–4:30 PM (campground office); 5 AM–9 PM March–October and 5 AM–6 PM November–February (park)
Handicapped Access: yes
Adult Admission: $10/person or $20/car (park)
Contact: Gulf Islands National Seashore, 1801 Gulf Breeze Pkwy., Gulf Breeze, FL 32563
Phone: (850) 934-2600
Email: none
Website: www.nps.gov/guis/

FURTHER READING

Bansemer, Roger. *Bansemer's Book of Florida Lighthouses*. Sarasota, FL: Pineapple Press, 1999.

Blank, Joan Gill. *Key Biscayne: A History of Miami's Tropical Island and the Cape Florida Lighthouse*. Sarasota, FL: Pineapple Press, 1996.

Cipra, David L. *Lighthouses, Lightships, and the Gulf of Mexico*. Alexandria, VA: Cypress Communications, 1997.

Clifford, Mary Louise, and J. Candice Clifford. *Women Who Kept the Lights: An Illustrated History of Female Lighthouse Keepers* (second edition). Alexandria, VA: Cypress Communications, 2001.

Collins, Toni C. *Cedar Keys Light Station*. Chiefland, FL: Suwannee River Publishing, 2011.

Dean, Love. *Lighthouses of the Florida Keys: A Short History and Guide*. Sarasota, FL: Pineapple Press, 1998.

De Wire, Elinor. *Guide to Florida Lighthouses* (third edition). Sarasota, FL: Pineapple Press, 2017.

Grant, R. G. *Lighthouse: An Illuminating History of the World's Coastal Sentinels*. New York: Black Dog & Leventhal, 2018.

Hairr, John. *Images of America: Florida Lighthouses*. Mount Pleasant, SC: Arcadia Publishing, 1999.

Henry, Ellen J. "The Lighthouse at Volusia Bar." *Keeper's Log*. US Lighthouse Society, July 2009.

Henry, Ellen J. *The Lighthouse Service and the Great War*. Ponce Inlet, FL: Ponce de Leon Inlet Lighthouse Association, 2013.

Henry, Ellen J. *The Ponce Inlet Lighthouse: An Illustrated History*. Ponce Inlet, FL: Ponce de Leon Inlet Lighthouse Association, 2018.

Holland, Francis Ross. *America's Lighthouses: An Illustrated History*. New York: Dover Publications, 1988.

Hurley, Neil E. *An Illustrated History of Cape Florida Lighthouse*. Camino, CA: Historic Lighthouse Publishers, 1989.

Hurley, Neil E. *Florida's Lighthouses in the Civil War*. Fort Lauderdale, FL: Middle River Press, 2007.

Hurley, Neil E. *Keepers of Florida Lighthouses*. Self-published, 1990. (Updated database of keepers available on CD-ROM.)

Hurley, Neil E. *Lighthouses of the Dry Tortugas: An Illustrated History*. Aies, HI: Historic Lighthouse Publishers, 1990.

Hurley, Neil E. *Lighthouses of Egmont Key*. Historic Lighthouse Publishers, 1995. (Updated edition available on CD-ROM.)

Hurley, Neil E. *Lighting Carysfort Reef, Volume 1: The Lightships*. Self-published, 2018.

Hurley, Neil E. *Lighting Carysfort Reef, Volume 2: The Lighthouse*. Self-published, 2018.

Kanekkeberg, Myrna Roberts. *Keepers of the Light: A History of the St. Marks Lighthouse and the Gresham Family*. Tallahassee, FL: Sentry Press, 2010.

Kruegler, Ralph. *An (Almost) Complete History of Hillsboro Inlet Lighthouse*. Self-published, 2019.

LeBuff, Charles. *Sanibel Island Lighthouse: A Complete History*. Sanibel, FL: Amber Publishing, 2017.

Levitt, Theresa. *A Short Bright Flash: Augustin Fresnel and the Birth of the Modern Lighthouse*. New York: W. W. Norton & Company, 2013.

McCarthy, Kevin M., and William L. Trotter. *Florida Lighthouses*. Gainesville, FL: University of Florida Press, 1990.

Noble, Dennis L. *Lighthouses and Keepers: The U.S. Lighthouse Service and Its Legacy*. Annapolis: US Naval Institute Press, 1997.

Ranson, Robert. *East Coast Florida Memoirs, 1837 to 1886*. Hobe Sound, FL: Florida Classics Library, 1988. (A short biography of lighthouse keeper Mills Olcutt Burnham.)

Roberts, William. *Lighthouses and Living Along the Florida Gulf Coast*. Bloomington, IN: Authorhouse, 2005.

Shelton-Roberts, Cheryl, and Bruce Roberts. *Lighthouse Families*. Birmingham, AL: Crane Hill Publishers, 1997.

Snyder, James D. *A Light in the Wilderness: The Story of Jupiter Inlet Lighthouse & The Southeast Florida Frontier*. Jupiter, FL: Pharos Books, 2006.

Spinella, Teri. *History of the St. Augustine Lighthouse*. Lake Buena Vista, FL: Artworks Florida, 1992.

Taylor, Thomas W. *Florida's Territorial Lighthouses, 1821–1845*. Self-published, 1995.

Taylor, Thomas W., and Gail Swanson. *Lore of the Reef Lights: Life in the Florida Keys*. Conshohocken, PA: Infinity Publishing Company, 2006.

Witt, Sonny. *The Discovery of Cape Canaveral & The Story of Who and What Came After.* Sarasota, FL: Sun Graphics, 2015. (This is an updated version of the author's *Drawn to the Light: The History of Cape Canaveral and Its People.*)

In addition to these books, there are two national lighthouse magazines. *Keeper's Log* is the quarterly publication of the US Lighthouse Society since 1984. *Lighthouse Digest* publishes every other month since 1992.

ABOUT THE AUTHORS

Harold J. "Hal" Belcher was a long-time resident of Fernandina Beach, a local historian, and founding president of the Amelia Island Lighthouse and Museum.

Chris Belcher is the son of Hal Belcher and a lifelong resident of Fernandina Beach. He followed in his father's footsteps as Amelia Island Lighthouse's representative to the Florida Lighthouse Association. He also served as president of the Florida Lighthouse Association from 2015 to 2019.

Joan Gill Blank has been a resident of Key Biscayne since 1951. She is a now-retired historian and author of *Key Biscayne: A History of Miami's Tropical Island and the Cape Florida Lighthouse* and editor of *Born of the Sun: The Official Florida Bicentennial Commemorative Book.*

Hibbard "Hib" Casselberry was a World War II veteran and one of Florida's most noted lighthouse enthusiasts. He was a founding member of the Florida Lighthouse Association, Hillsboro Lighthouse Preservation Society, and Florida Keys Reef Lights Foundation.

Love Dean (Winslow) was a resident of the Florida Keys, a noted historian, and author of several books about lighthouses, including *Lighthouses of the Florida Keys.*

Elinor De Wire is a nationally noted lighthouse historian and author of many lighthouse books, one of which, *Guide to Florida Lighthouses*, has become a standard.

Thomas M. Garner is the author of *The Pensacola Lighthouse* booklet and was the first Florida Lighthouse Association District Commissioner for the Florida panhandle.

Marilyn Hoeckel worked with the Barrier Island Parks Society, including the development of the Port Boca Grande Lighthouse Museum.

Neil Hurley is a retired Coast Guard officer. He is the longtime historian of the Florida Lighthouse Association and author of many books about Florida lighthouses and lighthouse keepers. He has also actively participated in many Florida lighthouse restoration projects.

Richard Johnson was president of the Egmont Key Alliance and secretary of the Florida Lighthouse Association when this book's first edition was published. He remains an active member of the Alliance.

Herman and Trip Jones are a father-and-son team who have been interested in the Gulf Coast lighthouses for many years and are major proponents of their preservation.

Janet and Scott Keeler were instrumental in the preservation of the Anclote Keys Lighthouse. Scott was a reporter for the *St. Petersburg Times*, and his photographs of lighthouses have been displayed around the state.

Craig Kittendorf is a ranger at St. Marks National Wildlife Refuge and the St. Marks Lighthouse representative to the Florida Lighthouse Association.

Charles LeBuff lived for many years in the keeper's quarters of the Sanibel Island Lighthouse. He is a noted local historian and author of two books about Sanibel's history.

John Lee was president of the Cape St. George Lighthouse Society and editor of the *Apalachicola Times* newspaper. He led efforts to save the lighthouse in the 1990s.

Andrew M. Liliskis founded the Mayport Lighthouse Association. He led a vigorous but unsuccessful campaign to restore permanent public access to the St. Johns River Lighthouse.

Josh Liller is the historian and collections manager at the Jupiter Inlet Lighthouse & Museum. He is Jupiter's representative to the Florida Lighthouse Association and a historian of the Florida Lighthouse Association.

Harry Pettit is a longtime member of the Florida Lighthouse Association and a former board member.

Danny Raffield and his family have been responsible for the preservation and restoration of the St. Joseph Point Lighthouse, which now serves as their private residence.

Barbara Revell was a major proponent of the preservation of the Crooked River Lighthouse and the first president of the Carrabelle Lighthouse Association.

Thomas W. "Tom" Taylor was historian at the Ponce de Leon Inlet Lighthouse, president of the Florida Lighthouse Association, founder of the Florida Keys Reef Lights Foundation, and editor of the first edition of this book.